Ulan Bator
NORTH KOREA
KOGURYO
JAPAN
Tokyo
Kamakura
Kyoto
Nara
Pyongyang
SILLA
Beijing
Seoul
Kyongju
Paekje
SOUTH KOREA
Luoyang
Xian
Nanking
Shanghai
INA
TAIWAN
UNNAN
Canton
Hong Kong
PACIFIC OCEAN
Hanoi
PHILIPPINES
VIETNAM
Dong Duong
CHAMPA
ND
Angkor
AMBODIA
Phnom Penh
SIA
SRI VIJAYA
Lumpur
SINGAPORE
BORNEO
embang
INDONESIA
Jakarta
JAVA
Borobudur

BUDDHISM AND BUDDHIST ART

AN ILLUSTRATED INTRODUCTION

By

CHARLES F. CHICARELLI

Silkworm Books

Copyright © 2004 by Charles F. Chicarelli

All rights reserved

No part of this publication may be reproduced, stored in a retrieval system, or transmitted, in any form or by any means, electronic, mechanical, photocopying, recording or otherwise, without the prior permission in writing of the publisher.

ISBN 978-616-215-137-8

First published in 2004 as *Buddhist Art: An Illustrated Introduction* by
Silkworm Books
104/5 M. 7, Chiang Mai–Hot Road, T. Suthep,
Chiang Mai 50200 Thailand
P.O. Box 296, Phra Singh Post Office, Chiang Mai 50205
info@silkwormbooks.com
http://www.silkwormbooks.com

Typeset in Garamond Premier Pro by Silk Type

Printed and bound in Thailand by O. S. Printing House, Bangkok

5 4 3

CONTENTS

PREFACE

Buddhist beliefs and their rich artistic legacy span the past twenty-five centuries and have had a profound impact on our world. The aim of this book is to introduce and briefly explore the principal elements of Buddhism and the subjects and themes frequently seen in Buddhist art, with photographs from temples, historical sites, museums, and private art collections. Hopefully general readers and experienced observers of Asian culture will find material here that is interesting and useful.

Many elements of Buddhist iconography share common roots and terminology with Hinduism, the ancient Indian religion whose pantheon of countless deities dates back four thousand years or more. One example is *mudra*—a Sanskrit word used to describe symbolic hand gestures. Another Sanskrit word—*asana*—classifies the positions of the lower body and limbs of figures, as well as the pedestals and thrones beneath them. Images are also sometimes defined by terms based on the word *bhanga*—the "posture" of a body. Appendix 1 provides further details about these terms and a selection of illustrations. Readers may find it helpful and interesting to review that appendix before proceeding with the main sections of this book.

Fig. 1. *Phra Bot* (*Buddhist temple banner*). *Top section shows Sakyamuni Buddha (center figure) with his two chief disciples, the monks Sariputra and Maudgalyayana. Lower section illustrates the shipwreck scene from the Mahajanaka Jataka*. Painting on cloth, 38⅝ x 106¼ in. (98 x 270 cm).

INTRODUCTION

The man who became *the Buddha*—the "Enlightened" or "Awakened" One whose teachings of wisdom, peace, and compassion are known as *Buddhism*—was born Prince Siddhartha Gautama of the Sakya people of Kapilavastu, a small Himalayan kingdom that straddled the borderlands of present-day Nepal and northeast India. One chronology tells that he was born in 623 B.C., another reckons 563 or 566 B.C.

At age twenty-nine he left his palace and his family, abandoned his royal privileges and material possessions, and became a monk. His goal was to find a way to liberate humankind from the miseries of pain and death. He sought out gurus, examined their teachings, and explored every imaginable approach to remedy humanity's ills. He learned advanced meditation techniques and made them a central component of his philosophy, useful for calming the mind, probing its true nature, and gaining heightened insights into the causes of suffering. One day, after six years of these efforts, he sat down and began meditating beneath a fig tree. He vowed not to move until he found a solution to suffering and death. As he sat meditating, focusing his concentration on the roots of human suffering, he reached a vivid understanding of *samsara*—the continuous, infinite cycle of birth, death, and rebirth. Everything that comes into existence must also decay and die. Nothing is permanent. All material possessions and physical pleasures are transient and must eventually perish or pass, so craving them is pointless and merely perpetuates attachment to the endless ordeal of existence.

One of Buddhism's defining acts, the story of Siddhartha conquering all aspects of craving and attaining enlightenment has been immortalized as a legend in

Fig. 2. *The Enlightenment of Sakyamuni Buddha*. Gilt bronze, Buddhist lineage, Tibet, 1600–1699.

which he is challenged by Mara, lord of the realm of desire and, in Buddhist mythology, a personification of evil. This legend tells that Mara was determined to foil Siddhartha's attempt to cast away human weaknesses such as greed, anger, and ignorance, which Mara uses to dominate sentient beings. First, Mara sent his three voluptuous daughters to tempt Siddhartha with sensual pleasures and material riches. Siddhartha ignored them. Mara then conjured up an army of demons, warriors, and ferocious beasts to attack Siddhartha and destroy his concentration, but they fell back, powerless against him. When Mara's tactics had all failed, as a final resort he announced that Siddhartha's efforts were in vain because no one had witnessed them, no one could give testament that Siddhartha had demonstrated the spiritual purity and supreme wisdom needed to defeat Mara and gain enlightenment. Siddhartha, still seated calmly and resolutely in meditation, extended his right hand out over the top of his right leg, palm against the knee, and touched the ground with his fingers to call the Goddess of the Earth to be his witness. The ground shook. The Earth Goddess emerged and affirmed that Siddhartha had conquered Mara and his defilements.

This event, particularly touching the ground with the fingers of his outstretched right hand to summon the Earth Goddess as his witness (*bhumisparsha mudra*), symbolizes Prince Siddhartha Gautama achieving enlightenment and becoming *the Buddha*, or *Sakyamuni Buddha*. He is also called *Gautama Buddha*. Known by various descriptive titles such as "The Enlightenment of Sakyamuni Buddha," "Buddha Calling the Earth To Witness," and "Buddha Subduing Mara," this pose has become Buddhism's principal icon—as shown, for example, in the statue of fig. 2.

After attaining enlightenment at age thirty-five, the Buddha spent the next forty-five years teaching his doctrine in northeastern India. When artists of the Indian subcontinent in approximately the first century B.C. began producing the first images showing his earthly form, they probably followed descriptions of him from the Buddhist scriptures and folk legends. When his teachings spread across frontiers and oceans, native craftsmen in other countries created new depictions of the great sage closely patterned after the poses, gestures, and proportions of Indian prototype artworks—but they often incorporated artistic motifs and embellishments based on their own physical characteristics, aesthetic ideals, and concepts of the spirit world. Stonecutters in Gandhara (an ancient state that included parts of today's Pakistan, India, and Afghanistan) reflected their strong stylistic heritage from Greece and Rome by producing Buddha statues with a European face. Sculptors in East Asia depicted him with their own Chinese, Korean, or Japanese features. Burmese and Thai painters represented him with their physical traits. And so on. A host of these regional variations are now hailed as masterpiece achievements. Most were produced anonymously, with no signatures or other identification of their creators—who, after all, worked mainly in pursuit of spiritual merit, not material gain. And while such icons have been produced throughout the past two millennia, the notion of Buddhist imagery as "works of art" is a very recent phenomenon.

Buddhist artworks fulfill important purposes for the faithful: they record a visual history of the Buddha's life and teachings, and they serve as physical substitutes for him, especially for veneration or worship. Certain images and amulets, reputedly endowed with spiritual energy, are believed able to grant blessings while warding off evil and misfortune. An enormous array of these likenesses carried the Buddha's doctrine from its cradle in ancient India across time and space to inspire and enrich hundreds of millions of human lives. Perhaps their most significant accomplishment has been to spark interest in the Buddha and his precepts among people with little or no prior knowledge of them. Moreover, the serenity and austere beauty of a Buddha image have as much relevance today as in past ages due to the growing use of meditation as a path to contentment and mental well-being.

The principal language spoken by the Buddha and his followers is believed to have been *Magadhi*, a dialect spoken in the ancient *Magadha* kingdom in northeast India where most of his travels and teachings occurred. Magadhi is closely related to *Pali*, the Indian language that monks in Sri Lanka used to record the first written transcripts of the Buddhist scriptures in the first century B.C. Pali lives on today as the voice of *Theravada Buddhism*—sometimes called "Southern Buddhism" as it is now widely practiced in Sri Lanka and mainland Southeast Asia. The sacred literature of *Mahayana Buddhism*—sometimes called "Northern Buddhism" as it is observed today principally in China, Korea, and Japan—is based largely on Sanskrit, the classical language of ancient India. *Dhyana Buddhism*, a branch of Mahayana which stresses the practice of meditation as a primary path to enlightenment, developed in China where it is called *Ch'an* or *Chan*, but is now best known internationally by its Japanese name, *Zen*. *Vajrayana Buddhism*, another branch of Mahayana, arose in India under the influences of Hindu and Tantric beliefs, and is now a major religion in Nepal, Bhutan, Mongolia, and Tibet.

Monks, pilgrims, historians, and scholars have translated texts of Buddhism's various branches into a multitude of languages and dialects.[1] Some terms then made their way into contemporary Western languages such as English via several parallel routes, giving our modern usage two or more spellings of the same word. For instance, the Buddha's teachings are known both as *Dharma*, from Sanskrit, and *Dhamma*, from Pali. Likewise, *karma / kamma* (actions that have bearing on our present and future circumstances), *nirvana / nibbana* (liberation from the cycle of birth, death, and rebirth), and *sutra / sutta* (a sermon or discourse attributed to the Buddha).

Since there is no single, universal system of transliteration for Buddhism's multilingual lexicon, and this book is not confined to any one language standard or Buddhist denomination, each foreign term is given here in what we believe to be its most familiar Romanized spelling, irrespective of its roots and doctrinal affiliations. For simplification, diacritical marks have been omitted. Additional information on word origins and definitions is included in the glossary. The terms *Burma* and *Burmese* are employed here because this book deals with past ages inextricably linked to those names—which may also be more familiar to the reader than the country's current official designation, *Myanmar*.

Throughout this book, the term "the Buddha" refers to *Sakyamuni Buddha*, the founder of Buddhism. Historical facts about him can be difficult to untangle from Asian mythology and folklore, partly because memorization and oral retelling, not the written word, were the principal means of preserving and transmitting his doctrine and life story for the first three or four centuries after his mortal life ended and he passed into *parinirvana*. It is also impossible to know if any facts have been altered or embellished during numerous phases of translation across the ages. The goal of this book is not to scrutinize those possibilities or to analyze Buddhism's supernatural aspects, but simply to introduce its core elements and the rich pageantry of its art.

Since Buddhist art is largely modeled after events concerning Sakyamuni Buddha's life and teachings, the first main section of this book traces his life story with artworks from the many regions where his doctrine has flourished. The second main section introduces the major schools of Buddhist thought which emerged as the teachings evolved and spread, and highlights the essential characteristics of their arts, especially as illustrated in the various Buddhas, bodhisattvas, and ritual objects found in each region. Buddhist beliefs and art spread from India by a number of paths: north to Central Asia, China, Korea, and Japan; northeast to Nepal and Tibet; south to Sri Lanka; east to Southeast Asia. Section Two therefore discusses those countries in that sequence. The bibliography lists some of the numerous works available for further study.

I.

THE LIFE AND TEACHINGS OF SAKYAMUNI BUDDHA

The Buddha's story begins with his birth as a prince, the son of King Suddhodana and Queen Maya, rulers of the Sakyas of Kapilavastu. The given and family names of the prince are recorded in Sanskrit as *Siddhartha Gautama*, and in Pali as *Siddhattha Gotama*. He achieved the title *Buddha*, or *Lord Buddha*, at age thirty-five when he attained enlightenment, the pure spiritual state of a fully awakened mind, liberated from all craving and attachment. His specific name and title—Sakyamuni Buddha (also spelled Shakyamuni Buddha)—distinguish him from the other enlightened masters said to have lived before him and the transcendent Buddhas who many believe reside in the heavens. Sakyamuni is also the "Historical Buddha"—the only Buddha whose lifetime in our physical world is known from material evidence.

Before his enlightenment he had been a *bodhisattva* ("enlightenment being")—a saintly individual who has accrued boundless wisdom, compassion, discipline, and spiritual merit through good deeds and exemplary conduct during an immense span of lifetimes and is thus destined to attain enlightenment and become a Buddha. In this context a bodhisattva can be defined as a "Buddha-to-be" or "Future Buddha."

The story of the Bodhisattva's life as Prince Siddhartha can be said to begin in the Tushita Heaven, a cosmic realm where he had been reborn as a *deva* (celestial being or god) following a previous lifetime on Earth, one of countless prior existences he had experienced in myriad forms. Although *devas* may enjoy an exalted level of existence in the heavens, they are still, like all beings, subject to the cycle of birth, death, and rebirth. (*Deva* is usually a male form, *devi* a female.) Since Buddhists contend that true enlightenment

Fig. 3. *Queen Maya's Dream.* Ink and colors on silk, 5⅞ x 6½ in. (15 x 16.5 cm). Dunhuang, China, Tang dynasty, 9th century.

and liberation from this cycle can only be achieved in the human realm, it was necessary for the Bodhisattva to have one final lifetime in our mortal world.

From his vantage in heaven, he considered when and where his final rebirth should occur, and chose Queen Maya to be his mother. He then appeared to the queen while she dreamed one evening, descending from the heavens in the form of a six-tusked white elephant and entering her sleeping body through her right side to achieve conception. A painting from Dunhuang, China shows the queen asleep in her palace chambers as the Bodhisattva appears (fig. 3). This interpretation pictures him as an infant seated atop a white elephant and accompanied by two celestial attendants.

When the queen spoke of her dream to her husband King Suddhodana, he summoned a group of learned Brahmins. They interpreted her vision as a sign that she was with child, a son who would one day become either a world monarch or a great spiritual leader.

Queen Maya gave birth to Siddhartha ten months later in a wooded grove called Lumbini, not far from the palace. Theravada tradition estimates the year was 623 B.C. Other biographies say 563 or 566 B.C. The queen is said to have given birth while standing beneath a *sala* tree, her right hand grasping a branch for support. Siddhartha was born from her right side in a painless delivery and was received by the gods Brahma and Indra, who presented him to his mother. Indra, king of the gods and lord of Trayastrimsa, Heaven of the thirty-three Gods, is also known to Buddhists as "Sakra" or "Sakka." Hindus say his complexion is golden; Southeast Asian art routinely pictures him green in color. Brahma, lord of creation, is especially recognizable, having four faces and four arms.

A gilt copper and brass statuette produced in Nepal early in the nineteenth century commemorates the moment of birth (fig. 4). The stylized form of the newborn Prince Siddhartha is seen emerging from Queen Maya's right side, his hands pressed together in the *anjali mudra* gesture of respectful greeting. In other portrayals of his birth, the Queen is sometimes attended by another lovely young woman, her sister Prajapati. They are shown together in a contemporary Thai painting of this event (see fig. 143).

Two streams of water flowed down from the heavens, one cool and one warm, to bathe the newborn infant. Lotus flowers sprouted up from the soil beneath his feet as he took seven steps. The lotus or water lily is an emblem of purity, rising up from roots in a muddy pond to blossom in the sun—and thus can be a surrogate for

the Buddha and his teachings, which rise above worldly defilements to guide humankind to liberation. The lotus can also serve as a badge of divinity. After surveying the Earth and seeing there was no one equal to him, the newborn Siddhartha pointed to the heavens and said, "I am the foremost in the world, the eldest in the world, the most excellent in the world. This is my last birth. No future births exist for me."

On the fifth day after Siddhartha's birth, King Suddhodana held a lavish palace festival to announce his son's name and royal rank. Among the Brahmin priests attending this event, eight who were skilled soothsayers examined the infant. They declared that Siddhartha possessed all of the thirty-two *lakshana* (major auspicious marks of perfection on the body) identifying a *mahapurusa* ("great man"). Seven of the priests offered a prophecy that when Siddhartha reached manhood he would have only two conceivable destinies. Either he would become universal monarch of a vast empire, or he would choose the religious life and become a Buddha, a great spiritual teacher who would release humankind from *duhkha*—the suffering and frustration that plague all beings. The eighth Brahmin, a young priest named Kaundinya, predicted as certain that the boy would take the religious path.

An elderly, revered sage named Asita also came to see the young prince. When King Suddhodana lifted Siddhartha toward him, the infant raised one foot to Asita's head. Tears came to the elderly man's eyes, and when he saw the king's worried expression he quickly explained there was no need for concern—all the signs did indicate that Siddhartha would grow to become a Buddha and teach the path to enlightenment—Asita was distressed only because he was already so old that he was not likely to live long enough to hear Siddhartha's teachings. In the following excerpt from *The Voice of the Buddha* (*Lalitavistara Sutra*), Asita describes for King Suddhodana the thirty-two *lakshana*, or major marks of perfection, as they appeared on the young prince's body:

Fig. 4. (Opposite) *Queen Maya Giving Birth to Prince Siddhartha, the Future Buddha*. Gilt copper and brass, inlaid with semiprecious stones, H: 21½ in. (54.5 cm). Nepal, early 19th century.

"What are these thirty-two signs? They are these, Great King, the head of the young Siddhartha is crowned with a protuberance of the skull. This sign is the first mark of a great man. Siddhartha's hair whorls to the right, is curly and blue-black and brilliant like a peacock's neck. He has a broad and smooth forehead. A tuft of hair, Great King, arises in the middle of his eyebrows, as bright as snow or silver. He has eyelashes like those of a heifer. He has deep black eyes and forty uniform teeth, closely set and perfectly white.

"He has a voice like Brahma's, O Great King, and an excellent sense of taste. He has a long and slender tongue, the jaw of a lion, and well-rounded arms. The seven principal parts of the body are lofty. His chest and shoulders are broad. He has fine, golden skin, and when he stands erect, his hands reach to his knees. His upper body is like a lion's. The young Sarvarthasiddha's [another name for Siddhartha] figure is like the trunk of the fig tree, O Great King. His hairs grow one by one, and they curl toward the right at their tip. His private parts are hidden in a sheath. His thighs are well-developed, and he has the legs of the king of gazelles.

"His fingers are long, the soles of his feet are broad, and his stride is long. His hands and feet are soft and delicate, and his toes and fingers are joined by a membrane up to the first joint. On the soles of the young Sarvarthasiddha's feet, O Great King, are two wheels—beautiful, luminous, brilliant, and white, each with a thousand spokes between hub and rim. His feet are even and well-placed.

"O Your Majesty, the young Sarvarthasiddha is endowed with the totality of the thirty-two signs of a great man. And, Great King, such signs are not those of a Cakravartin, but are those of a Bodhisattva.[2]

The *sutra* continues with Asita's description of the eighty secondary marks of a great man, all of which were also seen on Siddhartha's body. Many of the auspicious marks became standard characteristics for images of a Buddha. Most conspicuous and universally applied is the first mark, the *ushnisha*, a protuberance atop the Buddha's head signifying his immense wisdom. The *urna* (a tuft of hair, usually within a small mole) can appear between the eyebrows of Buddhas and bodhisattvas. It indicates superhuman vision and is comparable to the "third eye" on the forehead of many deities.

The possibility of Siddhartha abandoning their ancestral throne worried King Suddhodana. He wished his son would choose the first path and become a powerful, esteemed monarch, continuing their family's royal line. He therefore resolved to raise Siddhartha surrounded by luxury, insulated from any discomfort or pain that might spark interest in a spiritual quest. Queen Maya died seven days after giving birth—as the Buddhist scriptures say the mothers of all bodhisattvas do—and was reborn in the Trayastrimsa Heaven. Her younger sister Prajapati, also a consort of King Suddhodana, took up the responsibility of raising Siddhartha.

Prince Siddhartha came of age amid the pomp and splendor and worldly enjoyments of three palaces built for him by his father—one for the winter, one for the hot season, one for the rainy season. Beautiful female musicians entertained him; servants pampered him. He was given the finest education and excelled in every subject. Nevertheless, he often felt dissatisfied with life. On one occasion during his youth, while accompanying his father at a plowing ceremony in a farming area, Siddhartha sat in the cross-legged yoga posture beneath the shading branches of a *jambu* or rose apple tree and experimented with meditation. He achieved a deep meditative state lasting a good part of the day. Onlookers noticed that as time passed, the shadows cast from other nearby trees moved in their natural way, yet the shadow of the rose apple tree remained fixed in position around Siddhartha, shielding him from the hot sun. A variation of this legend tells that while meditating, Siddhartha floated up and levitated above those watching him.

At age sixteen, Siddhartha married a princess named Yasodhara.[3] Their marriage furthered his pleasant, insulated existence, but Siddhartha still felt restless, unfulfilled, disenchanted with life. When a son was born to them he named the child *Rahula*, a word meaning a fetter or constraint.

Prince Siddhartha's life reached a decisive turning point through a spiritual awakening known as the "Four Sights" or "Four Signs." Traveling outside the palace by chariot with an attendant named Chandaka, he saw for the first time a withered old man so feeble and bent he could only hobble along painfully leaning on a stick. Siddhartha asked Chandaka what was wrong with the man. Chandaka answered that this was simply an elderly person, different from them only by his many more years. It saddened Siddhartha to realize that every living creature must in due course suffer this deterioration of old age. Later they saw the second sight, a sick man lying helpless on the roadside, moaning in pain. Siddhartha was disheartened by Chandaka's revelation that this man was ill beyond help, and that such diseases and afflictions were unpredictable accidents of fate, which could strike anyone, young or old, commoner or royalty. Third and most jolting sight was a decaying corpse being prepared for cremation. This was the first time Siddhartha had ever seen a dead body, and he was shocked by Chandaka's explanation that all living things must meet this same end; all must eventually die. He then saw the fourth sight, a holy man, a wandering monk who had abandoned the material world to seek spiritual truths. The monk's tranquility and devotion to searching for enlightenment impressed and inspired Siddhartha. This man represented the hope of finding liberation from the miseries of pain and death.

Another version of this story tells that Siddhartha experienced these revelations on four separate trips outside the palace. In artworks, however, they are usually shown together, compressed into a single dramatic scene such as a Thai painting of Siddhartha in royal

attire atop his chariot, questioning Chandaka about the four men (fig. 5). According to yet another account, King Suddhodana always ordered the streets cleared of the sick and aged before his son traveled them—thus the old man, the sick man, the corpse, and the monk were illusions conjured by the gods to reveal life's dark realities to Siddhartha.

Fig. 5. *Prince Siddhartha Sees the Four Sights*. Acrylics on wood, 15⅛ x 10⅛ in. (38.4 x 25.6 cm). Thailand, 20th century.

The "Four Sights" and their profound influence on Siddhartha's view of existence led him to realize the pointless folly of pursuing material luxuries and fleeting pleasures. He decided to relinquish his wealth and royal privileges, become an ascetic himself and seek a solution to human suffering. Knowing his family would not agree with his decision, he arranged to leave the palace secretly that night. In fig. 6, we watch the evening of his Great Departure as painted in the folding pages of a nineteenth-century illustrated manuscript from Burma. The first scene is in the foreground, with Siddhartha giving a silent goodbye to his wife and young son, asleep in their quarters. Chandaka waits nearby holding Siddhartha's white horse, Kanthaka.

Fig. 6. *The Great Departure* (*Prince Siddhartha Leaving His Palace*). Illustrated manuscript, 18½ x 29⅛ in. (47 x 74 cm). Burma, 19th century.

Fig. 7. *The Great Renunciation* (*Prince Siddhartha Cutting Off His Hair*). Stone wall carving, Borobudur, Indonesia, circa 9th century.

The upper right corner shows the second scene—Siddhartha leaving the palace on horseback. Chandaka accompanies him, holding on to Kanthaka's tail. Four celestial beings muffle the sounds of the horse's hooves with their hands to avoid waking the palace guards as Siddhartha, now twenty-nine years old, rides away on his quest to solve the mysteries of universal suffering.

When he reached a forest near the Anoma River, Siddhartha dismounted from his horse. A relief carving on the stone walls of the enormous Borobudur Buddhist monument in Indonesia pictures Siddhartha at this moment, standing at the left, raising his sword with his right hand and cutting off his hair. This ritual, his Great Renunciation, confirmed his abandoning of all earthly attachments and marked his transition from crown prince to wandering ascetic (fig. 7). He stands upon a lotus pedestal, an indication of his divinity. Chandaka is seated at center, holding Siddhartha's discarded headpiece and scabbard. A celestial being witnesses this event, hovering overhead to receive the locks of Siddhartha's hair, which he will carry off and enshrine in the Trayastrimsa Heaven.

Siddhartha sent Chandaka back to the palace with his horse, to return his royal clothing and jewelry to his family, and to tell them not to worry for him. Some legends add that his horse Kanthaka died from grief when his master departed alone. From that day on, Siddhartha wore the humble yellow robes of an ascetic and was also known as Sakyamuni (Sage of the Sakya people).

He journeyed to Rajagriha city, capital of the Magadha kingdom, where he received food offerings. King Bimbisara, ruler of this state, met with him and was so impressed by his appearance, bearing, and noble origins that he offered him half the kingdom. Siddhartha declined, reaffirming his renunciation of worldly possessions and his determination to achieve spiritual liberation. He did agree to the king's request that he visit Rajagriha again after he had attained enlightenment.

Siddhartha applied himself to ascetic practices such as clenching the teeth while pressing the tongue to

Fig. 8. *Siddhartha Fasting.* Black stone, H: 33⅛ in. (84 cm). Gandhara, Pakistan, 3rd–4th centuries.

the palate, holding his breath for long intervals, and prolonged fasting. He mastered the techniques and use of meditation. Eventually he met five other ascetics. Eldest of the five was Kaundinya, the same priest who had seen Siddhartha as a newborn child and had predicted he would someday choose the religious life. The other four ascetics were named Vaspa, Bhadrika, Mahanaman, and Asvajit. All five joined Siddhartha and his regimen of austerities, believing he would lead them to spiritual enlightenment. They meditated for hours in the open air, purposely exposing their bodies to the extremes of heat and cold of the changing seasons. They existed on the fewest morsels of food and drops of water needed to sustain them.

This phase of Siddhartha's life is remembered in a stone statue from Gandhara (fig. 8). His emaciated body is sun-baked black and shrunken to skin and bones, his face is gaunt and constricted, with deep hollows under the eyes. The profound intensity expressed by this image is accentuated by the way its upper torso leans slightly to one side, as if nearing collapse from the strain of self-mortification.

Six years of this harsh regimen of self-denial and abstinence brought Siddhartha near to death from starvation. At this point, the god Indra intervened. Taking the guise of a wandering musician playing a three-stringed lute, Indra demonstrated how plucking a string which is too slack results in a sound that can barely be heard; a string too tight will break; but a well-tuned string produces beautiful sounds. This prompted Siddhartha to a realization that grew into a cornerstone of his teachings—that the most effective approach to life is to avoid both extremes of human behavior: unbridled self-indulgence, which is evil, destructive and pointless; and self-mortification, which is painful, degrading, and pointless. Follow instead the Middle Path, a path of moderation leading to awareness, wisdom, and enlightenment.

When Siddhartha announced he was ending his experiment with asceticism and would pursue a new philosophy of moderation, his five companions left him, thinking he was turning his back on the spiritual life to return to material comforts. Alone and weakened from intense fasting, he began his return to health by bathing in the nearby Nairanjana River, and accepted an offering of rice-milk in a golden bowl given by a young woman named Sujata (fig. 9). He ate the meal by the riverside, then sought a sign to confirm he was pursuing the correct path. He knelt beside the river's edge and released the empty bowl into the water: If it floated upstream against the current he would know he was following the true course to attaining supreme wisdom and becoming a Buddha. The bowl drifted out to the middle of the river and did float swiftly upstream, finally spinning in a small whirlpool which pulled it beneath the surface. It sank down into the underwater palace of a *naga raja* (Sanskrit: "serpent king")

Fig. 9. *Monk's Fan. Painted with Sujata offering rice-milk to Siddhartha. Reverse side tells the event that the fan commemorates.* H (overall): 36¼ in. (92.1 cm). Thailand, 20th century.

named Kala, coming to rest on the riverbed beside the bowls of three previous Buddhas of earlier times who had traveled the same route seeking enlightenment.

Siddhartha crossed the river and met a farmer carrying bundles of soft grass. The farmer gave him one bundle as an offering, to use as a mat. When Siddhartha reached a wooded grove, he spread the grass beneath a large fig tree's shading branches and sat down to meditate. He vowed to remain in meditation at that spot until he attained enlightenment and found a way to put an end to human suffering. A temple wall painting from Sri Lanka visualizes him seated beneath the tree in a classical yoga position—legs tucked together, right atop left in the *virasana* posture; hands joined on the lap, right atop left in the meditation pose known as *dhyana mudra*; body straight in bearing, motionless yet relaxed (fig. 10).

Fig. 10. *Siddhartha Meditating Beneath the Bodhi Tree.* Wall painting (detail), Cave #2, Maharajavihara, Dambulla, Sri Lanka, circa 1760.

Meditating under the fig tree, Siddhartha gained complete comprehension of the endless cycle of birth, death, and rebirth—and the impermanence of all things. That night he attained enlightenment and the Three Knowledges: During the night's first watch, early evening, he was able to recall details of his own countless prior lives spanning eons of time. In the second watch, the middle of the night, he was able to see the passing away and rebirths of multitudes of sentient beings. Each one's *karma*—the accumulated sum of their physical, verbal, and mental actions—determined their state of rebirth into one of the six *gati*, or realms of existence: hell-beings (*naraka*), hungry ghosts (*preta*), animals (*tiryagyoni*), humans (*manusya*), lower gods (*asura*), and gods (*deva*). In the night's third and final watch, the last hours of darkness, Siddhartha attained the knowledge of the destruction of defilements—he knew with certainty he had freed himself from the emotional attachments that bind all beings to the endless cycle of birth, death, and rebirth. He achieved enlightenment, nirvana in this world—pure and total detachment from all forms of craving. This would unquestionably be his final life, his final existence, and when it came to an end he would pass into *parinirvana*—complete and final nirvana, from which there is no rebirth. His enlightenment can also be described as an "awakening" to the true nature of things.[4]

Fig. 11 is a richly detailed Thai painting portraying his enlightenment in three conflated scenes. Beginning on the right side, Mara, the personification of evil, rides atop a war elephant and leads his army of archers, demons, and animal-like beings to attack Siddhartha in an attempt to destroy his concentration. Next, in the center, Siddhartha touches the ground (in this rare variation, with his left hand) and the Earth Goddess appears as his witness. She wrings her long black hair to unleash a flood of water that sweeps away Mara and his hordes. They are shown again in the final scene on the left, beaten back and swept away by the swirling deluge, their arrows and spears now transformed into

Fig. 11. (Opposite)
The Buddha Subduing Mara.
Oil on canvas (Detail),
65 x 27 in. (165 x 68.6 cm).
Thailand, 19th century.

Fig. 12. *The Enlightenment of Sakyamuni Buddha*. Gilt bronze, H: 16¼ in. (41.3 cm). Style of Lanna, Northern Thailand, 11th–18th centuries.

Fig. 13. *The Enlightenment of Sakyamuni Buddha*. Bronze, H: 57 in. (144.8 cm). Rangoon, Burma (Myanmar), circa 18th century.

Fig. 14. *The Enlightenment of Sakyamuni Buddha*. Silver, H: 15 in. (38.1 cm). Tibet, 19th century.

flowers by Siddhartha's purity. Asian custom often associates meritorious acts with the pouring of lustral water during religious ceremonies. The water stream gushing down from the Earth Goddess' hair thus equates to the vast store of merit accrued by Siddhartha through his myriad lifetimes as a bodhisattva—a fitting device to finalize his victory over Mara and mark the moment that he became the Buddha, or more specifically, *Sakyamuni Buddha*. In another version of this legend, the defeat of Mara occurs directly before the Enlightenment.

The menagerie of grotesque demons and vicious beasts populating Mara's army can be interpreted as embodiments of the addictive passions of the human mind such as lust, pride, cruelty, and envy that enable Mara to hold mankind in bondage. The anonymous painter employed a popular Southeast Asian formula that expresses this complex allegory with some license by including European soldiers with modern rifles among Mara's hordes. This conveys the timelessness and universality of the struggle between forces of good and evil—and suggests as well an Asian perspective of Europe's colonial powers. Such mixing of modern characters and devices with depictions of ancient situations had long been common in the visual arts. Other devotional paintings from Burma and Thailand, for instance, show the Buddha traveling by railway train and steamboat, sometimes encountering Westerners in costumes of the artist's era. Only in recent times did artists become concerned with accurately portraying historical minutiae in such compositions.

The image of Siddhartha touching the ground (nearly always with his right hand) to call the Earth Goddess to witness his enlightenment—and to mark his becoming the Buddha—is one of Asia's most widely celebrated pictorial traditions, again and again the main icon in Buddhist temples (figs. 12, 13, 14). The fig tree beneath which Siddhartha sat in meditation and became the Buddha was given the name Bodhi (Enlightenment) Tree. Its location came to be known as *Bodhgaya*.

The spot beneath the tree where the Buddha sat is usually pictured as a stylized pedestal called *Vajrasana* (Diamond Throne), a monument to the Buddha's enlightenment placed there by King Asoka in the third century B.C.

After attaining enlightenment, the Buddha continued meditating in the precincts of Bodhgaya for seven weeks. This period and the events that occurred then are sometimes referred to as the "Seven Stations of Enlightenment."[5] During the first week, he remained in seated meditation beneath the Bodhi Tree. The second week, he stood gazing at the tree while meditating. For the third week, he did walking meditation along a golden path. The fourth week was spent in seated meditation in a jeweled chamber. In the fifth week, he sat in meditation under a banyan tree belonging to a group of goatherds; some pictures of this interval include Mara's three seductive daughters again trying unsuccessfully to tempt him with worldly pleasures.

Sitting in meditation during the sixth week, the Buddha attained a state of deep mental absorption, unaware of a fierce rainstorm that was causing a flood. Muchalinda, a benevolent *naga raja* who lived nearby, feared for the Enlightened One's safety and lifted him up atop his own coiled body, above the rising flood waters, spreading his seven-headed hood overhead as a protective canopy to deflect the rain. This is replicated in a sandstone statue from Angkor, Cambodia (fig. 15). Other similar images give Muchalinda one, three, five, or nine heads; another rare version has him coiled completely around and above the Buddha's body to shield him from the storm and its cold winds. The downpour continued for seven days. When the sky cleared, Muchalinda gently withdrew his serpent's coils from around the Buddha, then magically transformed himself into the apparition of a young man. In this form, shown in a Tibetan gilt copper image, Muchalinda raised his hands in reverence and offered gifts to the Buddha (fig. 16).

Fig. 15. (Opposite) *Crowned Buddha protected by Muchalinda, the Serpent King.* Sandstone, H: 35¼ in. (89.5 cm). Angkor, Cambodia, approx. 1150–1175.

Fig. 16. *The Naga Raja in Human Form Offering Gifts to the Buddha*. Gilt copper, H: 23⅝ in. (60 cm). Southern Tibet, early 15th century.

In the Buddha's seventh week of meditations at Bodhgaya, the four *lokapalas*, guardian gods of the cardinal directions, each gave him a bowl for receiving alms and he applied his powers to meld the four bowls into one. Two merchants named Tapussa and Bhallika appeared and presented offerings of rice and honey to the Buddha and became his first lay followers, an event that can be recounted by seated images of him holding his alms bowl.

At this point the Buddha pondered whether he should reveal what he had learned to the rest of the world. He knew that some underlying concepts, such as the law of interdependent arising,[6] might be difficult for ordinary people to fathom. When the god Brahma encouraged him to spread his knowledge, the Buddha agreed, and decided to seek out the five ascetics who had been his companions and present the teachings to them. Knowing the five monks were staying in the vicinity of Sarnath, he walked there and met them in a Deer Park near the town. Initially the five agreed among themselves to avoid the Buddha, not to speak to him, believing he had abandoned the religious life for worldly pleasures. But when he told them of the knowledge he had acquired, they recognized it as the ultimate, irrefutable truth and accepted him as their teacher.

The foundation of the Buddha's teachings is built upon "The Four Noble Truths."[7] The first Noble Truth is suffering—birth is suffering, existence is suffering, decay is suffering, death is suffering. The second Noble Truth is that the cause of suffering is craving—sensual craving, craving to be, and craving not to be. The third Noble Truth is that suffering can be ended through the elimination of craving. The fourth Noble Truth is that the path to the elimination of craving and the end of suffering is the path to nirvana, and this is the Middle Path taught by the Buddha—the Noble Eightfold Path comprising: (1) right view, (2) right thought, (3) right speech, (4) right action, (5) right livelihood, (6) right effort, (7) right mindfulness, (8) right concentration.

A superficial reading of these teachings about suffering might give the mistaken view that Buddhism is pessimistic or negative about life. The Buddhist monk and teacher Rev. Dr. W. Rahula explains:

> First of all, Buddhism is neither pessimistic nor optimistic. If anything at all, it is realistic, for it takes a realistic view of life and of the world. It looks at things objectively (*yathabhutam*). It does not falsely lull you into living in a fool's paradise, nor does it frighten and agonize you with all kinds of imaginary fears and sins . . . a true Buddhist is the happiest of beings. He has no fears or anxieties. He is always calm and serene, and cannot be upset or dismayed by changes or calamities, because he sees things as they are. The Buddha was never melancholy or gloomy. He was described by his contemporaries as "ever-smiling" (*mihitapubbamgama*). In Buddhist painting and sculpture the Buddha is always represented with a countenance happy, serene, contented and compassionate.[8]

The Buddha's teachings are referred to as the *Dharma*, a Sanskrit word whose interpretation depends on context and can apply to topics such as law, doctrine, justice, and truth. The Pali language form is *Dhamma*. The Buddhist Dharma can be symbolized by a *chakra* (wheel) or *dharmachakra* ("Wheel of the Law")—often shaped with eight spokes to represent the Noble Eightfold Path. In India, the *chakra* has long been emblematic of a powerful emperor or *chakravartin* ("wheel ruler"— an extraordinary monarch whose chariot wheels roll everywhere unobstructed). *Chakravartin* has been applied by some as an epithet for a Buddha and the universal application of his precepts.

A famous fifth-century sandstone sculpture from India's Gupta period depicts the Buddha preaching his first sermon in the Deer Park (fig. 17). Both hands are raised in front of his chest, index finger and thumb touching, to indicate the *dharmachakra mudra* of

Fig. 17. (Opposite) *The Buddha Preaching His First Sermon*. Sandstone, H: 63 in. (1.60 m). Sarnath, India, Gupta period, 5th century.

Fig. 18. *The Buddha Preaching His First Sermon*. Carved, painted and gilded teakwood, 98 x 46 in. (2.48 x 1.17 m). Wat Palelai Temple, Singapore.

"Turning the Wheel of the Law," or "Setting the Wheel of the Law in Motion." Artworks picturing him with just his right hand raised, index finger and thumb touching in the *vitarka mudra* (teaching or discussion gesture), can represent the first sermon as well. One example is the carved and gilded teakwood door of a Singapore temple showing the Buddha preaching to the five ascetics (fig. 18).

Kaundinya was first of the ascetics to comprehend the teachings and was ordained by the Buddha as the first Buddhist monk (Sanskrit, *bhikshu*; Pali, *bhikkhu*) in what came to be the *Sangha*, the community of monks, nuns, and novices.[9] The remaining four ascetics received further instruction and were then ordained. From Sarnath the Buddha journeyed to other areas, initiating new followers to the Dharma, ordaining those who wished to become monks and sending them on to spread the doctrine for the benefit and welfare of all people. Some of his precepts could be termed revolutionary. He opposed slavery and India's caste system and all other kinds of injustice and oppression. He repudiated the magical rites and animal sacrifices practiced by Brahmin priests of the time. While acknowledging the existence of gods and other celestials, he stressed that each mortal being possesses the spiritual power to control his own destiny without divine intervention. And that a god, upon the depletion of his meritorious karma, might be reborn in one of the lowest realms of existence, while a human being, by leading a pure life and amassing merit, has the capacity to be reborn as a god.

Remembering his promise that after attaining enlightenment he would again visit King Bimbisara, the Buddha traveled to Rajagriha accompanied by many monks and supporters. The king led a throng of people in welcoming them, and donated a bamboo grove called *Veluvana* to be the first monastery to shelter the Buddha and his followers.

Also staying in Rajagriha at the time were two young ascetics whose names are recorded in Sanskrit as

Sariputra and Maudgalyayana. Pali texts call them Sariputta and Moggallana. These two young men had been close friends since childhood, had come of age together, and had given up comfortable existences in their wealthy families to seek spiritual fulfillment as wandering monks. Sariputra happened one day to meet the *bhikshu* Asvajit, one of the Buddha's first disciples. As a result of that meeting, Sariputra and Maudgalyayana went to the bamboo grove to hear the Dharma. After listening to the Buddha's sermon, Sariputra and Maudgalyayana were ordained into the Sangha. Soon afterwards, both young men acquired an understanding of the Dharma beyond all others in the clergy, and became two of the Buddha's chief disciples. Artworks often picture them as attendants standing at his sides (see fig. 1).

At about this same time another monk was ordained. His given name was Pippali, but he became known as Mahakasyapa when he joined the Buddha's following. He would eventually become the senior monk in the Sangha and play a significant role in preserving and propagating the Dharma after the Buddha's death.

While the Buddha was residing and preaching at Rajagriha, his father King Suddhodana sent an envoy to invite him to Kapilavastu for a visit with their family. The messenger arrived in Rajagriha and found his way to the field where the Buddha was delivering a sermon. Upon hearing the Dharma, the messenger was converted and received ordination into the monkhood. Since monks avoid worldly affairs, he did not present the king's invitation. King Suddhodana dispatched one more representative, and another, and yet another—with the same outcome nine times. The message was at last delivered to the Buddha by a friend named Kaludayin. In one rendition of this legend, each of King Suddhodana's nine emissaries is accompanied by a thousand men, all of whom take the monastic vows.

The Buddha accepted his father's invitation and traveled to Kapilavastu with an entourage of attendants and disciples. When they arrived at the city, the local

people treated them with a lack of interest and respect, unaware of the Buddha's attainments since leaving their land as a young prince years earlier. Deciding it was appropriate to demonstrate his powers, the Buddha performed what became known as the "Miracle of the Pairs." He floated up and levitated above the crowd, flames radiating from his upper body, torrents of water spraying out from the lower part (fig. 19). Suddenly the paired flows of fire and water reversed—flames appeared from his lower body and water flowed from his upper torso. Then the paired elements changed again—fire came from his right side and water streamed from his left. In all, there came twenty-two different formations of the fire and water pairs, after which King Suddhodana joined the gathering in offering reverence to his son.[10] One commentary suggests the words "fire" and "water" used in this description may refer to

Fig. 19. *The Buddha Performing Miracles at Kapilavastu*. Mural painting (detail), Wat Rajasittharam, Thonburi, Thailand, 18th century.

brilliant red and blue rays of light radiating from the Buddha's body.

Next morning, the Buddha led his monks about the city with their alms bowls, receiving offerings of food from the townsfolk (fig. 20). King Suddhodana was upset to hear his son seemed to be begging for food. He hurried to the Buddha and asked why was this happening, why was his princely son born of royal lineage taking charity like a beggar? The Buddha explained that this was now his way of life, the way of the Buddhas, to accept alms from those wishing to offer them. The king then escorted him to the palace where ministers and the royal family welcomed him with reverence. Accompanied by two monks and members of his family, the Buddha also met with Yasodhara,

Fig. 20. (Left) *The Buddha with His Alms Bowl.* Gilt wood, H: 11⅜ in. (28.9 cm). Cambodia, 18th century.

Fig. 21. (Below) *The Buddha visits his Family in Kapilavastu.* Oil on canvas, 23½ x 34½ in. (59.7 x 87.6 cm). Burma (Myanmar), 19th century.

his wife before his renunciation. An oil painting from Burma interprets this event (fig. 21).

Other noteworthy situations occurred during that visit in Kapilavastu. Nanda, younger half-brother of the Buddha, was to be confirmed as heir to the throne and given a bride, but after hearing the Buddha teaching, he abdicated his royal position and ordained as a monk. A day or two later, Yasodhara told her young son Rahula a palace tale describing a rich royal treasure said to be held by his father, the Buddha. She brought Rahula to meet the Buddha and prompted the boy to ask for the treasure as his inheritance. The Buddha listened to his young son's request, then explained his own conviction that wealth and possessions do not generate happiness, that true contentment comes only from wisdom and insight. Instead of giving material riches to Rahula, he had the boy ordained as the first novice monk. A stone narrative sculpture from Gandhara shows this scene (fig. 22). The Buddha is seated at center. On the left, Yasodhara holds Rahula on her lap as his hair is cut for the ordination

Fig. 22. *The Buddha visits his Former Wife and their Son*. Phyllite, 10½ x 16½ in. (26.7 x 41.9 cm). Gandhara, Pakistan, approx. A.D. 100–300.

ceremony. In the picture's right side, the newly ordained Rahula is kneeling in reverence. The Corinthian pilaster on the far left was a common motif for dividing narrative scenes in Gandharan sculpture, another reminder of the strong Hellenistic influence on this school of art.

News of Rahula's admission to the monkhood troubled King Suddhodana. He confided to the Buddha that all three of his sons had left him for the religious life: his first son, the Buddha; his second son, Nanda; and now his grandson, Rahula—and he felt this was an unfair burden for one man to endure. The Buddha sympathized with his father and established a rule which stands today in the Sangha—that every young man desiring to join the order of monks must have the consent of his parents (or wife, if married) before he can ask to be ordained.

Fig. 23. *Standing Buddha, "Stopping his Relatives from Quarreling over Water."* Gilt bronze, H: 28¾ in. (73 cm). Ayutthaya, Thailand, 17th century.

During the fifth year of the Buddha's ministry, King Suddhodana passed away. Soon afterward, their Sakya clan of Kapilavastu became embroiled in a dispute with the Koliyas of a neighboring city over water rights to the Rohini River, which flowed down from the Himalayas' southern peaks, irrigating farmlands in both territories. The conflict escalated and threatened to result in bloodshed. The Buddha was kin to both factions since his mother, Queen Maya, had been a Koliya princess, so he was trusted and respected by all concerned. He met with leaders from the two clans and counseled them that water was indeed valuable, but not near the worth of human life. The Sakyas and the Koliyas accepted his compromise solution of sharing the river equally to settle their feud. Images such as a gilt bronze statue from Ayutthaya, Thailand, with the Buddha raising his right hand in the *abhaya mudra*, are often associated with this event and referred to as "Stopping his Relatives from Quarreling over Water" (fig. 23).

Another famous episode in the Buddha's biography occurred in a village beside the Nairanjana River while he visited three brothers—Uruvilva Kasyapa, Nadi Kasyapa, and Gaya Kasyapa—leaders of a cult of fire-worshiping ascetics. In the course of his time with them, the Buddha tamed a fierce, fire-breathing *naga* serpent; was greeted reverently by the four *lokapala* guardian gods; and read Uruvilva Kasyapa's thoughts. He performed a host of miracles as well, most notably stopping the rising waters of the nearby river, which had flooded the village during a severe rainstorm. Witnessing these marvels and hearing the Buddha preaching, the Kasyapa brothers and their one thousand followers asked to be ordained. This series of events is usually remembered by images of the Buddha standing with his left and right hands raised in *abhaya mudra*, stopping the flood or "Calming the Waters," as shown by a gilt wood statue from Laos (fig. 24).

The two legends just described—"Stopping his Relatives from Quarreling over Water" and "Calming the Waters"—are at times confused with one another, understandably perhaps since both concern river themes and can be represented by standing portrayals of the Buddha's "granting protection" gesture of *abhaya mudra*. Such standing images are therefore associated somewhat interchangeably with either of these two events, whether the pose has one or two hands raised. Both forms are extensively seen on statues in Southeast Asian temples, more so the version with the Buddha's two hands raised, an icon now sanctified into a universal symbol of reconciliation and peace.

Fig. 24. *Standing Buddha, "Calming the Waters."* Gilt wood with glass inlay, H: 74¾ in. (1.90 m). Laos, 1700–1900.

Fig. 25. *Anathapindada Purchasing the Jetavana Park*. Mural painting, Kamsan-sa Temple, Kyongju, Korea.

Sometime after King Suddhodana's death, his widow Prajapati petitioned the Buddha, whom she had raised as her own son, to allow women to join his monastic order and to ordain her as the first female member. The Buddha initially refused. He cited potential difficulties like distraction and sexual temptation that might arise if women were admitted to the Sangha. Still, Prajapati persisted. She cut off her hair, clothed herself in yellow robes and repeated her request several times. Ananda, a senior monk and cousin of the Buddha who served as his personal attendant, interceded by voicing support for Prajapati's request. Finally the Buddha consented and allowed the admission of women, provided they comply with all codes and regulations of the Sangha and abide by eight additional rules of conduct. Prajapati accepted and became the first woman to be ordained as a Buddhist nun (Sanskrit, *bhikshuni*; Pali, *bhikkhuni*).

Another *vihara* or monastic dwelling place to shelter the Buddha and his disciples was established at Sravasti, capital city of the northeast Indian kingdom of the Kosalas. Costs to buy the land and construct this *vihara* were sponsored by a wealthy merchant known as Anathapindada, a staunch supporter of the Buddha. The location was a beautiful secluded park called Jetavana. Its original owner, a prince, initially refused to sell the tract. Anathapindada was only able to purchase the land by paying the prince an amount of gold sufficient to cover the park's entire grounds. In a Korean temple painting of this occasion, the prince is greeted by Anathapindada, whose workers are unloading gold sheets from the back of an elephant and positioning them on the ground (fig. 25).

Sravasti became a fashionable gathering place where ascetics, pundits, and religious leaders of all doctrines debated metaphysics and philosophy. When two rivals of the Buddha confronted him there with a challenge to display his powers, he accepted, saying he would perform a miracle near a large mango tree. Conniving supporters of the rival ascetics heard this news and tore up all the

Fig. 26. *The Miracle of Sravasti*. Mural painting (detail), Wat Suthat Thepwararam, Bangkok, Thailand, 19th century.

Fig. 27. *The Buddha Descending from Heaven*. Mural painting (detail), Wat Thong Thammachat, Thonburi, Thailand, 19th century.

mango trees in that area. When the Buddha arrived and found the grounds bare, he asked an onlooker to bury the pit of a mango fruit in the earth; then he poured water from his own hands onto the soil. A mango plant sprouted up from the ground, rapidly growing into a tree of full height with hundreds of images of the Buddha emblazoned across its branches. His rivals attempted to duplicate the miracle by hastily raising a makeshift wooden scaffold, but it collapsed, tossing them to the ground—as shown in the right-center part of the Thai temple painting of this "Miracle of Sravasti" in fig. 26. At this time the Buddha also repeated the "Miracle of the Pairs," levitating above the gathering while flames and streams of water radiated from his body in varying combinations, as he had done when visiting his family at Kapilavastu.

Shortly after performing the miracles at Sravasti, the Buddha applied supernatural powers to ascend into the Trayastrimsa Heaven to visit his mother, Queen Maya, who had passed away when he was just seven days old. He remained there for the three-month rainy season, explaining the Dharma to her. We see them together in the top section of a Thai temple painting (fig. 27). The boldly colored zigzag bands are a compositional device used to separate the scenes. At the picture's middle, the Buddha is returning to our world, descending from heaven down a triple staircase created by the gods. He walks down the central staircase, made from green gems; the gold and silver steps on either side are for the gods Brahma and Indra.

During the Buddha's sojourn in heaven, King Udayana of Kausambi was saddened by his absence and therefore assigned a renowned artist to produce a sandalwood statue of him. The sculptor was able to follow the Buddha up to heaven but could not directly observe his form because of a brilliant golden light radiating from his body. The sculptor had to carve the image while viewing shimmering glimpses of the Buddha's reflection in a celestial pool of water. Soft ripples over the water's surface were replicated in the statue as U-shaped, symmetrical rows of fine pleats cascading down its robes. This fabled image, which many faithful believe was the first likeness of the Buddha ever created, miraculously rose and hovered in mid-air to greet him when he returned to Earth. Neither that legendary statue nor any other depiction of the Buddha survives from his lifetime, still, the symmetrically stylized folds frequently seen on the monastic robes of early standing images are widely thought to be patterned after that sandalwood image, or copies of it.

A fine example of a "Udayana-style" standing statue from China has the Buddha's right hand raised in *abhaya mudra* and the left posed in *varada mudra* (bestowing a blessing or charity), a popular pairing convention in East Asian art (fig. 28). This statuette stands atop a base of lotus petals shaped as if rising from the celestial pool, which is represented by a band of waves between two rows of pearls. Tibetan influences are apparent in the face and hair being painted: "This practice of painting features on sculpture serves to bring the image to life—and, when consecrated, Tibetan images are considered to be living embodiments of deities."[11] The Chinese refer to this image style as *Zhantan* ("Red-sandalwood") *Buddha*, after the original sandalwood statue, which they believe was carried from India to China during the Tang dynasty (618–906). One Southeast Asian folk legend adds that, when the Buddha returned from the Trayastrimsa Heaven and the sandalwood image rose up to greet him, the Buddha gestured for the image to remain on its pedestal. This gesture, rarely seen in artworks, is indicated by the Buddha standing with his left hand raised in *abhaya mudra* and his right hand lowered to his side.

In about the tenth year of the Buddha's ministry a schism arose in the Sangha regarding certain rules of conduct when a monk at Kausambi was suspended for an infraction he did not acknowledge. This led to heated debate over interpretation and enforcement of the monastic rules. The Buddha tried to mediate in the

Fig. 28. *Udayana Style Buddha Image*. Gilt bronze, H: 7½ in. (19 cm). China, Yongle period (1403–24).

dispute but was not fully successful. Finally, he went alone for three months' retreat in the nearby Parileyyaka forest, where he was attended to and protected by its animals. One or more monkeys bringing him honey from a beehive for food usually represents this occasion. This "Miracle of the Monkeys" was painted into a palm leaf manuscript from Bihar, India (fig. 29). Especially favored in forest monasteries, depictions of this scene sometimes include a small elephant offering a gourd of drinking water to the Buddha.

Fig. 29. *Miracle of the Monkeys*. Segment of a Prajnaparamita manuscript, palm leaf, H: 2 in. (5.0 cm). Bihar, India, circa 1075–80.

A vicious thief and murderer was perhaps the most hardened scoundrel who found spiritual regeneration through the Dharma. He was called *Angulimala* ("Garland of Fingers") because he hacked a finger off the hand of each of his victims and wore them on a string around his neck. To flaunt his ruthlessness, he was about to kill his own mother as his one-thousandth victim. A contemporary Korean temple painting shows the Buddha intervening to save the woman (fig. 30). Angulimala then tried to chase and slay him instead,

Fig. 30. *Angulimala and the Buddha*. Mural painting, Chogye-sa Temple, Seoul, Korea, 20th century.

but was thwarted by the Buddha's powers. Soon afterward, Angulimala was converted and ordained as a monk. Some monks and lay people were appalled by his presence in the Sangha and attacked him with stones. The Buddha counseled Angulimala that this was his karma, the direct result of his past deeds, which he would have to endure to achieve spiritual liberation.

Vast numbers flocked to the Buddha and his teachings, yet he did encounter as well some detractors and jealous opponents. One cruel and vengeful antagonist was his cousin, a man named Devadatta. In the palaces of Kapilavastu during their childhood together, a sibling rivalry began when Devadatta used a bow and arrow to shoot down a white swan. The Buddha, then known as Prince Siddhartha, saved the bird by removing the arrow and intended to set it free. Devadatta angrily insisted the bird belonged to him since he had brought it down. Their conflict was settled by the royal family; they agreed with Siddhartha's plea that saving an animal's life is nobler than destroying it for sport.

When Siddhartha attained enlightenment, became the Buddha, and founded his monastic order, Devadatta followed him and was ordained. For a while he was a respected monk, but eventually the sour rivalry of their youth festered within Devadatta until he became so obsessively envious of his gifted relative that he attempted to wrest control of the Sangha. When this scheme failed, he plotted to kill the Buddha. First he sent a gang of archers to assassinate the Buddha, but when they heard his exposition of the Dharma, they joined his following. Devadatta then tried personally to kill the Buddha by hurling a large boulder down at him from atop the mountain known as Vulture's Peak, however just a fragment of the rock struck the Buddha's foot. Devadatta later attempted to slay the Buddha by unleashing a killer elephant named Nalagiri to attack him. A mural painting from a temple in Sri Lanka shows the Buddha taming the animal (fig. 31). Devadatta spent the brief remainder of his life

Fig. 31. *The Buddha Taming the Elephant Nalagiri.* By Soliyas Mendis. Mural painting, Kelaniya Rajamaha Vihara, Gampaha District, Sri Lanka, 1946.

agitating dissension in the Sangha, until one day he died. He sank down into the earth and was said to be reborn in the hell states.

Belief in reincarnation is a core tenet that Buddhism shares with Hinduism and other religions. But the doctrine of rebirth taught by the Buddha is unique in that it denies the existence of any eternal soul, teaching instead that what passes from one life to the next is a continuing energy stream comprising five transitory, ever-changing groups or aggregates: form, feeling, perception, volition, and consciousness. The Buddha sometimes explained this concept through *jataka* tales, recollections of his own prior lifetimes. Hundreds of *jataka* stories are described in the scriptures and in folk legends and are illustrated in narrative artworks. See, for example, fig. 43, a scene from the Vessantara *Jataka*—the story of the Buddha's previous lifetime as Prince Vessantara.

The Buddha continued teaching the Dharma into his eightieth year, by which time his health had declined considerably. He became seriously ill while traveling with Ananda and a group of other monks, and paused to rest amid a grove of *sala* trees belonging to the Malla clan of the northeast Indian town of Kusinara. Ananda prepared a couch for him to rest upon, between two trees. The Buddha then announced he would pass away that night and described multitudes of *devas* assembled around them, grieving that his death would soon come. Ananda asked the Buddha, how might his followers offer reverence to him once he had passed away. The Buddha named four places the faithful could visit in pilgrimage: his birthplace at Lumbini; the location where he attained enlightenment at Bodhgaya; the site of his first sermon in the Deer Park near Sarnath; and the place where he would attain *parinirvana*. He also gave detailed instructions on how, upon his death, his mortal remains were to be treated and cremated.[12]

Attended by a congregation of monks and devotees and Malla men and women offering their respects, the Buddha spent his final hours resting in the wooded grove near Kusinara. Among the gathering was an ascetic named Subhadra, who had some knowledge about the Buddha's teachings and wished to meet him to learn more. Ananda initially refused to allow this, not wanting to disturb the Buddha's rest, but the Buddha overheard their conversation and beckoned Subhadra to speak with him. The Buddha explained the Dharma and answered Subhadra's questions. At the end of their talk, he granted Subhadra's request to be admitted into the monkhood. Subhadra was the last disciple converted by the Buddha.

Fig. 32. *The Parinirvana of the Buddha*. Blue-gray schist, 10½ x 17½ in. (26.7 x 44.4 cm). Gandhara, Pakistan, 2nd–3rd centuries.

The Buddha's final words were a gentle yet clear exhortation to his followers: "All living things are subject to decay, but the truth remains forever. Work with diligence towards your salvation." He passed away on the full-moon day of the fifth lunar month (corresponding to April/May) in his eightieth year, entering *parinirvana*, the complete and final nirvana from which one is never reborn. This calendar date is now observed worldwide as the holy day *Vesak*, commemorating his birth, enlightenment, and *parinirvana*. The year of his passing is recorded in Theravada doctrines as 543 or 544 B.C. Other biographies place it between 483 and 486 B.C.

Indian literature frequently attaches the Sanskrit / Pali word *maha* ("great") as a prefix to the names of honored persons, places, and events; as in *maharaja* ("great king"). Queen Maya is often remembered as *Mahamaya*; her sister Prajapati, the Buddha's maternal aunt and stepmother, as *Mahaprajapati*. And the Buddha's *parinirvana* is often called the *Mahaparinirvana*.

Works of art commemorating his *parinirvana*, such as a stone sculpture from Gandhara (fig. 32), usually portray the Buddha reclining on his right side atop a couch or pedestal in a highly stylized pose of serenity. His head rests upon a pillow and his right hand, which suggests a final gesture of *abhaya mudra*. The left arm rests directly atop the left leg and it atop the right leg, almost as if the image had been created in a standing position, then gently laid down on its right side. This particular sculpture is unusual for having the feet angle away from each other; all but a few images of this kind continue the stylization by placing the left foot squarely atop the right. Larger statues frequently have the bottoms of his feet formed as perfectly flat surfaces engraved with sacred emblems or symbolic wheels of a thousand spokes, as described by the thirty-two *lakshana*.

Subhadra, the last convert, is seated in meditation in front of the couch. Vajrapani ("Thunderbolt Bearer"), a Mahayana bodhisattva often pictured as the Buddha's companion and guardian, stands left of the couch. Vajrapani was a beloved character in Gandharan art, which usually patterned him after the Greek hero Hercules, with thick curly hair and a muscular physique, and wielding an abbreviated *vajra* thunderbolt weapon in one hand. Standing at far right is the monk Mahakasyapa, speaking with the ascetic who informed him of the Buddha's death. The four figures in the background are apt to be Malla nobles expressing their regrets, or they could be deities.

That this sculpture marks the end of the Buddha's mortal life is confirmed by the grieving mourners. Nevertheless, the word "death" is not generally used to describe this event because, although the Buddha's physical body had passed away, he had attained *parinirvana*, the culmination of his achievements, a complete release from the world of suffering. *Parinirvana*, the ultimate goal of Buddhism, is said to transcend the cycle of birth, death, and rebirth, and can be called the "deathless" or "undying" state. Devotees of the Buddha often say that such images show him resting or lying down in meditation. Some likenesses in this vein do portray him at rest or in reclining meditation, usually indicated by a relaxed pose with his feet loosely separated and his robes draping down casually.

The clergy and lay followers present at the *parinirvana* were aided by the Mallas in arranging the Buddha's funeral. For six days they gave reverence to his remains with offerings of music, dancing, flower garlands, and scented oils. On the seventh day, they carried the body to a shrine east of Kusinara and prepared it for cremation according to instructions the Buddha had given to Ananda. The Malla chieftains placed the body atop the funeral pyre, but when they attempted to light the pyre, it would not catch fire. One of the monks identified the problem—Mahakasyapa, senior monk at the time, was in journey with several hundred other members of the Sangha, and the gods would not allow the cremation to begin until those senior disciples had paid their last respects. When Mahakasyapa reached the funeral site, he walked reverently round the remains three times, then bowed. The monks accompanying him did the same. When they completed this ritual the funeral pyre ignited. At that moment, the earth trembled and the trees released a shower of blossoms and leaves which covered the forest floor.

After the cremation, a dispute arose over disposition of the ashes. The Malla elders insisted that the Enlightened One's remains should be interred there in Kusinara, where he had passed away. But envoys from other clans who venerated the Buddha demanded portions of his relics and ashes to enshrine in memorial stupas in their states. This led to an incident known as "The War of the Relics," actually a confrontation between archers and soldiers from the various factions. The matter was finally settled peacefully, with a Brahmin named Dona dividing the cremated remains and ashes into eight portions that he distributed among the tribes and clans of followers.

Approximately three months later at Rajagriha, the monk Mahakasyapa convened and presided over the First Council, a gathering of five hundred senior monks who recited and systematized the Buddha's teachings in an oral compilation that became the original Buddhist Canon. Its first section, the *Vinaya Pitaka* ("Rules of Discipline Basket"), guides the behavior of members of the Sangha. Its second section, the *Sutra Pitaka* ("Sutras Basket"), is a compilation of the Buddha's sermons, as recited by his chief attendant, Ananda. Each *sutra* begins with Ananda's words, "Thus have I heard . . ." A third section, the *Abhidharma Pitaka* ("Higher Dharma Basket"), comprising commentaries, subcommentaries, and analyses on the doctrine, was added later and completed the *Tripitaka* ("Three Baskets"), as the Canon came to be called. Using the word *pitaka* in this context likely stems from a tradition of that era of keeping or carrying books in baskets, even though the Canon began as an oral compilation that was first written down in Sri Lanka around 83 B.C.

With the passage of time, some groups of followers developed different interpretations of the Buddha's teachings, and formed into schools and sects with a diversity of beliefs, rituals, and artistic traditions. A substantial body of new *sutras* appeared among proponents of what came to be known as the Mahayana movement, which in turn branched into schools such as Vajrayana and Zen. Still, all Buddhist denominations and lineages share common roots in the Four Noble Truths, the Noble Eightfold Path, and the *Triratna* ("Triple Gem"): the Buddha, the Dharma, and the Sangha. These core beliefs can be expressed in an affirmation of faith that is often recited as a chant or prayer: "I take refuge in the Buddha; I take refuge in the Dharma; I take refuge in the Sangha."[13]

II.

BUDDHIST ART AND BUDDHIST BELIEFS: THERAVADA, MAHAYANA, VAJRAYANA, AND ZEN

INDIA

The senior monks who participated in the First Council preserved the original Buddhist Canon by reciting and memorizing its component parts. Together with other *bhikshus* and *bhikshunis* of their era and successive generations who wore the yellow robes, they sustained and propagated the scriptures by oral retelling for the next several hundred years, a time when much of northern India experienced frequent periods of foreign invasion and political turbulence.

Alexander the Great and his Macedonian army invaded the Indus Valley in 326 B.C. Their brief occupation of some western parts of the subcontinent resulted in a Greek colony being established at Bactria, in what is now northern Afghanistan, and energized the flow of trade and cultural exchange between the Mediterranean and the Orient. Soon after Alexander's death, his army retreated from India, largely at the hands of a coalition led by King Chandragupta, founder of the Maurya dynasty based in the eastern city of Pataliputra.

During the third century B.C., Chandragupta's grandson, King Asoka the Great, extended the Mauryan realm across much of the subcontinent, expanding it into the first major Indian empire. But in the eighth year of his reign, after one especially bloody battle that vividly articulated the grief and carnage of war, Asoka converted to Buddhism and became its most prominent patron. He sent missionaries throughout his territories and as far as Sri Lanka and Southeast Asia to spread the Dharma and proclaimed his devotion through stone pillars inscribed with the Buddha's doctrinal ideals. These pillars, decorated with a variety of animal emblems such as lions and

Fig. 33. (Opposite) *The Great Stupa of Sanchi (Stupa 1) and its West Torana.* H: 54 ft., 1 in. (16.5 m). Sanchi, India, original brick core constructed 3rd century B.C., enlarged 1st century B.C.

elephants and the Wheel of the Law, are the earliest known artistic representations of the Dharma. Asoka is also said to have collected the Buddha's ashes from their eight reliquary sites and enshrined them in eighty-four thousand new stupas where the faithful could pay homage.[14] One example was the original core construction of the Great Stupa of Sanchi, about sixty-four kilometers north of the central Indian town of Bhopal.

Early stupas were plain, dome-shaped constructions whose design had evolved from the Buddha's own funeral mound. Around the first century B.C., a momentous progression occurred when the first known Buddhist figural art was created as stone relief sculptures to decorate the railings and gateways of stupas at Sanchi and Bharhut. Fig. 33 is a view of the Great Stupa of Sanchi (Stupa 1) and the outer face of its intricately carved west *torana* (gateway), comprising a pair of stone pillars supporting three horizontal beams with spiral ends. These early expressions of Buddhist art are elaborate, sophisticated compositions in stone using human and animal imagery to depict key events from the Buddha's biography and the *jataka* stories of his previous lives. They are enlivened with popular themes from Indian mythology such as male *yaksha* and female *yakshi*—supernatural beings embodying the forces of Nature. These lavish, sensuous interpretations of life surround and stand in vivid contrast to the stupa itself—a large and solid but essentially unadorned dome emblemizing the Buddha's attainment of *parinirvana*. The top of the dome holds a square stone fence protecting a three-tiered umbrella symbolizing the Triple Gem: the Buddha, the Dharma, and the Sangha.

The Buddha himself, though, was not yet shown in his human form. He was instead represented by aniconic symbols of notable happenings in his life.[15] A scene carved into the south *torana* of Stupa 3 at Sanchi, for example, pictures the First Sermon in the Deer Park near Sarnath, with the Buddha indicated by a Wheel of the Law atop a pillar, surrounded by deities and worshipers (fig. 34). Other symbols were

Fig. 34. *The First Sermon, with the Wheel of the Law representing the Buddha.* Sanchi Stupa 3, south torana, west pillar, north face. Sanchi, India, 1st century B.C.

also used extensively as surrogates for his presence in early works of art: a prominent pair of stylized footprints in front of an empty seat or throne; a fiery pillar, sometimes placed behind the empty throne; the Bodhi Tree, where he attained enlightenment; a pair of deer, for the Deer Park where he preached his first sermon; and the traditional stupa, representing his *parinirvana*.

Interestingly, no tangible evidence survives today of any statues or portraits of the Buddha having been created in the course of his lifetime, or for approximately four hundred years after his decease—even though the doctrine he taught and the monastic order he founded have both flourished since his time. The reasons are elusive. One theory is that he may have forbidden his disciples from making images of him, to encourage their spiritual self-reliance and to stress that he was a teacher, a guide, a human being who discovered and taught the truth about existence. He did not claim to be a god or a creator. Another possibility is that his early followers were respecting the Buddhist concept which denies the existence of an eternal self or soul, believing that after he had passed away and attained *parinirvana*, no earthly likeness could adequately represent his formless essence. Or, perhaps the Buddha was once considered too sacred to be depicted by imagery. Of course it is imaginable that portraits of him were made during those early years and they simply have not yet been unearthed; or they might all have been fashioned from perishable materials and no longer exist.

Tradition says that by the third century B.C. there were eighteen Buddhist sects. The oldest one arose soon after the Buddha's *parinirvana* and has preserved his original teachings to today—*Theravada* (Pali: "Teachings of the Elders"). Hence, the term Theravada is often applied collectively to all orthodox schools and lineages. In the early orthodox congregations primary focus was on the monks, who, with material support from the laity, pursued the holy life as a means to reach nirvana as quickly as possible. The monks in turn provided spiritual sustenance, guiding their initiates to lead good lives and accrue merit which would enable them to be reborn under favorable conditions in future births.

But a significant new step in Buddhism's evolution was also beginning with the rise of fresh interpretations of the Dharma. Proponents of this new movement eventually adopted the name *Mahayana* ("Great Vehicle") to emphasize their liberal aspiration of helping all sentient beings to attain *bodhichitta* ("enlightened mind"). They considered traditional doctrines such as Theravada too conservative and incomplete, and referred to them disparagingly as *Hinayana* ("Lesser Vehicle").

One cornerstone of the Mahayana faith is its vast body of *sutras*, sacred writings that in some instances arose from mysterious origins. Mahayana tradition maintains that their *sutras* include advanced teachings of Sakyamuni, the historical Buddha, which he entrusted to the *nagas* for safekeeping until the proper time came to reveal them to humankind. And that these teachings were brought to light by the great Buddhist philosopher Nagarjuna, who discovered them in the *nagas*' undersea palace in about the second century A.D. Mahayanists therefore feel their faith is a vital extension of earlier orthodox doctrines. Theravada scholars, however, generally consider the Mahayana *sutras* to be the creation of poets and holy men, not the words of the Buddha.[16]

Mahayanists revere all Buddhas as omniscient, transcendent beings possessing *trikaya* (Sanskrit: "three bodies"), consisting of: (1) *Dharmakaya* ("great teachings body" or "essence body"), the pure, eternal, true nature of the Buddha; (2) *Sambhogakaya* ("enjoyment body"), the form that resides in a paradise abode, enjoying the fruits of enlightenment; and (3) *Nirmanakaya* ("transformation body"), the Earthly body which a Buddha assumes to expound the Dharma to all sentient beings.[17] In addition, "the word *kaya* when used of the Buddha can refer to his actual body, primarily the physical body, and also to any group or collection of elements which make up or in some sense pertain to the Buddha."[18] Thus Sakyamuni Buddha was recognized as a supramundane being who appeared in our world in his *nirmanakaya* form, and while that human manifestation did dissolve at his death, his spiritual essence continues to aid all beings on the path to liberation. From this perspective, it could be possible for skilled meditation masters to employ a trance-like state of mental absorption to achieve spiritual communion with him and other celestials, and receive new precepts from them, revelations that might then have been recorded in Mahayana *sutras*.[19]

Some Mahayana *sutras* revealed previously unknown celestial Buddhas and bodhisattvas who joined Sakyamuni in the growing pantheon worshiped by the Mahayana movement. A prominent case developed from the two *Sukhavativyuha* ("Land of Bliss") *Sutras*, wherein Sakyamuni tells about a bodhisattva known as *Dharmakara*, who lived on Earth eons earlier and is now a Buddha named *Amitabha*, presiding over a celestial paradise called *Sukhavati*.[20] Sukhavati is described as a heavenly realm in the western reaches of the cosmos, fertile with fragrant flowers and fruits, resplendent with golden and silver trees bearing gems not found anywhere else—a "Pure Land" whose inhabitants dwell in unbounded bliss. Members of the Pure Land branch of Mahayana contend that Amitabha, Buddha of Infinite Light, created Sukhavati as a heavenly refuge for beings who are not yet able to attain enlightenment but desire release from *samsara*, the endless cycle of birth, death, and rebirth. Devotees are said to be reborn in the Pure Land of Sukhavati when their mortal lives end if they faithfully recite this invocation, particularly as they approach the moment of death: "Veneration to Amitabha Buddha" (Sanskrit, *Namo Amitabhaya Buddhaya*; Chinese, *Namo Amituofo*; Japanese, *Namu Amida Butsu*). They can then remain in the Pure Land as long as they wish, continuing their spiritual progress and eventually attaining nirvana. A "Pure Land" is sometimes called a "Buddha Land" or "Buddha Field" (Sanskrit, *Buddhaksetra*).

Several terms are in current usage for describing celestial Buddhas such as Amitabha, including: Jina ("Conqueror"); *Dhyani* ("Meditation") *Buddha*; *Cosmic Buddha*; and *Tathagata*—roughly "Thus gone (to nirvana)," an epithet Sakyamuni Buddha frequently used when referring to himself. But this concept is best rendered in English as "transcendent Buddha"—an omniscient celestial who transcends all aspects of time, space, and form.

Mahayanists also give greatly expanded roles to bodhisattvas. In earlier orthodox schools, the primary activity of a bodhisattva was to nurture and advance his own spiritual growth with the aim of achieving Buddhahood and final nirvana. By contrast, Mahayana tradition focuses largely on transcendent bodhisattvas—saintly, self-sacrificing celestials who have attained enlightenment but voluntarily postpone entering final nirvana so they may assist other beings on the path to liberation. Transcendent bodhisattvas serve as benevolent intermediaries between mortals and the Buddhas, receiving our prayers and providing divine intervention to the faithful. The most widely known and worshiped is Avalokitesvara, Bodhisattva of Compassion. It is said that during one occasion, while deep in meditation, Amitabha Buddha emitted from his right eye a beam of white light from which Avalokitesvara was born as his spiritual son. Avalokitesvara can appear in any of thirty-three different manifestations. He is worshiped as *Lokesvara* (South Asia), *Guanyin* (China), *Kwanseum Posal* (Korea), *Matsyendranatha* (Nepal), *Chenrezig* (Tibet), and *Kannon* (Japan).[21] Likenesses of him frequently include in the front of his headdress a small image of his spiritual father, Amitabha Buddha, seated in meditation.

Another venerated member of this celestial family is the goddess Tara (Sanskrit; Tibetan, *Dolma*), a female emanation of the Bodhisattva Avalokitesvara. A variety of legends describe Tara's origins. One tells how Avalokitesvara, disheartened by humankind's immense suffering, shed a tear from which a lotus flower arose. When its petals opened, Tara appeared and vowed to serve him in aiding humankind. Tara is seen in twenty-one different forms, distinguished by color, pose, and physical attributes. These range from the savioress Green Tara, said to be the original ideal from which all her other forms emanated, to the wrathful Yellow Tara.[22] A Tibetan variation of these legends tells that "the Buddha Amitabha saw the need to increase his activity toward benefiting others. From his right eye he emitted a beam of white light and from his left a ray of green. From these sprang forth respectively the manifestations of the deities Chenrezig [a Tibetan name for Avalokitesvara] and Tara."[23]

Theravadins generally do not acknowledge Mahayana's transcendent Buddhas and bodhisattvas, yet the two schools do agree that Sakyamuni was one in a series of *manushi* (human) Buddhas who have lived and expounded the Dharma in our world. The two schools also share the belief that one day in the future, when knowledge of the teachings has been lost, a bodhisattva named *Maitreya* will appear, become the next Buddha and teach the Dharma. According to the *Lalitavistara Sutra*, a Sanskrit biography of the Buddha's life, prior to his birth as Prince Siddhartha he and Maitreya resided together in the Tushita Heaven, where Maitreya now waits for the appropriate occasion to be born to a final lifetime in this world and become the next Buddha.

Evidently, the emergence of the Mahayana movement was a key impulse leading to popular demand for images of the Buddha, which the faithful could use for spiritual devotions. Additionally, the process of creating such images came into vogue as a means of gaining religious merit. "Eventually the point was reached where the real Buddha was thought to reside in his image; by the 'eye-opening' rite and by depositing sacred objects inside the image, it was believed that the latter could acquire a numinous vitality and even a magical miracle working power."[24]

It was probably late in the first century B.C. when the first images were created of the Buddha in his human form. This apparently occurred at about the same time in two locations within northern India's Kushan Empire: Mathura, in north-central India near Delhi; and Gandhara, a region in the northwest that was centered around the city of Taxila and included parts of modern-day Pakistan and Afghanistan. Did artists in Mathura, or in Gandhara, produce the first anthropomorphic images depicting the human person of the Buddha? This question has been extensively researched and debated by art historians and scholars, yet neither of these two regional art styles has been conclusively proved to predate the other.[25]

Sculptors from Mathura certainly did create the first purely Indian portraits of the Buddha in figural form, drawing inspiration from pre-existing native art models such as *yaksha* and the stylistic treatments of stone narrative carvings at the stupas in Sanchi and Bharhut. Early images from Mathura typically portray the Buddha with massive yet realistically rendered physical characteristics and posed in traditional yoga postures (fig. 35). His hair is smoothed back around a small spiral topknot representing the *ushnisha* on the crown of his head. This design was later transformed into a stylized formula of short, snail-like curls of hair covering the head and *ushnisha* that became a standard mark of the Buddha's appearance. Other *lakshana* of a great man are displayed as well, especially the *urna* mole between the eyebrows. Another emblem of the Buddha—incorporated here and on virtually every likeness of him regardless of school or style—is distended earlobes. Stretched by the weight of elegant earrings worn during his youth as a Sakya prince and now elongated though unadorned, his long earlobes remind us of his renunciation of royal entitlement and the material world. Also traditional and universally seen are the three parallel skin lines circling his neck. He wears a sheer monk's robe over the left shoulder, open on the right side.[26] The lion throne beneath him confirms his royal ancestry. The halo behind his head and two celestials hovering above indicate his divinity. Branches and leaves of the Bodhi Tree in the background recall his enlightenment. "Another interesting feature of this relief is that it appears to be an early example of the trinity in Indian art; the attendants presumably may be identified as Indra and Brahma, who later are replaced by Bodhisattvas."[27]

Devotional art from Gandhara, although contemporary with that of Mathura, had quite different origins. Positioned as northwest India's gateway to Central Asia and the Silk Road—a far-flung network of

Fig. 35. *Buddha Seated on a Lion Throne.* Red sikri sandstone, H: 27⅛ in. (69 cm). Katra, India, Kushan period, circa 2nd century A.D.

Fig. 36. *Gold stater of Kanishka I.* Diameter: 25/32 in. (2.0 cm), weight 7.04 g. Ahinposh, Jalalabad District, Afghanistan, issued circa A.D. 100–123.

ancient caravan trade routes that carried commerce and cultural exchanges between China, the Indian subcontinent, the Middle East, and the Mediterranean—Gandhara was a crossroads for a broad spectrum of cultural currents. Hellenistic and Roman cultural energies were especially strong in this region, largely as a heritage from nearby Bactria. Consequently, Gandhara engendered a unique, hybrid school of Buddhist art based on the harmonious blending of classical Greco-Roman stylistic conventions and Indian subject matter.

Ancient coins can be a rich source of facts and clues about the cultures of their realms. Among the oldest surviving Buddha images is the Gandharan-style likeness on a rare gold stater issued about A.D. 100–123 by Kanishka I, ruler of the Kushan Empire (fig. 36). Pictured on the left is the coin's obverse side, with Kanishka making a sacrifice at a small altar. He wears the Kushan royal headpiece and diadem while holding a spear and an elephant goad. Greek letters are used for the Bactrian language inscription "king of kings Kanishka Kushan," a sign of the vigorous Greco-Roman influence in that region and time. Pictured on the right is the coin's reverse side, with a standing view of the Buddha in monastic robes, which he holds with his left hand while gesturing the *abhaya mudra* with his right hand.

Fig. 37. *Meditating Buddha. Schist*, H: 12¾ in. (32.4 cm). Gandhara, Pakistan, Kushan period, A.D. 200–300.

The Bactrian inscription is "BODDO," with Kanishka's dynastic symbol in the right-hand field. This was one in a series of gold and bronze Kushan coins bearing images of Persian, Greek, and Indian divinities.[28]

A schist stone statue of the Buddha seated in meditation similarly reveals the strong Hellenistic ambiance in Gandharan art (fig. 37). The face is European, resembling the god Apollo; the robe is heavy, with thick folds more akin to a Greek toga than to the sheer fabrics worn by Indian holy men; the *ushnisha* protuberance atop the head is covered by wavy hair in a Greek adaptation. Yet despite these Greek stylings, the subject clearly is the Buddha. His divinity is indicated by the nimbus or halo behind his head, rendered in a plain disk design seen on many sacred images from Gandhara. This widely applied characteristic (like the halo in Christian iconography) probably evolved from ancient forms of sun worship, such as early Vedic imagery where a golden disk symbolized the sun.

The mountains of Gandhara provided an abundant supply of this fine-grained schist stone in colors ranging from gray to blue-black. It could be polished to a smooth finish that endured well, and became the preferred medium for statuary. Smaller images were produced in volume from terracotta. Bronze castings were also made later in the period. Caravans traveling the Silk Road brought technical innovations aplenty from Europe and the Middle East, including the introduction of stucco as yet another material for sculpture (fig. 38). Traces of gold are often found on these pieces, suggesting most were once gilded. In this polyglot land traveled by pilgrims, nomadic tribesmen, and itinerant merchants from a diversity of cultures, Gandharan artworks were a highly effective medium for propagating the Buddha's teachings and illustrating memorable episodes in his life (see figs. 8, 22, and 32).

Buddhist statuary of this period is largely Mahayanist, and the compelling importance that doctrine extends to bodhisattvas was boldly expressed in Gandharan art. Images of Prince Siddhartha, the historical

Fig. 38. *Head of the Buddha*. Stucco, H: 7⅛ in. (18 cm). Gandhara, Pakistan, 4th–5th centuries.

bodhisattva (up to the day he attained enlightenment and became a Buddha), usually show him dressed in the jeweled regalia of the Sakya nobility, and apparently spurred a predilection for depicting virtually all bodhisattvas in royal jewelry and robes. Revered teachers of the Dharma and benevolent leaders who worked for the spiritual betterment of their people may have been viewed as bodhisattvas too. The convention of including a small Buddhist emblem on the front of the headdress of some bodhisattvas may have started with Indian rulers who wore Buddha images on the faces of their crowns to affirm their faith—and, conceivably, to aspire to the title of bodhisattva.[29]

Details of the headdress design and the items held in a bodhisattva's hands or carried on the body will often identify the subject.

Images of the Bodhisattva Maitreya—said to be residing in the Tushita Heaven awaiting the auspicious time to be reborn in our world and become the next Buddha—usually have him carrying a *kalasa*, a small bottle containing a magical elixir (Sanskrit, *amrita*; Pali, *amata*). A beverage of the gods churned from the depths of the ocean, *amrita* is said to give eternal life, and is comparable to the Greek drink *ambrosia*. Both words mean "no death," and probably share ancient origins. *Amrita* can also be considered a symbol of the Dharma, a "prescription" formulated by the Buddha to cure humankind's spiritual ills.

A stone statue of Maitreya modeled with a European face and a powerful torso mark the Greco-Roman style of Gandhara (fig. 39). His left hand holds the bottle of *amrita*; his right hand, now lost, would have been raised in the *abhaya mudra* of dispelling fear. He wears thick robes prominently ridged, and princely bracelets and amulets. Especially interesting is the necklace of Greek centaurs worn around his neck.

Evidently, ateliers in Mathura and Gandhara gradually influenced each other. Bulky, toga-like robes on early Gandharan Buddhas evolved into a sheer garment draped over the left shoulder of later statues, leaving the right shoulder bare, as frequently worn by South Asian monks. Mathuran images lost some of their early massiveness, maybe inspired by the athletic appearance regularly seen in Gandharan sculptures. Gandharan art reached full flower around the third century A.D. and faded in the fifth century when the White Huns invaded from the north, destroying Buddhist monasteries and monuments across the region.

Buddhism continued to gain ground in the early centuries of the first millenium A.D. During that span a famous center of Buddhist learning flourished in the southeast of India, around the monasteries of Nagarjunakonda, home of the revered philosopher

Fig. 39. *Bodhisattva Maitreya*. Schist, H: 41 in. (1.04 m). Gandhara, Pakistan, A.D. 100–300.

Nagarjuna, who was one of the Mahayana movement's founders. The Buddhist art that developed in this region drew inspiration from the styles of both Mathura and Gandhara. Named after the southeastern city of Amaravati, capital of the Andhra Empire, this school is especially noted for delicate relief carvings of busy, crowded scenes and an expressive energy calling to mind India's lively dance and drama traditions. A stone relief carving from Amaravati pictures two elephants, likely representing local royalty, kneeling in worship of a stupa that signifies the Buddha attaining *parinirvana* (fig. 40). Coiled around the stupa's dome are two intertwined *nagas*, traditional protectors of the Buddha and the Dharma. The Andhra Empire operated a substantial maritime trading network which helped to carry Buddhist teachings and an abundance of artworks from Amaravati to seaports across the south of Asia, imprinting their flavor on the devotional art created by artisans in Sri Lanka and the lands of Southeast Asia.

A golden age of Indian civilization was reached during the Gupta period from A.D. 320 to approximately the mid-seventh century. Marked by widespread prosperity and prodigious achievements in science and the arts, the Gupta era attained a high classic style of Buddhist art. "In the iconography and style of painting and sculpture we find the establishment of a norm that

Fig. 40. *Relief Carving of a Stupa and two Elephants.* Stone, 12⅜ x 25⅝ in. (31.25 x 65 cm). Amaravati, India, 2nd century.

Fig. 41. *Head of the Buddha*. Sandstone, H: 10¼ in. (26.0 cm). Sarnath, India, Gupta period, 5th century.

lent itself to adaptation in the hands of all the peoples who followed the Buddhist religion. The paintings and sculptures of Gupta India are more than prototypes for the religious art of Asia; they occupy a position corresponding to that of Greek and Roman art in the West."[30]

At the dawn of the Gupta period, the Theravada and Mahayana movements both flourished in India alongside the Hindu faith. But Mahayanist beliefs, now well developed, became the dominant influence in religious art. The Gupta Buddha image evolved directly from early Mathura prototypes, and the city of Mathura continued as a prominent center of art and culture throughout the Gupta period.

A Gupta-period statue of the Buddha preaching his first sermon, carved in high relief from stone in the fifth century at Sarnath (see fig. 17), another active artistic center during this era, exemplifies the profoundly spiritual artworks inspired by the Mahayana movement. The fully opened eyes on early Mathura images have evolved here into a serene gaze of half-closed eyes suggesting meditation. The monastic robe is so smoothly textured as to appear nearly transparent, yet still exhibits a subtle accent from Gandhara in the way it wraps about the chest to cover both shoulders. In the lower section of this sculpture, the Wheel of the Law is flanked by worshipers and two kneeling deer, reminders of the Deer Park where the first sermon was given. This type of classical Gupta Buddha image blends spiritual perfection, a delicate sense of detached calm, and sublime humanity into an idealized vision of the great sage that would serve as a model for later schools of art across much of Asia.

Another stone carving from Sarnath gives a closer view of Gupta detailing (fig. 41). The hair is configured as stylized rows of snail-shell curls, each coiling left to right as specified by the thirty-two *lakshana*, and covering the head and *ushnisha*—a design innovation that became universally applied to Buddhist portraiture. The shape of the *ushnisha* is narrow but prominently raised. The earlobes are large and fully distended.

Artists of Sarnath and of Mathura apparently worked exclusively in sandstone from local quarries. A rare Gupta-era standing image of the Buddha cast from a copper alloy in northern India incorporates styling elements from both cities (fig. 42). Its standing posture with somewhat elongated legs, the positions of the arms, the clearly marked parallel folds cascading down the front of the robe—all are reminiscent of stone statuary from Mathura. However, the facial characteristics and slender, delicate rendering of the torso are more akin to images from Sarnath. The figure's outstretched left hand holds the end of the upper robe. The right hand, raised in *abhaya mudra*, is webbed between the fingers, another *lakshana* specification Gupta artists were first to illustrate. But Gupta artworks usually do not include the small *urna* protuberance that normally appears above a Buddha's eyebrows, as is noticeable in the examples shown here.[31]

Notable among ancient India's artistic marvels are the rock temples, carved by hand from stone mountains in several regions of the country. The earliest were excavated by Theravada Buddhists in the Barabar hills of Bihar during the reign of King Asoka. Later examples were built by members of the Hindu and Jain religions. In the Gupta period, Mahayana Buddhists constructed additional caves, many grandly decorated with statues of Buddhas and deities. Some existing older sites were modified by adding fresh paintings and elaborate carvings of transcendent Buddhas and bodhisattvas to accommodate Mahayanist worship rituals.

Of the more than one thousand rock-cut monasteries constructed in India, the most artistically significant belong to a series cut into the Western Ghats, a mountain chain lying parallel to the western coastline. Hollowed out of mountains and hillsides by stone cutters and sculptors, these man-made caves served as *viharas* (residence halls for monks) and *chaityas* (sanctuaries for worship). The arrangement of the *vihara* caves resembled conventional monastic quarters, but the *chaitya* halls were given a unique new design.

Fig. 42. (Opposite) *Sakyamuni Buddha*. Copper alloy with color, H: 15½ in. (39.4 cm). Uttar Pradesh (?), India, Gupta period, late 6th century.

Generally, the term *chaitya* is synonymous with stupa, both referring to outdoor, dome-like burial mounds or funerary monuments honoring the Buddha or other venerated icons. But most rock-cut temples have a stupa constructed inside a communal worship hall, usually carved from solid stone in the center of the room to allow circumambulation rituals by the faithful. Definitions in this application are therefore modified: the word *chaitya* refers to the worship hall, and *stupa* to the dome-shaped monument within it. Each *chaitya* chamber's ceiling was shaped into a rounded vault with finely chiseled stone surfaces sculpted in meticulous imitation of the beams and rafters of conventional wooden architecture. An ample number of these chambers were richly decorated with statuary, ornamental carvings, and wall paintings.

A complex of twenty-eight caves excavated between the second century B.C. and the seventh century A.D. at Ajanta, in Maharashtra state overlooking the Waghora River, is especially remarkable for its vibrantly colored murals of *jataka* tales and other Buddhist themes. Many are masterpieces in design and execution that skillfully employ dramatic poses and gestures to convey the mood of a scene and maintain its narrative flow.

> Every wall and ceiling at the Ajanta monastery was covered with lavish painted decoration, made possible by the largesse of the wealthy and influential patrons of the monastery who employed several workshops of painters. Stone walls were left unpolished to provide a suitable base for two layers of mud plaster, which was then overlaid by lime wash. Colours were not added while the lime was still wet, which would have given it the durability of fresco; instead, painters waited for the wash to dry before executing their work, using red paint for outline sketches. Colours were mostly from local minerals: red and yellow ochres, lampblack, white lime and kaolin, and mineral green; only lapis lazuli for blue was imported, coming from Afghanistan.[32]

Fig. 43. *Scene from the Vessantara Jataka*. Mural wall painting in Cave 17, Ajanta, India, 5th–6th centuries.

A wall painting from Cave 17 at Ajanta depicts a scene from the Vessantara Jataka (fig. 43). This story, the most popular and chronologically last of the *jataka* tales describing the Buddha's prior lifetimes, tells of his existence as Prince Vessantara, a paragon of compassion and generosity, the culmination of striving for perfect wisdom in the course of his innumerable prior lives. So generous was Vessantara that he never hesitated to give away any possession to whoever might request it. But when he gave away his kingdom's sacred white elephant to some Brahmins from another land, his father the king was compelled to banish him to live in the forest. We see in this painting the palace interior, with the dark-skinned Prince Vessantara informing his wife of his banishment. She swoons upon hearing this terrible news, her head falling to one side. Vessantara tries to comfort her with a cup of wine brought by the green-jacketed manservant standing behind them and leaning forward with a concerned air. The couple appears again in the next scene to the left, commencing their departure from the palace. During their exile in the forest, Vessantara continued his pursuit of perfect compassion, giving away everything he possessed, even his wife and two children. Ultimately, the gods acknowledged his perfect generosity and restored his family and position to him. After this incarnation, he dwelt in the Tushita Heaven as a *deva* and subsequently was born again on Earth in his final life as Prince Siddhartha.

The decline of the Gupta dynasty, starting in the sixth century A.D., led to India's medieval period, with the subcontinent dividing into numerous small states. By this time, Buddhism was on the wane in much of India, continuing as a major spiritual movement only in the northeastern region of today's Bengal and Bihar. There the Pala and Sena dynasties sustained the faith through libraries and centers of learning, most notably the famous monastic university at Nalanda, which accommodated thousands of students from across Asia. Spanning the eighth to twelfth centuries, the Pala-Sena period was heir to cultural traditions of the Guptas, yet also saw the rise of complex new artistic expressions of Hindu, Jain, and Buddhist beliefs.

Artists of the Pala-Sena period created elaborate sculptures featuring a number of subsidiary components grouped around one or more central subjects, all carved in deep relief, with sumptuous ornamentation covering most connecting surfaces. Typical is a twelfth-century stone stele (fig. 44) re-enacting "Eight Great Miracles" in the Buddha's life, an expansion of the earlier tradition that celebrated the four key episodes of his birth, enlightenment, first sermon, and *parinirvana*. The large seated likeness of the Buddha in the center wears a rich crown and regal jewelry, a style popularized during the Pala-Sena period and which alluded to both his royal ancestry and the Mahayanist view of him as a supramundane being. This theme of depicting the Buddha "in royal attire" may have originated from devotees adorning early statues with actual diadems, bracelets and other jewelry, and later became

Fig. 44. *Eight Great Miracles in the Buddha's Life*. Stone, H: 18 in. (47.5 cm). Eastern India, Pala-Sena period, 12th century.

fashionable in other countries as well. Here, seated on a double lotus throne and touching the earth to signify his enlightenment, he is surrounded by seven smaller images to illustrate the eight important events in his life. As with nearly all compositions of this kind, the scenes are placed by aesthetics, not chronology. Beginning at top-center and viewing clockwise, we see: (1) the Buddha reclining, passing away into *parinirvana*; (2) preaching his first sermon; (3) taming the elephant, Nalagiri; (4) receiving honey from the monkey; (5) being born as Prince Siddhartha, son of Queen Maya, shown here grasping a tree branch while giving birth; (6) descending from heaven after visiting his mother; and (7) the Miracle of Sravasti. Beneath the lotus base are two heraldic lions and three attendant figures.

Craftsmen of this time mastered the lost-wax process of metal casting as well, and produced bronze statuary in a wide range of designs and sizes. The Pala-Sena period also saw the rise of a major new form of Buddhist thought: Tantric Buddhism, an extension of the Mahayana movement seeking spiritual salvation through a doctrinal system of meditation, *tantra* (sacred texts which aid meditation), *mantra* (mystical invocations) and esoteric rituals. The secretive nature of these techniques requires novice practitioners to be initiated by a trained master. The Tantric school of Buddhism adopted many traits of the Hindu religion and became known as *Vajrayana*. As explained in appendix 1, the word *vajra* has two interpretations. Its original meaning comes from Hinduism, where *vajra* is the divine "thunderbolt" weapon of the god Indra. In the Buddhist context, *vajra* can also symbolize the indestructible and is thus translated as "diamond" or "adamantine." *Vajrayana* then translates as "Diamond Vehicle" or "Diamond Path." This doctrine is sometimes called *Mantrayana* or *Tantrayana*.

The Vajrayana faith formalized a pentad of five transcendent Buddhas: Vairochana, the Resplendent Buddha; Amitabha, the Infinite Light Buddha; Akshobhya, the Immovable Buddha; Ratnasambhava, the Jewel Born Buddha; and Amoghasiddhi, the Infallible Buddha. All Buddhas are said to share the same physical and spiritual perfections and to be identical in appearance. So images of the transcendent Buddhas might seem indistinguishable from one another and from those of Sakyamuni, the historical Buddha. Still, identification is often possible based on the context and attributes of an image, especially since each transcendent Buddha is normally depicted in one designated *mudra* pose. Additionally, each is affiliated with specific iconographic symbols, is said to reside in a celestial paradise in a certain sector of the cosmos, and is associated with a particular bodhisattva. These characteristics are summarized in appendix 2. Many of them can be seen in the Nepali sutra cover of fig. 83, the Tibetan mandala of fig. 92, and the Tibetan lama's crown of fig. 97.

Some Vajrayana sects add a sixth transcendent Buddha, a primordial, supreme being known as *Adi-Buddha*, an eternal essence from which all things are believed to emanate, including all other Buddhas. He is also called *Samantabhadra*, *Svayambhu*, *Vajradhara*, or *Vajrasattva*. When the *Adi-Buddha* is represented, he usually wears a crown and royal regalia, and holds a vajra scepter in his right hand and a *ghanta* bell in his left (see figs. 82 and 128). His arms are sometimes raised and crossed at the wrists in his distinctive *vajrahumkara mudra*.

Vajrayana Buddhist beliefs and rituals were exported to Southeast Asia, Nepal, Tibet, and China, where they blended with, or absorbed, existing indigenous faiths. Vajrayana also has roots in the Kashmir region of the Indian subcontinent's far north. A bronze sculpture from Kashmir has as its central subject *Lokesvara* ("Lord of the World"), a form of Avalokitesvara worshiped in certain Tantric sects (fig. 45). Similarities with Hindu deities are visible in his having six arms, which hold attributes such as a small bottle of the magical *amrita* elixir, a bow, and a lotus flower near his left shoulder. The prominent figurine of Amitabha Buddha carved into the headdress is found on many manifestations of Avalokitesvara. Here, Lokesvara sits in *lalitasana* (relaxation posture), his right leg raised, his left leg resting upon a lotus footstool. He is flanked by two Tara figures in the same pose. At his right side is the Green Tara, his principal consort, in a somewhat unusual pose whereby her right arm conceals much of her upper body. She is usually modeled in a more open fashion to emphasize her graceful, full-bodied feminine form. On his left side is Bhrikuti, the wrathful Yellow Tara, identified by an extra eye in the center of her forehead and the large lotus bud held against her left arm.

Fig. 45. *Lokesvara Seated between Two Tara Images and Two Donor Figures.* Bronze alloy inlaid with silver and copper, H: 13⅝ in. (34.5 cm). Kashmir, India, late 10th or early 11th century.

At the lower corners of the rectangular base are male and female donors. From their features and dress, they seem to be foreigners, Persian perhaps. The artist used the technique of differentiating figures by scale and position to indicate their relative importance: the two Taras are half the size of the center bodhisattva; the two donors are smaller still. This piece was probably created in northwestern India in the tenth or eleventh century. Lokesvara's head bears traces of cold gold painting, the process of brushing on a mixture of gold powder and a gelatin adhesive. A common practice in Tibet, this suggests the statue may have been placed in a Tibetan monastery as an offering.

Another technique once employed widely in Asia for applying a gold finish to an object is the chemical process known as fire gilding. The object's surface is coated with a paste of powdered gold and mercury. When heated, the mercury vaporizes, leaving upon the surface a fine layer of gold that can be burnished and waxed to heighten its color. Today gilding is mostly accomplished by treating the surface with an adhesive such as paint, then attaching thin sheets of gold leaf, or brushing on coats of gold paint.

Throughout the first millennium A.D., Indian Buddhism underwent significant doctrinal changes, with its original fundamentals losing much of their relevance as increasing attention was focused on mysticism, rituals, and faith in benevolent deities. This evolution was reflected in artistic trends, with representations of Sakyamuni, the historical Buddha, appearing less frequently, while likenesses of the transcendent Buddhas and bodhisattvas and other deities gained in appeal. Distinctions between Buddhism and Hinduism gradually diminished, particularly after the Hindus deified Sakyamuni Buddha in about the fifth century, elevating him to their pantheon as the ninth *avatara* or divine incarnation of the god Vishnu.

Since the Gupta dynasty, royal patronage had been shifting in favor of Hinduism, which eventually absorbed Indian Buddhism. Another decisive setback to Buddhism came from a succession of invading armies that swept over much of the subcontinent, destroying monasteries and terrorizing the monks. By the thirteenth century, Buddhism had virtually disappeared from India.

Fortunately, Buddhist pilgrims from other countries had been visiting India since the Gupta period, or earlier, translating the scriptures into their own languages and carrying them home along with devotional artworks to propagate the Dharma in their own lands. Accounts of their expeditions became valuable historical records of life and culture in India, where invaders had largely destroyed local archives. Fa-Hien, the first known Chinese pilgrim to study Buddhism in India, also visited Sri Lanka and some twenty-eight other south Asian states during the fifth century. His travel record *Fo-kuo chi*, translated into English as "A Record of Buddhistic Kingdoms," offers first-hand observations of the status and activities of Buddhism at that time. Hiuen Tsiang, a Chinese monk who studied at the Buddhist university at Nalanda from A.D. 629–645, compiled detailed surveys of Buddhist holy places in India, then devoted himself to translating the scriptures into Chinese.[33]

The great irony is that while Buddhism was waning and would nearly vanish in its birthplace in India, it was at the same time evolving and growing across many other parts of Asia, taking firm root in a host of countries where it blended successfully with indigenous belief systems and became the personal faith of hundreds of millions.

CHINA AND CENTRAL ASIA

Buddhist beliefs and art traveled from India to Central Asia and then into China mainly via the caravan trails of the Silk Road. From about the second century B.C. until the fifteenth century A.D., when mercantile sea lanes began replacing them, these overland trade routes brought cultural flavors from every direction, making Central Asia a cosmopolitan meeting ground for religious and artistic currents of countless types. By the third century A.D., this region had become an influential base for the propagation of Buddhist teachings.

At the start of Buddhism's spread northward, India's primary gateway to Central Asia was through Gandhara, the Kushan Empire's northern hub. Gandharan aesthetic styles and conventions had a prominent impact on Central Asian art. Among the most impressive samples were a pair of colossal Buddha statues at Bamiyan, Afghanistan, once a prosperous intersection of trade routes some 130 kilometers west from Kabul. Measuring about 120 feet (36.6 meters) and 175 feet (53.3 meters) tall, respectively, these two giant standing images were carved from the Bamiyan valley's sandstone cliffs inside deeply recessed niches. Both were fashioned in the stylistic traditions of north Indian art, enlarged on a grand scale befitting the Mahayanist view of the Buddha as a cosmic, supramundane being. The larger statue was originally covered with layers of clay and plaster applied over strands of rope to replicate the folds in the Buddha's robes, then finished in polychromy (fig. 46). The vaulted ceilings and walls of its niche were decorated with painted likenesses of Mahayana deities. Vandalism, gunfire from marauding armies, and centuries of weather erosion severely damaged the two statues, their painted surfaces, and the man-made network of corridors and chambers connecting them. Most regrettably, both of these colossal monuments, along with innumerable other artworks

in Afghanistan, were totally destroyed intentionally by the Taliban movement in March 2001.

Moving eastward across Central Asia, the Silk Road divided at Kashgar, branching into northern and southern routes that linked oasis settlements along the edges of the vast Taklimakan Desert, converging again at Dunhuang, a strategic military and commercial center in northwest China. Buddhism first reached China via these trails sometime in the early years of the Han dynasty (206 B.C.–A.D. 220). A famous legend tells of Buddhism's introduction in A.D. 65, the result of Emperor Ming of the Eastern Han dynasty (A.D. 25–220) having dreamed about a golden deity floating in the air at the front of his palace.[34] When he looked for interpretations of this vision, one of his ministers told him about the Buddha, a holy man from the west reputedly endowed with supernatural powers. He thereupon sent emissaries to India to investigate and they brought back a Sanskrit copy of the *Dvachatvarimshatkhanda Sutra* ("Sutra in Forty-two Sections") and devotional images. The emperor is said to have constructed the *Baimasu* ("White Horse") Monastery in the city of Luoyang to house these sacred images and the *sutra*—the first Buddhist text known to be translated into Chinese. Missionary activity began in earnest around the middle of the second century A.D., when monasteries in Central Asia translated many more *sutras* into Chinese texts, which their monks brought to China's western provinces to teach the Dharma.

Buddhist devotees dug hundreds of caves into hillsides and mountain cliffs along the Silk Road to create monastic cells and shrines where travelers could pray for a safe journey, prosperity, and other blessings. Pilgrims and local congregations sought spiritual merit by contributing to the construction of the caves and endowed them with a priceless heritage of Buddhist statuary and mural paintings.

Fig. 46. (Opposite) *Colossal Buddha of Bamiyan.* Carved sandstone, H: circa 175 ft. (53.3 m). Bamiyan, Afghanistan, 5th–6th centuries; destroyed 2001.

The Mogao Grottoes, commonly called the Cave-temples of the Thousand Buddhas, are the biggest group

Fig. 47. *Ksitigarbha with the Ten Kings of Hell*. Ink and colors on silk, 35½ x 25¾ in. (91 x 65.5 cm). Dunhuang, China, Five Dynasties, mid-10th century.

> of ancient rock-cut temples in China. According to the tablet *Restoration of the Mogao Grottoes,* erected by Li Huairang in 698 A.D., work on the Mogao Grottoes began in 366 A.D., and by the time of the Tang Dynasty there were over a thousand caves and niches. In Mogao today 492 grottoes are extant. . . . With over 45,000 sq. m. of murals, more than 2,000 statues, and five timber structures belonging to the Tang and Song periods, this group of grottoes is one of the world's biggest treasure houses of ancient Buddhist art.[35]

Votive banners honoring esteemed deities were also popular, carried by travelers for worship during a journey and frequently given as offerings to grace the sanctum walls of shrines they visited along the way. Banners were made in a variety of materials, techniques, and sizes to match the financial resources of all levels of donors. Some were modest paper drawings. The finest examples were done with ink and colors on silk, such as a painting of the Bodhisattva Ksitigarbha with the Ten Kings of Hell, illustrating the Chinese Buddhist belief in the judgement of souls after death (fig. 47). This concept originated in the Mahayanist lore of India, telling how forty-nine days after death each soul is brought before Yama, judge of the dead and ruler of a nether world comprising a series of hot and cold hells. Aided by his sister Yami, overseer of the female departed, Yama interrogates and passes judgement on the deceased, sending each of them to be reborn in one of the six *gati*, or realms of existence, as a hell-being, hungry ghost, animal, human, lower god, or god.

The Sutra of the Ten Kings, a composition of uncertain authorship that appeared in China during the tenth century, elaborates on this format, describing ten successive stages in the underworld that each departed soul must pass through before attaining rebirth. Every stage has a presiding king sitting in judgement. Each soul is judged by the first seven kings at seven-day intervals, by the eighth king on the hundredth day, by the ninth king one year after death, and by the tenth king three years after death.

Ksitigarbha is venerated by the Chinese as *Dizang,* a savior able to rescue souls from the torments of hell. He is shown seated in the center of this painting, flanked by the ten kings, each of them represented as a mandarin magistrate aided by clerks and attendants. Ksitigarbha holds two identifying attributes: in his right hand a *chintamani,* or wish-fulfilling jewel, which radiates light across the realms of hell to calm the souls in torment there; and in his left hand a *khakkara,* or monk's staff, with six metal rings strung upon its end to signify he is ready to aid beings in all six realms of existence. This staff also functions as his magical key to unlock the gates of hell. A large halo around Ksitigarbha's head indicates his divinity; its flaming edges signal his powers in the underworld. Below Ksitigarbha is a protector lion, another of his symbols. Left of the lion is the priest Daoming, who journeyed to hell and returned to our mortal world to describe it. Beneath them stands an ox-headed jailer leaning on a large club. He holds the chains of a man whose neck is locked in a wooden yoke while he is forced to watch a mirror reviewing the evil deeds of his life; at this moment it recalls him killing an ox.

At the time of Buddhism's introduction into China, two native philosophies prevailed there: Daoism (Chinese, *Dao*: "the Way"), a belief system that stresses harmonizing the fundamental energies of Nature as a way to attain longevity and spiritual immortality; and Confucianism (teachings of the sage *Kung Fu-tse*; Chinese, *Ru-chia*: "School of Scholars"), a system of social ethics and secular values primarily concerned with preserving morality and order in society. In China, as in Central Asia, Mahayana (Chinese, *Dacheng*) became the dominant path of Buddhist thought. This movement's remarkable flexibility enabled it to adapt to and absorb many aspects of Daoist philosophy, and to enrich certain spiritual beliefs of Confucianism, such as ancestor worship. One offshoot from the commingling of these three worldviews was a syncretic concept known as the "Unity of the Three Religions," an attempt to blend what the Chinese saw to be the most practical and attractive precepts of Buddhism, Confucianism, and Daoism.[36]

Tales of magical powers and miraculous deeds associated with Mahayanist beliefs enhanced that doctrine's allure among the Chinese. One prominent example commences with the *Saddharmapundarika Sutra* ("Lotus of the True Law Sutra" or "Lotus Sutra"), which, many Mahayanists contend, is the final and most comprehensive of Sakyamuni Buddha's discourses, expounded by him to a large gathering of devotees atop Mount Gridhrakuta (Vulture Peak) near Rajagriha, India. Through this *sutra*, Sakyamuni explained in detail the path to enlightenment and revealed his own eternal nature by successfully summoning another Buddha named *Prabhutaratna* who had lived eons earlier. Prabhutaratna miraculously traveled through time and space and appeared seated inside a stupa overflowing with gold and gemstones, which materialized in the sky above the congregation. Sakyamuni rose magically and sat beside Prabhutaratna; the two then engaged in a discussion of philosophy and metaphysics. This scene is reproduced in a gilt bronze statuette from the Northern Wei dynasty (A.D. 386–534) in fig. 48. Its inscription gives a date corresponding to A.D. 518 and records that it was presented as an offering by donors on behalf of their deceased relatives. The elongated, angular features of the two smiling Buddhas; the elaborate detailing of their long, flowing robes which fall into flaring points; the leaf-shaped aureoles adorned with stylized flames behind the figures—all are traits of Northern Wei sculptors marking the emergence of a distinctly Chinese style of Buddhist art. This popular and influential episode was often portrayed in such small images, as well as on large-scale, rock-carved likenesses.[37]

Amitabha Buddha (Chinese, *Amituofo*) has been widely worshiped in China since about the fourth century A.D., perhaps due in large measure to the appealing prospect of a blissful afterlife in Sukhavati, his bountiful Western Paradise, or Pure Land, where

Fig. 48. *Sakyamuni Buddha and Prabhutaratna Buddha.* Gilt bronze, H: 10⅛ in. (25.7 cm). China, Northern Wei dynasty, 518.

Fig. 49. *Greeting the Soul of a Righteous Man on the Way to the Pure Land of Amitabha*. Mineral pigments painted on canvas, 56⅛ x 37 in. (142.5 x 94 cm). China, Tangut State of Xi Xia, Khara Khoto, 12th–13th centuries.

the faithful are said to be reborn. By roughly the mid-seventh century, Amitabha had surpassed Sakyamuni as the primary object of devotion in Chinese Buddhism and today is still the paramount deity in East Asia. Two connected themes serve as the principal subjects in devotional paintings of this faith: diagrammatic illustrations of the Pure Land, some rendered as mandalas; and Amitabha Buddha descending to Earth to greet devotees at their moment of death and guide them to rebirth in his Pure Land. A painting from twelfth to fourteenth-century Khara Khoto shows Amitabha in brightly colored robes, accompanied by the Bodhisattvas Avalokitesvara and Mahasthamaprapta. They are carrying a golden lotus throne on which Amitabha will install the soul of a deceased righteous man, who can then be happily reincarnated (fig. 49). The deceased is represented as a naked boy, rising before them in a white ribbon of light that flows from Amitabha's *urna*. A monk, seated beneath a tree at the lower left corner of the picture, witnesses the ritual.

China applied a host of innovations and variations to Buddhist ideology and iconography. Beginning around the tenth century, Chinese artists frequently added a small round jewel or mound within the front portion of the *ushnisha* on the heads of images of Sakyamuni and other Buddhas.[38] Sometimes called a "mound of light" representing a Buddha's luminosity, this adaptation is often colored red—as on the painting of Amitabha Buddha in fig. 49. It can also take the form of a small bald spot just above the forehead.

Early in the sixth century, a revered Indian monk named *Bodhidharma* arrived by sea in China and founded a branch of Buddhism there that became known as *Chan*—from the Chinese pronunciation of *dhyana,* a Sanskrit word for meditation. In striking contrast to the splendors associated with the Pure Land of Sukhavati, the Chan movement focuses on attaining enlightenment as a direct, personal experience through a disciplined practice of meditation and detachment from worldly comforts. Chan Buddhism is considered a branch of Mahayana, but minimizes the use of rituals, scriptures, and the worship of deities. In due course, the Chan doctrine spread to Korea, where it is called *Son*, and to Japan, where it is known as *Zen*.

> As the Ch'an [Chan] sect matured in China, it inevitably lost much of the Indian ideology and mythology that were part of early Buddhism, and, equally inevitably, it took much from Taoism [Daoism], a Chinese system of belief that predated Chinese Buddhism . . . "meditation" was radically redefined. In effect it came to refer not so much to sitting motionlessly as to a state of mind—or, we might better say, a state of no-mind or of unselfconsciousness—which characterized one's daily business, that is, a state of mind one maintained even when chopping wood or sweeping. . . . Ch'an Buddhism, then, moved away from the Indian Buddhist emphasis on withdrawing from the world by means of relatively ascetic practices, and moved toward a Taoist view of uniting the self with the underlying principle of nature. . . . If one sees one's own nature (in Taoist terms, if one returns to the source), one perceives the unity of all things and experiences enlightenment (Chinese: *wu*; Japanese: *satori*).[39]

Fig. 50. *Tamo* (*Bodhidharma*). By Guo Fa Cheng. Carved wood, H: 23¼ in. (59 cm). China, 1999.

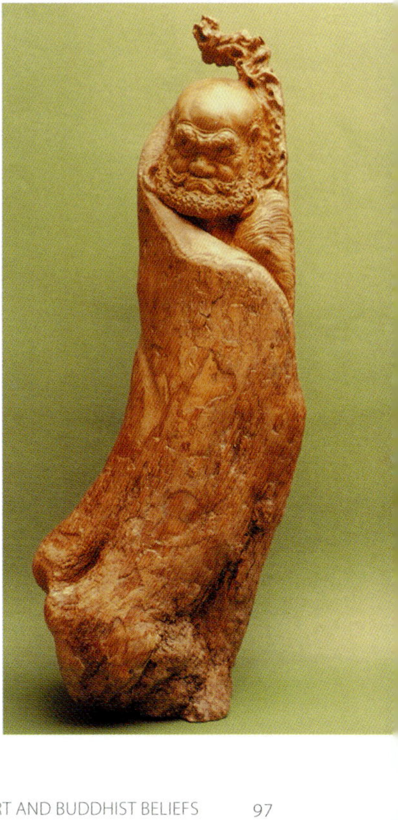

In Chinese the monk Bodhidharma's name is *Pu'-ti-tamo,* or *Tamo*; in Japanese, *Bodaidaruma,* or *Daruma*. He gained renown across East Asia for reputedly sitting in deep meditative absorption in front of a stone wall for nine years, thereby acquiring superhuman powers and, according to one legend, living to the age of 150 years.[40] His followers revere him as the twenty-eighth patriarch of the Indian lineage of Buddhism which began with Sakyamuni Buddha, and as first patriarch of the Chan / Zen movement. East Asian artists have immortalized Bodhidharma as having a fierce, wide-eyed stare, a thick black beard, and bushy eyebrows, and always wearing a heavy white robe (fig. 50). Shaolin Temple, a monastery in the hills of central China where Bodhidharma lived and taught, won additional fame from the distinctive *kung-fu* martial arts perfected by its monks as a regimen of spiritual development and self-defense.

The Chan movement also popularized an icon of the Buddha reminiscent of images from Gandhara picturing him as an emaciated, bearded ascetic (see fig. 8). Chan practitioners refer to this kind of likeness as "Sakyamuni Coming Down from the Mountain," based on East Asia's mystical association of remote mountain peaks with places of spiritual retreat. In the Chan context, it commemorates his attaining enlightenment and returning to society to teach the Dharma. This theme was also adopted in Japanese Zen paintings patterned after Chinese prototypes (see fig. 75).

The Chinese have historically known their country as *Zhongguo*—the "Middle Kingdom" positioned at the center of the universe and surrounded by uncivilized barbarians. Thus it is not surprising that Buddhism was initially viewed with suspicion by much of China, as an alien faith pursuing abstract principles quite different from their own revered, ancient traditions. Still, the Chinese gradually absorbed the core elements of Buddhist ideology and art, eventually creating their own unique patterns of Buddhist culture which flowered into a high classic era during the Tang dynasty (618–906). Tang artists are especially known for their remarkable technical skills that produced graceful, fully formed statuary. "Suave, rhythmic drapery patterns follow the form of the body so closely that one senses the texture, weight and fall of the cloth. As the figures became more substantial and often plump, there was an ever-increasing tendency towards rich detail, complexity of forms and restless movement in the sweeping curves of the drapery folds."[41]

Fig. 51 is a classic Tang statue of the Buddha sculpted from white marble with traces of polychromy. He sits in the full lotus posture upon an ornately embroidered cloth atop a tall, octagonal pedestal. His left hand rests upon his left thigh. His missing right hand would have been raised in *abhaya mudra*, where the palm faces out and all fingers are pointing skyward. This *mudra* usually

Fig. 51. (Opposite) *Sakyamuni Buddha.* White marble with traces of polychromy, H: 30 in. (76.2 cm). China, Tang dynasty, 618–906.

Fig. 52. *Lokapala.* Painted pottery, H: 24¾ in. (62.8 cm). China, Tang dynasty, 8th century.

indicates "granting protection" or "dispelling fear," but the Chinese routinely employed this pose to mean "teaching," in place of the *vitarka mudra* normally associated with teaching or discussion. This statue's head and unusually large *ushnisha* are covered by a unique arrangement of wave-like swirls of hair; a design probably derived from early Gandharan works of art. The face is modeled realistically, softly rounded to exude both humanity and spirituality.[42]

During the Tang dynasty a number of Buddhist traditions and rituals were absorbed into mainstream Chinese culture. For instance, statues of *lokapalas* became popular as guardian gods in monasteries and tombs, typically arrayed in sets of four, one positioned at each cardinal direction. Ancient Indian cosmology tells that the dwelling place of the gods is Mount Meru—the World Mountain positioned at the center of the universe. In Buddhism, the realms of hell-beings and hungry ghosts are located beneath Mount Meru; its base holds the human realm; above its peak is a progression of celestial paradises. Each of Mount Meru's four sides is protected by a specific *lokapala* (Sanskrit: "world protector"; Chinese, *lishi,* or *tien-wang*; Japanese, *shi-tenno*). Additionally, the *lokapalas* defend the Buddha and his teachings, appearing repeatedly in key episodes of his life.

They supplied him with four bowls to receive alms from his first lay followers, Tapussa and Bhallika. In the course of his visit with the Kasyapa brothers, they greeted the Buddha reverently and attended him. Some commentaries mention the four *lokapalas* in other situations—for example, identifying them as the four celestials who lifted and muffled the hooves of the horse that carried the Future Buddha from his palace on the night of his Great Departure.

Lokapalas are typically pictured as fierce warriors wearing armor and crown-like helmets. A fine example from the Tang period, modeled in ceramic form and painted, wears a feathered headdress and elaborate covers over his chest, stomach, arms, and legs (fig. 52). He stands on a rocky pedestal, vanquishing an unidentified demon.[43] In some instances, *lokapala* and other guardian deities are known as *devaraja* (Sanskrit: "god-king").

Fig. 53. *Dvarapala*. Carved wood, H: 92⅛ in. (2.34 m). China, 18th century.

Another form of guardian figure is the *dvarapala* (Sanskrit: "gate protector"), derived from the *yaksha* beings of Indian mythology. Different from the *lokapala*, who wears the body armor of a soldier, the *dvarapala* is usually pictured naked from the waist up, displaying powerful muscles and a fiercely scowling expression (fig. 53). Each *dvarapala* holds a *vajra* thunderbolt weapon in his hand. They normally go in pairs,

Fig. 54. *Maitreya, the Future Buddha.* Gray limestone, H: 32½ in. (82.6 cm). China, Tang dynasty, dated 705.

guarding the entrances to temples and other sacred places.

The Bodhisattva Maitreya is also known and worshiped in China (Chinese, *Miluo Fo*), particularly among cults aspiring to be reborn in their next life with him, either in the Tushita Heaven where he is said to reside now, or in this world when he appears here as the next Buddha. In South Asia, Maitreya is usually depicted wearing the traditional regal robes and headdress of a bodhisattva. But in East Asia he is sometimes given the attributes of a Buddha, and may be seated on a tall throne with both legs extending down to the floor in *bhadrasana* ("auspicious posture"), which some call the "European sitting position"—for example the Tang dynasty limestone statue of fig. 54.[44] Here he wears the robes of a Buddha and has a large, round *ushnisha*, covered by a hairstyle of wave-like swirls similar to fig. 51. The Chinese inscription on the base of this Maitreya statue tells that it and two more bodhisattva images were dedicated in the year A.D. 705 by a disciple named Yan Zong in honor of his parents and family. Unfortunately, much monumental art from the Tang era was destroyed during a campaign of political persecution against Buddhism in 843–845.

Fig. 55. *The Monk Budai.* Glazed stoneware with paint, H: 9⅜ in. (23.8 cm). China, 20th century.

Maitreya is also associated with a legendary itinerant Chinese monk called *Budai,* or *Pu-tai* (a pun on his "Big Belly" and the "Hemp Sack" he carried on his back).[45] Budai lived in the tenth century and is remembered as a laughing, rotund, wandering miracle worker who spread happiness and good cheer. Just before his death, Budai revealed that he was an incarnation of the Bodhisattva Maitreya. Since then, images of this beloved "Laughing Buddha" have been favored as good-luck charms and can be found in nearly every Chinese temple. His huge belly is a token of prosperity; his jolly smile suggests happiness and contentment (fig. 55).

China is credited with inventing paper (in A.D. 197) and printing ink (A.D. 400). By the ninth century A.D., Chinese Buddhists had achieved a remarkable technical proficiency using carved wooden blocks to print multiple

Fig. 56. *Frontispiece of a Chinese Translation of the Diamond Sutra.* Block printed on paper, H: 9⅞ in. (25 cm). Found at Dunhuang, China, dated A.D. 868.

copies of illustrations and pages of texts. Fig. 56 is the frontispiece of a Chinese woodblock print of the *Vajrachchedika Prajnaparamita Sutra* ("Diamond Cutter of Perfection of Wisdom Sutra" or "Diamond Sutra") bearing a date corresponding to May 11, 868 A.D.—the world's oldest dated printed book.[46] Separate woodblocks were used to print the Chinese text and the illustration of the Buddha seated on a lotus throne behind a small table, preaching to an elderly disciple known as Subhuti. Marked on the center of the Buddha's chest is a swastika (from Sanskrit, *svastika*: "auspiciousness sign"), an ancient Indian mark of good fortune that can also symbolize the Buddhist teachings, especially the esoteric doctrines. Included in the scene are an entourage of monks, guardian deities, a pair of protector lions, and two celestial maidens (Sanskrit, *apsara*; Chinese, *tian-nu*) floating overhead on clouds. The printed sheets were attached to a backing strip and rolled into a scroll over sixteen feet long.

Avalokitesvara, the Bodhisattva of Compassion, is widely worshiped in China as a divinity named *Guan Shih Yin*, or *Guanyin* (also spelled *Kuan-yin*). Avalokitesvara / Guanyin was initially depicted by the Chinese in traditional masculine form, often as a savior aiding those in distress.[47] During the Tang dynasty, likenesses of Guanyin began to appear which were endowed with feminine features. Apparently this iconographic transformation to female form occurred gradually, the result of Tantric Buddhist and Daoist influences, and, perhaps, an inclination by the Chinese to associate loving compassion and gentle nurturing with the tender heart of a woman.[48] Since about the tenth century, the female personage of Guanyin has been one of East Asia's most revered deities, worshiped as a benevolent goddess, savioress, and provider of children to women desiring offspring—and therefore is frequently pictured holding a child. She traditionally wears long flowing robes and carries in her hand a flask of *amrita*, the elixir of immortality.

A superb, over-life-size polychrome wood statue from the eleventh or twelfth century shows the feminine form of Guanyin (fig. 57). She is seated in a variation of *rajalilasana* (royal ease posture) atop a moss-covered ledge suggesting a grotto by the sea. She wears the ornate headdress, jewels, and flowing scarves typically associated with bodhisattvas, and a long, lavishly decorated skirt flaring out about the feet as if tossed by an ocean breeze.

Plenty of ancient legends allude to Guanyin's origins. One version says she was born as *Miao Shan*, a saintly princess who rejected the life of royalty and privilege to join a monastery. Her father, *King Miao Zhuang*, imprisoned her as punishment and, when she refused his demand that she return to the palace, ordered her execution. Through her immense piety she was saved and escaped to a remote mountain cave where she gained supernatural powers through devoted study of the Dharma. When her father became desperately ill, she cut off one of her own arms and plucked out

one of her own eyes to make a magical potion that saved him from death. To express his gratitude the king ordered a statue made honoring her likeness, specifying that it should have "complete" arms and eyes—but the sculptor misunderstood and portrayed her with a thousand arms and eyes. This form of Guanyin image is everywhere in East Asia and much of Southeast Asia, her multiple arms holding various symbols for the countless ways she alleviates humanity's suffering. These likenesses range from modest images found in shrines and household altars (fig. 58) to monumental statuary erected in major temples (see fig. 71). Is Avalokitesvara, or Guanyin, inherently male, or female? Neither. A bodhisattva can manifest in any form, realm, and physical location as appropriate to help sentient beings in distress.

Fig. 58. *Bodhisattva Guanyin*. Stoneware with polychrome glazes, H: 8¼ in. (20.9 cm). China, 19th century.

The esoteric precepts and rituals of Vajrayana gained believers in China too. This movement, which emerged in northeast India during the Pala-Sena period, arrived via Central Asia and Tibet. In the Yuan dynasty (1279–1368), the Tibetan form of Vajrayana achieved widespread recognition among the Chinese and was given imperial patronage from the ruling Mongol court, which embraced it as the state religion. A glimpse of Vajrayana's impact on Chinese Buddhism is visible in the head of a Guanyin statue from northern China wearing a crown displaying the five transcendent Buddhas (fig. 59), a design similar to headdresses worn by

Fig. 57. (Opposite) *Bodhisattva Guanyin*. Wood with paint, 95 x 65 in. (2.41 x 1.65 m). China, Northern Sung or Liao dynasty, 11th–12th centuries.

Fig. 59. *Head of Bodhisattva Guanyin with Five Transcendent Buddhas in the Headdress.* Gray marble, H: 24⅜ in. (62 cm). North China, 14th–15th centuries.

Tibetan lamas while performing Tantric rituals (see fig. 97).

The Ming dynasty (1368–1644) is celebrated for the beauty and quality of its porcelain and the classic lines of its wood furniture. Masterpieces of metal sculpture were also produced by commission of the Ming emperors. One fine sample is a gilt bronze Udayana-style Buddha statue from the Yongle period (1403–1424) of that dynasty (see fig. 28).

Fig. 60. *A Luohan Seated in Meditation.* Earthenware with 3-color lead glaze, 40 x 31 x 26 in. (102 x 78.7 x 66.0 cm). China, Liao dynasty (907–1125) to Jin dynasty (1115–1234).

Another Chinese subject of note is the *luohan* (from Sanskrit, *arhat*; and Pali, *arahant*: "worthy one"), a monk or other follower of Buddhism who has attained enlightenment by devotion to the Dharma. The *luohan's* individual pursuit of wisdom and liberation has come to be associated with practitioners of the Chan and Zen schools. Chinese temples often contain collections of *luohan* statues grouped in various auspicious numbers. This began as ten, honoring those said to be the Buddha's ten great disciples during his lifetime in India: Mahakasyapa, Ananda, Sariputra, Maudgalyayana, Subhuti, Purna, Katyayana, Aniruddha, Upali, and Rahula.[49] In East Asia, prominent local monks were added, expanding the number to twelve, then sixteen, and sometimes eighteen. A few bigger temples have sets of five hundred statues—for the five hundred senior monks who participated in the first Buddhist Council in India and compiled the original Canon. Chinese *luohan* images reflect a medley of Buddhist and Dao traditions, rendered with strikingly realistic human features absorbed in meditation (fig. 60) and other poses, for example performing superhuman feats such as taming tigers and dragons.[50]

The long and complex processes of cultural assimilation, adaptation, and innovation enabled the Middle Kingdom to evolve its own unique, Sinicized assemblage of Buddhist beliefs, traditions, and artistic conventions—which was propagated with great success to neighboring lands, particularly Korea and Japan.

KOREA

Buddhism was introduced to Korea from China late in the fourth century A.D., during the Korean peninsula's "Three Kingdoms" period. The first recorded appearance was in the year 372, when a Chinese monk brought devotional images and copies of the scriptures to the northern Korean kingdom of Koguryo (37 B.C.–A.D. 668), which shared a common land border with China. At that time the dominant native religion of the Koreans was Shamanism, a type of animism that worships spirits thought to dwell within living beings and certain inanimate objects. The tenets of Chinese Mahayana Buddhism complimented and mingled with Shamanist beliefs to create a Korean form of Buddhism that gradually propagated down the peninsula.

Fig. 61. *Sakyamuni Buddha.* Gilt copper, H: 5½ in. (14 cm). Korea, Koguryo period, mid-6th century.

Early arts and culture in Koguryo developed under the hegemony of neighboring China's Northern Wei and Northern Qi Empires. A gilt copper, standing image of Sakyamuni Buddha from Koguryo in the mid-sixth century bears features echoing the designs of northern China (fig. 61). Solid cast in the round with heavy mercury gilding, its robe drapes down below the chest in U-shaped, symmetrically arranged Udayana-style folds that flare outward in pointed edges. The right hand is raised in the *ạbhaya mudra* of dispelling fear; the left hand is lowered in the *varada mudra* of bestowing a blessing—a favored iconographic pairing in Chinese images of Sakyamuni preaching the Lotus Sutra. Here the fourth and fifth

fingers of the lowered left hand are bent upward, a Korean design innovation frequently seen in Koguryo and Paekche imagery from the sixth century. A large, inverted lotus sculpted in a rolling wave pattern covers the base. On the back of the image is a single-hole loop, indicating it once included a nimbus, or halo, now missing. This rare statuette is of additional interest for having undergone a three-year research study by the Smithsonian Institution that confirmed its antiquity through a series of tests including atomic absorption spectroscopy, X-ray fluorescence, and metallographic and lead isotope ratio analyses of its gilding, corrosion, and malachite encrustation.

The kingdom of Paekche (18 B.C.–A.D. 663), in the southwest corner of the Korean peninsula, was introduced to Buddhism in A.D. 384 through its links with the Eastern Chin dynasty of southern China.[51] By 535, Buddhism was well established too in the southeastern Silla Kingdom (57 B.C.–A.D. 668) which eventually conquered the entire peninsula and consolidated the Three Kingdoms into the first united Korean nation.

Among the most ubiquitous devotional images in Korea are those of the Bodhisattva Maitreya (Korean, *Miruk*), the Future Buddha, seated in contemplation. A large gilt bronze statue from the seventh century is pictured in fig. 62. Maitreya's right leg rests horizontally across the knee of his left leg, which extends straight down to a small lotus-base footstool. His left hand holds the right leg in place. His head and shoulders lean forward with intense concentration, while the fingers of his right hand are raised to his right cheek in a delicate and distinctive expression of contemplating the suffering of humankind and his future mission as the next Buddha. This "contemplative" or "pensive" posture dates to Indian statuary from Mathura and Gandhara, which evidently served as prototypes for adaptations created in Central Asia and China. This genre occurs in Japanese iconography as well, but the enormous popularity in Korea of the Maitreya image in this contemplative pose has made it an emblem of Korean Buddhism.

Fig. 62. (Opposite) *Bodhisattva Maitreya*. Gilt bronze, H: 36⅞ in. (93.5 cm). Korea, Three Kingdoms period, 7th century.

Fig. 63. *Sakyamuni Buddha.* Granite, H (statue): 11 ft., 2⅞ in. (3.42 m). Sokkuram, Kyongju, Korea, Unified Silla period, circa 751.

Buddhism was embraced as a state religion and flourished as a cornerstone of Korean culture during the Unified Silla period (668–935). One of Korea's most remarkable national treasures is a man-made grotto known as *Sokkuram* ("Cave of the Buddha"), constructed in about 751 atop Mount Toham near Kyongju, the Unified Silla capital. Shaped as a thirty-foot-tall domed rotunda, the interior walls are sculpted with bodhisattvas, *arhats*, guardian figures, and other deities. Ten small niches cut into the top of the circular wall of the main chamber were fitted with additional carvings. Placed at the center of the chamber as its principal icon is a splendid granite statue of Sakyamuni seated, calling the Earth Goddess to witness his enlightenment, a favorite topic in the Unified Silla period (fig. 63). "The central Buddha of the main hall is both imposing in size and majestic in posture, radiating a feeling of inner strength and spiritual expansion. The stoutly built body is broad-shouldered and superbly proportioned. To it clings a monastic robe with a minimal number of folds, gathered in front between the legs in an unusual fan-shaped arrangement."[52]

Fig. 64. *Amitabha Buddha*. Stone, H: 114¼ in. (2.90 m). Korea, Unified Silla period, 719.

Korean Buddhism is essentially Mahayanist, with much devotion focused on Amitabha Buddha (Korean, *Amita-bul*), apparent from a large stone statue of the Unified Silla period (fig. 64). The Buddha *Bhaisajyaguru* (Sanskrit: "Medicine Teacher"; Korean, *Yaksayorae*), a Mahayana deity worshiped in China since the sixth century, also has cult followings in Korea and Japan. He is said to have lived eons ago, but now reigns in an eastern paradise and symbolizes the healing capabilities of the Dharma. Fig. 65 is a gilt bronze standing image of Bhaisajyaguru cast in the eighth century. His large round *ushnisha* is topped with a three-tier crown; the solemn expression of the face and the softly modeled, harmonious proportions of the body are characteristic of the late Silla period, which gained fame from its sophisticated metal creations. Bhaisajyaguru Buddha is usually identified by carrying a small medicine bowl and a myrobalan fruit (cherry plum), known in Asia for its health-giving properties. Both symbolize his healing powers. This statue may have originally held one of those objects in its left hand.

Vairochana Buddha is also known and worshiped in Korea (Korean, *Pirochana-bul*). The iron statue in fig. 66 was cast during the Koryo dynasty (918–1392), from which the name "Korea" is derived. This statue incorporates some distinctive traits of Korean Buddhist art that had developed by the ninth or tenth century: the head and hands are large in proportion to the torso; the face is broad and youthful with a narrow, smiling mouth; the *ushnisha* is wide yet round. Iron was commonly used to create such large-scale statuary during this period owing to the scarcity of copper and other metals. Vairochana Buddha is customarily portrayed with his hands posed in the *dharmachakra mudra*. The variation we see here is often encountered in East Asia, with one hand clasping the raised index finger of the other hand in the *bodhyangi* (fist of wisdom) *mudra*, sometimes called *bodhyagiri* (supreme wisdom) *mudra*. This *mudra* is a euphemistic substitute for the sexually explicit *yab-yum* (Tibetan: "father-mother") pose

Fig. 65. (Opposite) *Bhaisajyaguru Buddha*. Gilt bronze, H: 9¼ in. (23.5 cm). Korea, Unified Silla period, 8th century.

Fig. 66. *Vairochana Buddha displaying the Bodhyangi Mudra*. Cast iron, H: 44⅛ in. (1.12 m). Korea, Koryo dynasty, 10th–11th centuries.

expressing the spiritual union of masculine and feminine energies in the Tantric imagery of Nepal and Tibet. In such depictions, a male *yab* deity, representing compassion, unites with his *sakti* (female counterpart), a *yum* deity representing wisdom. An example of the Tantric *yab-yum* pose is seen in fig. 92, a Tara mandala from Tibet.

In the formative years of the Chosun dynasty (1392–1910) the ruling class redirected their patronage

Fig. 67. *Fourth of the Ten Kings of Hell*. Ink and paint on silk, 47¼ x 34 in. (120 x 86.4 cm). Tongdosa Temple, Korea, 1775.

to a Korean form of Confucianism patterned from the Ming dynasty of China. Buddhism suffered a period of oppression and decline, yet endured among the common people. During this span Buddhist art survived chiefly through folk art traditions, as simple images carved from wood and brightly colored brushwork that decorated the walls of rural temples.

A rare set of ten silk paintings from the Chosun period depicts the Ten Kings of Hell. That of the Fourth King appears in fig. 67. For a long span in Korea, as in China, the Bodhisattva Ksitigarbha (Korean, *Chijang Posal*) had been venerated as a protector of the dead who were suffering the torments of hell. However, in both countries some devotional focus gradually shifted from Ksitigarbha to the Ten Kings.[53] This painting illustrates how Korean iconography adopted the Chinese belief in the judgement of souls after death. The king is seated at the center, his importance made clear by rendering him much larger in scale than all the attendants, secretaries, and servants assisting him. In the bottom portion of the picture, one wrongdoer is being lowered into a fiery cauldron of boiling water, while other unfortunate souls await their punishments. To soften this nightmarish view of judgement and grisly torture after death, Korean painters included a touch of comedy relief in the form of a "friendly ogre." In this painting, he is the rascally, bald caricature of a horn-headed devil squeezing his way among the smiling female attendants at the king's left hand.

The Choson dynasty ended in 1910 with the Japanese occupation of Korea. When this period of colonization by Japan concluded in 1945, Korean Buddhism began a great revival. The Chan / Zen doctrine, introduced from China during the Unified Silla period, had by this time absorbed most other schools of Korean Buddhism into its Chogye Order, which continues today to have the largest congregations. Known as *Son* in Korean, this doctrine blends Mahayanist ideals of personal development through spiritual discipline and the practice of meditation as a path to enlightenment.[54]

JAPAN

Official chronicles say the Dharma was introduced to the islands of Japan in the year 552, when King Song of the Korean state of Paekche presented a gilt bronze image of Sakyamuni Buddha and copies of some scriptures to the Japanese court of Emperor Kimmei. This was a period of increasing contacts between Japan and Korea, with Korean monks, scholars, painters, and metalsmiths arriving to promote Buddhist studies, rituals, and art. Even so, Korea was mainly an intermediary, relaying to Japan what was essentially Chinese Buddhism.

The principal native religion of Japan at that time was *Shinto* ("Way of the Gods"), a form of animism that worships Nature divinities called *kami*. Some *kami* are said to inhabit natural places such as trees, stones, rivers, waterfalls, and mountains; others are believed to be the spirits of mythological figures and esteemed historical personalities.[55] After an initial period of opposition from some Shinto cults, Buddhism achieved ascendancy during the reign of Empress Suiko (r. 592–628). She proclaimed Buddhism the state religion in 594, then became a Buddhist nun. Her nephew Prince Shotoku ruled as her regent, fostering a new Japanese tradition which blended elements of Mahayana Buddhism, Shinto, and Chinese Confucianism.[56] Harmonious coexistence of Shinto and Buddhism was attained by identifying various *kami* deities as manifestations of Mahayana bodhisattvas and Buddhas (Japanese, *bosatsu* and *Butsu*), thereby achieving a pantheon shared and worshiped by both faiths. Prince Shotoku also launched a vigorous national modernization movement based largely on increased contacts with China, whose Buddhist ideology, system of writing, methods of government administration, advancements in science and medicine, and myriad other institutions were adopted by the Japanese.

Fig. 68. *Amida Nyorai (Amitabha Buddha) Flanked by Two Bodhisattvas—(right) Kannon (Avalokitesvara) and (left) Daiseishi (Mahasthamaprapta)*. Gilt bronze, H (center figure): 14⅛ in. (35.7 cm). Japan, Hakuho/early Nara period, 7th century.

During the Nara period (645–794), named for the southern city which became the first permanent imperial capital in 710, cultural exchanges were expanded with China's Tang dynasty, a rich source of styles and techniques of artistic expression that were imported, studied, and copied by the Japanese. In Japan, as in China, the branch of Mahayana worshiping Amitabha Buddha (Japanese, *Amida*), lord of the Pure Land or western paradise of Sukhavati, became the most widely practiced religion. *Nyorai*, Japanese for "Tathagata," is frequently included with the names of Buddhas, for example, *Amida Nyorai*.[57]

The Pure Land faith is often represented by the Amitabha trinity (Japanese, *Amida sanzon*), the three deities portrayed in a seventh-century gilt bronze statue from the early Nara, or Hakuho period (645–710) (fig. 68). Amitabha Buddha, the center figure, is seated "European style." At his sides stand his two attendant bodhisattvas: at the right of this picture, Avalokitesvara (Japanese, *Kannon* or *Kwannon*), identified by a headdress containing a small seated image of Amitabha; and, at the left, Mahasthamaprapta (Japanese, *Seishi* or *Daiseishi*). Mahasthamaprapta, a symbol of wisdom, is rarely depicted alone. He can usually be recognized by a small vase at the front of his headdress. In this piece, each of these two bodhisattvas stands atop a lotus whose curling stalk rises from the central base—a reminder of the promised afterlife where faithful devotees are transported inside lotus buds through a sacred pond and reborn in Amitabha's celestial Pure Land.

Yakushiji Temple in Nara, one of Japan's most revered Buddhist sites, is dedicated to Bhaisajyaguru (Japanese, *Yakushi Nyorai*), the "Medicine Teacher" Buddha. This temple's three main icons are larger than life-size bronze statues forming the Yakushi (Bhaisajyaguru) triad, a national treasure from the Hakuho period (fig. 69). The central, seated statue of Bhaisajyaguru Buddha has seven smaller images of him arrayed upon the mandorla behind his back. They symbolize the seven bodies or forms in which he can manifest. Two attendant bodhisattvas stand at his sides: Chandraprabha, Bodhisattva of the Moon (Japanese, *Gakko*) at left of the picture; and Suryaprabha, Bodhisattva of the Sun (Japanese, *Nikko*) at right of the picture.

> The history of Yakushiji is a Japanese tale of two cities.
> In 680 Emperor Tenmu pledged to build the temple

> when his consort Jito was afflicted with an eye disease and it was feared that she might go blind. For some reason the actual building of the temple was deferred until after Tenmu's death in 686, but it appears to have been completed by 697, when the eye-opening ceremony was held for the principal statues. This ritual was essential, because by drawing in the eyes of a statue, the wood or metal was converted from base material into a divinity.[58]

The early decades of the eighth century were a turbulent period in Japan, marked by frequent violent clashes between rival clans vying for control of rural areas, and devastated by a deadly epidemic that struck much of the country. Buddhism had long been associated with magical powers, a strength that had drawn the interest and support of a profusion of royal courts and governments, so it is not surprising that Emperor Shomu (701–756) looked to stabilize and protect Japan by

Fig. 69. *Yakushi Triad*: (left) *Gakko, Bodhisattva of the Moon* (*Sanskrit, Chandraprabha*); (center) *Yakushi Nyorai* (*Sanskrit, Bhaisajyaguru Buddha*); (right) *Nikko, Bodhisattva of the Sun* (*Sanskrit, Suryaprabha*). Yakushiji Temple, Nara, Japan, Hakuho/early Nara period, 697.

expanding imperial patronage of the Buddhist church. He donated huge tracts of land to erect a temple in every province and sponsored construction in Nara of a *Daibutsu* ("Great Buddha"), a gigantic bronze statue of Vairochana Buddha (Japanese, *Birushana Butsu*, or *Rushana*).[59] Nine years were needed to gather the necessary copper and other materials and cast this enormous statue portraying Vairochana seated on a lotus base, his right hand raised in a variation of *abhaya mudra* that has one finger slightly bent forward, his left hand resting palm upward in *varada mudra* on his left leg (fig. 70). Consecrated in 752, the statue later suffered extensive damage during a fire that destroyed the Todaiji Temple, which contained it. The statue has been repaired several times, and is today believed to be the largest of its kind in the world, measuring 18.02 meters from the bottom of the base to the top of the head. It is housed in the rebuilt Todaiji Temple, the biggest wooden edifice in the world—although just

Fig. 70. *Birushana-butsu, the Great Buddha of Nara* (*Vairochana Buddha*). Bronze, H: 49 ft., 3 in. (15 m). Todaiji Temple, Nara, Japan, 752.

Fig. 71. *Senju Kannon Bosatsu* (*Thousand-armed Bodhisattva Avalokitesvara*). Dry lacquer over a wooden core, H: 17 ft., 7 in. (5.36 m). Toshodaiji Temple, Nara, Japan, 8th century.

two-thirds the size of the temple's original wooden structure that was destroyed by fire.

Vairochana, the Resplendent Buddha, is the supreme deity of Japan's esoteric sects such as Tendai and Shingon. He is also known in Japan as *Dainichi* (Great Sun), with his solar aspects equated to those of the Shinto sun goddess, *Amaterasu Omikami*, from which the Japanese imperial family is believed to have descended. When Emperor Shomu began planning Todaiji and its immense statue of Vairochana Buddha, he was careful to maintain harmony between Buddhism and Shinto: "An imperial messenger was sent to Ise [an imperial shrine at Honshu dedicated to Amaterasu] to ask the will of the sun goddess. As reported, her response was favorable; she allowed that she and this buddha were aspects of the same reality."[60]

In 754, the Tang dynasty sent a venerated Chinese monk named Chien Chen to Japan at the invitation of Emperor Shomu. Chien Chen (Japanese, *Ganjin*) spent the rest of his life in Japan, teaching the Dharma to lay people, priests, and members of the imperial family. He established the Japanese Ritsu school of Buddhism and, in 759 with sponsorship by the Emperor, founded a new temple called Toshodaiji in the city of Nara. An immense, dry-lacquer-over-wood statue of a thousand-armed Bodhisattva Avalokitesvara (Japanese, *Senju Kannon Bosatsu*) stands in the main hall of Toshodaiji (fig. 71). This national treasure is the only extant Japanese sculpture of this deity constructed with one thousand separate arms. Forty-two are full-size, displaying attributes and gestures associated with Avalokitesvara; 911 smaller arms are also intact; all are attached directly to the body of the figure. This statue reflects the flavor of Tang dynasty sculpture from China, its upper body and thick cloth sash modeled with elegant naturalism. The lower robe's heavy folds are stylized yet realistic; an intricately carved, openwork halo positioned behind the head confirms the figure's divinity.

A new imperial capital was established in 794 at Heiankyo, today called Kyoto. The Heian period

(794–1185) saw growing devotion to Buddhism, by the court and the masses, particularly the esoteric beliefs and rituals freshly imported from China and disseminated by the Tendai and Shingon schools. A cavalcade of bodhisattvas and wrathful deities previously unknown in Japan were introduced with the esoteric teachings (Japanese, *Mikkyo*) and related through secret rites and pictorial diagrams called *mandala* (Sanskrit: "circle"; Japanese, *mandara*).

Increasing numbers of devotees, donors, and artisans in provincial areas brought renewed activity in sculpting religious images from wood, especially Japanese cypress. A perennial problem in carving a large image from a single solid block of lumber (Japanese, *ichiboku zukuri*) is that its outer sections typically lose moisture and contract faster than its core, especially in the dehydrated environment of a heated building. In time, this can cause cracks and splits that mar the statue's surface. One way to minimize this problem is to cut or chisel into its bottom or backside and remove wood from the core, thus enabling the wood to dry out more evenly. Wooden plugs are later cut and attached to cover the access holes. Japanese sculptors in the Heian period perfected yet a more effective technique: Several separate wooden blocks were rough-shaped, hollowed out and joined together, then detailed into the final product (Japanese, *yosegi zukuri*).[61] This allowed the creation of wooden sculptures grander in size and ornamentation, yet safe from the old problem of cracking surfaces. Additionally, sacred relics and prayer sheets could be placed inside each statue's hollow core during its consecration ritual to empower it with spiritual energy. One example of this technique is a wood carving of *Jizo Bosatsu* (Bodhisattva Ksitigarbha)—its head, front, and back of the body formed from three separate blocks of wood, then joined and finished (fig. 72). As this statue demonstrates, East Asian art often depicts Ksitigarbha as a monk, while other bodhisattvas are dressed in princely robes and jewelry.

Fig. 72. *Jizo Bosatsu* (*Bodhisattva Ksitigarbha*). Carved wood, H (figure only): 57 in. (1.46 m). Japan, late Heian period, late 11th–early 12th century.

The Heian era saw a rise in power of tribal clans and the emergence of a new breed of aristocratic warriors called *samurai*. This period closed with five years of civil war between two powerful samurai families: Taira and Minamoto. In 1185 the Minamoto faction won a decisive victory and established a military government, the Kamakura shogunate, first in a lineage of shoguns who would control most of feudal Japan until the Meiji Restoration re-established imperial rule in 1868.

The Kamakura period (1185–1333) began with a national program of reconstruction to repair damage inflicted by the war. Old Buddhist temples were restored and more were built. Although the imperial capital remained at Kyoto, political power shifted to Kamakura, a coastal town southwest of modern-day Tokyo. It was there that followers of Amitabha and his Pure Land faith donated funds to create a colossal statue of him which became known as *Amida Daibutsu*, the Great Buddha of Kamakura (fig. 73). The original statue was constructed from wood in 1243. When it was damaged by a storm, donors replaced it with an enormous bronze statue that was consecrated in 1252 and still stands today. This monumental seated image, 37 feet, 3 inches (11.36 meters) in height, has both hands resting in the lap, fingers folded up and pressed together in a distinctive variation of the meditation *mudra* that has come to be associated with Japanese likenesses of Amida / Amitabha Buddha. His head is inclined slightly forward and bears a thin, finely engraved moustache. The other features are traditional among Buddha images: the hair is composed of individual stylized curls; the earlobes are distended; the fingers are mildly webbed; a prominent *urna* is centered on the forehead; a broad, round *ushnisha* rises atop the head. An immense wooden hall once housed this statue but was destroyed by a tidal wave in 1495. Since then, the statue has stood in the open air.

Japan's earliest contacts with the Chan Buddhism of China probably occurred in the seventh century when Japanese monks visiting the mainland likely first encountered that newly developing school. In the

Fig. 73. *Daibutsu, the Great Buddha of Kamakura* (*Amitabha Buddha*). Bronze, H: 37 ft., 3 in. (11.36 m). Kotoku-in Temple, Kamakura, Japan, 1252.

course of the Kamakura period, Chan beliefs became firmly rooted in Japan under the name *Zen*, and grew to be an integral part of the national psyche. Zen is essentially a branch of the Mahayana movement, but has evolved into a unique spiritual tradition well described by its advocates in these four lines:

> A special transmission outside the scriptures;
> No dependence upon words and letters;
> Direct pointing at the soul of man;
> Seeing into one's nature and the attainment of Buddhahood.[62]

Zen masters see their doctrine as the ultimate truth and Zen consciousness as the path to a life of freedom and contentment. As with other Buddhist schools, the goal of Zen is enlightenment, here called *satori* (from the Japanese verb, *satoru*: "to know"), a sudden and profound spiritual awakening that can only be achieved through one's personal experience of Zen, not from just the knowledge and logic found in books and scriptures. An uninitiated observer or beginning student may first find the Zen experience puzzling, contradictory, even incomprehensible. Their teacher, usually a *roshi* (venerable Zen master), may help their understanding along with parables, some illustrated by calligraphy and Zen paintings (Japanese, *Zenga*). One popular series unfolds the path of Zen by "Ten Oxherding Pictures" (Japanese, *Jugyu-zu*). These first appeared in China in the eleventh century and have since then been reinterpreted in drawings, verse, and commentaries. As shown in a set of ten ink paintings by Master Gyokusei Jikihara (fig. 74), the ox herder is a person seeking spiritual enlightenment. The ox represents his mind, or true self, which he must tame and transform. The corresponding ten stages of Zen practice that lead the herder to enlightenment are described in a translation of verses attributed to the Chinese Master K'uo-an Chih-yuan (circa 1150; quote with permission from the publisher), followed by comments based on contemporary interpretations.

Fig. 74. *Ten Oxherding Pictures. By Master Gyokusei Jikihara*. Ink paintings on paper, each 30 x 24 in. (76.2 x 61.0 cm). Zen Mountain Monastery, Mt. Tremper, New York, 1983.

(1) The Search for the Ox

In the pasture of the world, I endlessly push aside the tall grasses in search of the ox.
Following unnamed rivers, lost upon the interpenetrating paths of distant mountains,
My strength failing and my vitality exhausted, I cannot find the ox.
I only hear the locusts chirping through the forest at night.

The herder is about to begin his spiritual quest. He stands amid Nature's beauty and bounty, yet feels unsatisfied, anxious, confused. He does not realize that the ox—his true self, the Buddha-nature within every living being—is not lost; he simply fails to notice it because of his confusion.

(2) Discovering the Footprints

Along the riverbank under the trees, I discover footprints!
Even under the fragrant grass I see his prints.
Deep in remote mountains they are found.
These traces can no more be hidden than one's nose, looking heavenward.

The herder sees footprints, an indication of his first awareness of Buddhist teachings and meditation as the path to liberation. Yet this is but a tentative discovery; he is only beginning to understand.

(3) Perceiving the Ox

I hear the song of the nightingale.
The sun is warm, the wind is mild, willows are green along the shore -
Here no ox can hide!
What artist can draw that massive head, those majestic horns?

The herder is no longer confused; he has found the path. All of his senses have merged harmoniously, enabling him to clearly perceive reality.

(4) Catching the Ox

I seize him with a terrific struggle.
His great will and power are inexhaustible.
He charges to the high plateau far above the cloud-mists,
Or in an impenetrable ravine he stands.

The herder uses a rope to catch the ox, but it struggles to break free and run wild. The herder has begun to practice meditation but his mind wanders, jumping from one thought to another.

(5) Taming the Ox

The whip and rope are necessary,
Else he might stray off down some dusty road.
Being well-trained, he becomes naturally gentle.
Then, unfettered, he obeys his master.

The ox is no longer wild; the herder can now guide it gently with a loosely held rope. Through dedicated meditation practice, the herder has tamed his mind, yet remains disciplined and vigilant lest it stray again.

(6) Riding the Ox Home

Mounting the ox, slowly I return homeward.
The voice of my flute intones through the evening.
Measuring with hand-beats the pulsating harmony, I direct the endless rhythm.
Whoever hears this melody will join me.

This struggle is over; the ox has been tamed. The herder sits serenely upon its back, joyfully playing a tune on his flute as they ride home. The herder has become one with his true self.

(7) The Ox Transcended

Astride the ox, I reach home.
I am serene. The ox too can rest.
The dawn has come. In blissful repose,
Within my thatched dwelling I have abandoned the whip and ropes.

The herder rests contentedly in his hut. He no longer needs to think about the ox—it was only a means for realizing his own true nature.

(8) Both Ox and Self Transcended

Whip, rope, person, and ox - all merge in No Thing.
This heaven is so vast, no message can stain it.
How may a snowflake exist in a raging fire.
Here are the footprints of the Ancestors.

All desires, all attachments, all burdens have disappeared. Both ox and self have vanished, merged with Emptiness, which is represented by a simple black circle the Japanese call enso. "Emptiness" is a translation of the Sanskrit term sunyata (Pali, sunnata; Chinese, chen-kung; Japanese, shinku), a central principle of Buddhism that is not a negative concept; rather, it is the ultimate reality which makes possible all existence, including the Buddha-nature.[63]

(9) Reaching the Source

Too many steps have been taken returning to the root and the source.
Better to have been blind and deaf from the beginning!
Dwelling in one's true abode, unconcerned with that without -
The river flows tranquilly on and the flowers are red.

Oneness with Nature is a prime component of Zen ideology and artistic expression, with certain natural elements and forest creatures symbolizing ethical ideals and spiritual insights.[64] Plum blossoms, bamboo, and rocks—"three worthy ones" to the Chinese and Japanese—are traditionally associated with purity and strength of character. The sparrow exemplifies freedom. This idyllic woodland scene may then represent the herder's enlightened spirit, part of the perfect unity of all things.

(10) In the World

Barefooted and naked of breast, I mingle with the people of the world.
My clothes are ragged and dust-laden, and I am ever blissful.
I use no magic to extend my life;
Now, before me, the dead trees become alive.

The herder leaves his material possessions and worldly concerns behind. He applies himself to helping others on the path to liberation, following the example of China's legendary monk Budai (Japanese, Hotei)—shown in this sketch happily wandering from place to place with his hemp sack and stick.[65]

Zen thrived and permeated the national culture largely because many of its precepts were compatible with the military mindset of the shoguns who ruled feudal Japan. While this association might seem to contravene Buddhism's non-violent spirit, it did happen that samurai warriors and Zen masters shared ideals such as discipline, courage, austerity, and the transcendence of life and death. *Bushido* ("Way of the Warrior"), the samurai's moral code, embraced those tenets of Zen Buddhism, Confucianism, and Shinto that served its goals. Buddhism's teachings on rebirth were useful in calming the soldier's fear of death, and Zen methods of mental training had practical applications in the martial arts.

As mentioned earlier, the Chan movement in China created likenesses of the Buddha as an emaciated, bearded ascetic "Coming Down from the Mountain" to represent his enlightenment and his return to society to teach the Dharma. A Japanese ink-on-paper scroll of this theme from the Kamakura period was likely patterned after a Chinese prototype and exemplifies the Chan/Zen approach to painting (fig. 75). Pictorial elements are kept to a minimum and rendered in a simple, austere, natural style depicting Sakyamuni (Japanese, *Shaka*) as a man, not a deity. Stylization, symmetrization, allusions to the supernatural, pigments, gilding, and other decorative motifs—techniques applied everywhere in traditional Buddhist iconography—are all absent here. Still, Sakyamuni's special identity is maintained by the subtle display of his *urna* and *ushnisha*. His finely drawn face bears a serene, contemplative expression. Six difficult years of asceticism and meditation that culminated in his enlightenment are signified by his beard, a trait liked by Zen artists but rarely seen elsewhere. His windswept robe is pictured with broad, rough brush strokes emphasizing the composition's angular perspective—all together an effect unique in religious portraiture.[66]

Named for a district in Kyoto from which the Ashikaga shoguns ruled, the Muromachi period (1392–1573)

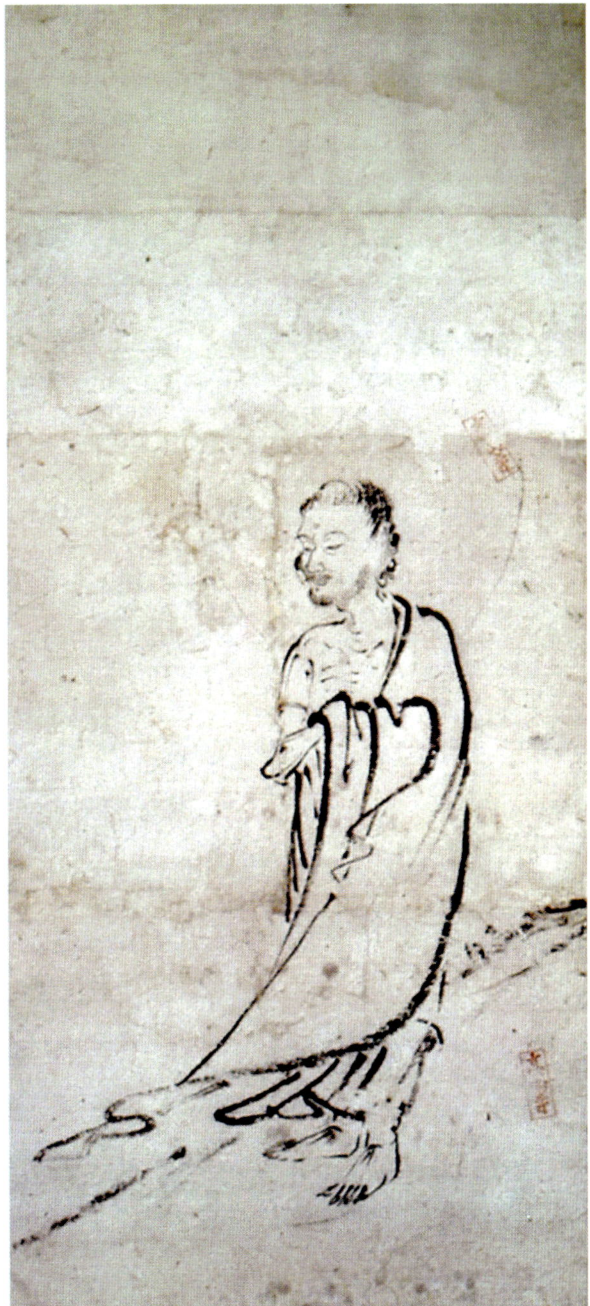

Fig. 75. *Shaka (Sakyamuni) Coming Down from the Mountain*. Ink on paper scroll, 35¾ x 16 in. (90.8 x 41.9 cm). Japan, Kamakura period, circa 1300.

saw Buddhist influences widening in secular as well as religious art and literature. Bodhidharma (Japanese, *Bodaidaruma*, or *Daruma*), the Indian monk revered as founder and first patriarch of the Zen school, was by then a favored subject for artists. A renowned fifteenth-century painting by Sesshu Toyo illustrates the legend of "Hui-k'o Presenting His Arm to Bodhidharma" (fig. 76).[67] Bodhidharma, sitting in meditation facing a cave wall at the right of the picture, is conspicuous by his stern expression, wide-eyed stare, and familiar long white robe with its hood pulled up over his head. He had ignored the pleas of a Chinese monk named Hui-k'o, who earnestly wished to become Bodhidharma's disciple. As a final, grim demonstration of his devotion and resolve, Hui-k'o cut off his own left hand at the forearm and offered it to Bodhidharma, as we see in this painting. Bodhidharma then accepted Hui-k'o as a pupil and eventually appointed him to be his successor and second patriarch of the Zen school.

Another Chinese Buddhist tradition observed in Japanese temples was to erect statues of the four fierce guardian gods, or *lokapalas* (Chinese, *lishi*, or *t'ien-wang*; Japanese, *shi-tenno*). Outfitted with body armor and a variety of weapons and symbolic attributes, they stand as sentinels at their respective cardinal directions giving divine protection. *Bishamonten* (or, *Tamonten*, both Japanese names for the Guardian of the North) traditionally holds a trident and a miniature stupa (fig. 77). This stupa represents a shrine in the *nagas'* undersea palace where Nagarjuna is said to have discovered the advanced teachings of the Buddha so important in the Mahayana, and attests to Bishamonten's role as a protector of the Dharma. To the Japanese, *Zochoten* is guardian of the south; *Jikokuten*, the east; and *Komokuten*, the west.

The Edo period (1615–1868), named for the city that came to be called Tokyo in 1868, saw the rise of mass attraction to a uniquely Japanese craft: *netsuke*—miniature carvings fashioned from wood, ivory, and

Fig. 76. *Hui-k'o Presenting His Arm to Bodhidharma* (*Japanese, Daruma*). By Sesshu Toyo. Ink and colors on paper, 78¾ x 44⅞ in. (2.00 x 1.14 m). Sainenji, Aichi prefecture, Japan, Muromachi period, 1496.

Fig. 77. (Right) *Bishamonten* (or *Tamonten*), *Guardian of the North, One of the Four Lokapala.* Wood, copper and pigments, H: 52 in. (1.32 m). Japan, 18th–19th centuries.

Fig. 78. (Below) *Netsuke of Bishamonten and a Tiger. By Kokoku*. Boxwood, ebony and ivory, inlaid with tortoise shell, gold, and silver, H: 1¾ in. (4.3 cm). Japan, Meiji period.

79. (Right) *The Western Paradise of Amida* (*Amitabha Buddha*). Ink and gold and colors on silk, 27⅛ x 20½ in. (69 x 52 cm). Japan, 19th century.

animal horn. Their original form was a small, plain piece of wood having two holes through which a cord was threaded, then attached to a pouch, medicine case, or other object to be carried on the *obi* (sash) of the traditional Japanese kimono, which had no pockets. Later carved examples of netsuke depicted animals, deities, and famous persons. Some are exquisitely constructed masterpieces, such as a miniature portrait of Bishamonten, Guardian of the North, his body sculpted from boxwood, boots from ebony, and ivory pieces shaped as his face, hands, stupa, and the companion tiger crouching by his side, with gold, silver, and tortoise shell inlay (fig. 78). An interesting comparison with the life-size statue of the same deity in fig. 77.

Shogun domination of Japan ended in 1868 when the military government was overthrown and imperial rule was restored under the young emperor Meiji, ushering in the Meiji period (1868–1912). Then, as now, the Pure Land sect that worships Amida/Amitabha Buddha was the largest religious denomination in Japan. A painted silk scroll from the nineteenth century uses ink and gold and dazzling colors to depict the Pure Land as a majestic paradise in the style of a Chinese temple complex (fig. 79). Amida/Amitabha Buddha sits on a lotus throne at the center of the main hall. His right hand is raised, index finger and thumb touching, which in Japanese imagery indicates he is welcoming faithful devotees reborn from lotus buds in the sacred pond facing the main hall. He is flanked by the bodhisattvas Avalokitesvara (Kannon) and Mahasthamaprapta (Seishi). Around them are a retinue of beautiful female attendants and celestial musicians and dancers. Overhead are the colorful clouds that carry Amitabha and his heavenly host when they descend to Earth. Such paintings assist worshipers to visualize and pray for rebirth in the Pure Land. This type of iconography is called *henso* (Japanese: "transformed configuration" or "transformed picture") and is often categorized in Japan as a mandala (Japanese, *mandara*).[68]

The Western Paradise of Amida/Amitabha is the best known and most sought of Buddhism's Pure Lands. Yet each of the Mahayana's numerous transcendent Buddhas (and many bodhisattvas) is said to preside over his own celestial paradise. Some are listed in the chart of characteristics of the transcendent Buddhas in appendix 2. Bhaisajyaguru Buddha (Japanese, *Yakushi*) reigns over a Pure Land in the eastern reaches of the cosmos. The celestial realm of the Bodhisattva Maitreya (Japanese, *Miroku*) is the Tushita Heaven, where he now dwells, preparing to be reborn on Earth one day in the future and become the next Buddha.

NEPAL

It is a point of great national pride among Nepal's people that their country was the birthplace of Sakyamuni, the historical Buddha. So it is not surprising that scenes depicting his birth are popular in their art. The gilt copper and brass statuette of Queen Maya giving birth (see fig. 4) exudes charm and elegance, picturing her in the gently swaying pose known as *tribhanga* ("triple bending" of the body). She grasps a branch of the *sala* tree for support as her newborn son, the Bodhisattva Prince Siddhartha, the Future Buddha, appears from her right side, his hands clasped in the *anjali mudra* of respectful greeting. Elegantly inlaid with colored gemstones, this image exemplifies the fondness for sumptuous, finely detailed ornamentation and the high order of metalworking skills that are hallmarks of the Newari, a Kathmandu ethnic group whose craftsmen produce the bulk of Nepal's religious artworks.

Although the Buddha was born and came of age in what is now the Kingdom of Nepal, the principal events regarding his teaching of the Dharma occurred in northeastern India. Those teachings and the fabric of what we know as Buddhism were likely introduced from India into Nepal primarily by the missionary efforts of King Asoka in the third century B.C.

> During the fifth and sixth centuries the contacts of Nepal were with the Indian schools of sculpture in Mathura and central India. Whether Indian sculptors from these centers taught in Nepal, or Nepali sculptors came to India to work under Indian masters, or whether sculptures reached Nepal in that period cannot be answered at present.
>
> Traits of these several Indian schools mingled in Nepal, but whichever components prevail they are subsumed to a whole which is Nepali. Its form is harder, the line more consciously drawn. Watchfully, daintily, and with firmness the sculptor has groomed his presentation.[69]

Fig. 80. *Bodhisattva Manjusri.* Silver, H: 6½ in. (16.5 cm). Nepal, 19th century.

Since ancient times Nepal has maintained trade links with and absorbed cultural influences from neighboring India, adopting its multiple forms of Hinduism, Buddhism, and other belief systems. Today about 90 percent of Nepal's population practice Hinduism and 5 percent are Buddhist, but the worship of certain deities, as well as innumerable rituals and ceremonies, are shared by the two religions, so the demarcation between them is not sharp. For example, in Nepal the Bodhisattva Avalokitesvara is known as *Padmapani*, and as *Matsyendranatha*—and is worshiped by Buddhists and Hindus alike.

Manjusri, Bodhisattva of Wisdom in the Mahayana pantheon, receives special veneration in Nepal. A silver statuette depicts him seated atop a double lotus base, his left hand raised in the *vitarka mudra* of teaching (fig. 80). It also shows his two main identifying

attributes: a double-edged, flaming sword in his right hand, which he uses to destroy ignorance; and a lotus flower in his left hand supporting the *Prajnaparamita Sutra* ("Perfection of Wisdom Sutra"), an important Mahayana text. In other imagery he sometimes has four arms, the added pair wielding a bow and arrow, another of his weapons for destroying ignorance.

Fig. 81. *Svayambhu Mahachaitya*. Kathmandu, Nepal, original brick and clay core constructed circa 4th century A.D.

The *Svayambhu Purana*, a circa-fifteenth-century holy text describing Nepal's history, tells that Manjusri traveled from his home in China on a pilgrimage to Nepal to worship at a shrine of the Adi-Buddha (Nepali, *Svayambhu*: "First" or "Self-originated" Buddha). The shrine consisted of a sacred flame emanating from a lotus flower on a lake called *Nagarasa* (also *Naga Daha*), after the *naga* serpents that inhabited it. Access to the shrine was difficult because of the lake's vast waters and the mountains surrounding it, so Manjusri swung his magical sword and cut the Chobar gorge that drained the lake and created the Kathmandu Valley, enabling humans and other creatures to live there. He is then revered by many as the founder of Nepali civilization. Manjusri is worshiped in China, too, as a bodhisattva named *Wenshu*, frequently shown riding atop a lion. He and the Bodhisattva Samantabhadra (Chinese, *Puxian*), whose mount is an elephant, sometimes appear together as attendants forming a trinity with Sakyamuni Buddha.

Legends also say that when Manjusri drained the great lake and created the Kathmandu Valley, the lotus shrine of the Adi-Buddha was transformed into a hill, and the sacred flame became the stupa known as *Svayambhu Mahachaitya*, one of the valley's most revered sites (fig. 81). Across the centuries, this stupa has been damaged or destroyed and rebuilt several times. Its top is now crowned by a spire with thirteen golden rings signifying the thirteen stages of development in Tantric Buddhism. Each of the four sides of the square structure between the dome and the spire displays the "All-seeing Eyes of the Buddha," an icon related to the Vajrayana pentad of five transcendent Buddhas. Each of four of the Buddhas is worshiped at a shrine at the stupa positioned according to the location in the cosmos of his paradise, or Pure Land: Amitabha at the west; Akshobhya at the east; Amoghasiddhi at the north; and Ratnasambhava at the south. The fifth Buddha, Vairochana, said to preside over a paradise at the center of the cosmos, has a shrine

next to that of Akshobhya and is represented by the "All-seeing Eyes." The Adi-Buddha is also known as *Vajrasattva* ("Thunderbolt" or "Diamond" Being). Vajrasattva is always shown wearing a crown and royal robes, holding a *vajra* scepter in his right hand and a ghanta bell in his left hand (fig. 82). The five transcendent Buddhas are visualized through other media as well,

Fig. 82. *Vajrasattva*. Carved wood, gilded and painted, H: 42⅛ in. (107 cm). Nepal, 19th or 20th century.

for example, as painted on the wooden cover of a Nepali *sutra* (fig. 83).

Theravada and Mahayana traditions teach that Sakyamuni, the historical Buddha, was one in a series of mortal Buddhas who have appeared in our world and taught the Dharma. Both traditions also acknowledge the *jataka* stories spanning a number of "world cycles" (Sanskrit, *kalpa*; Pali, *kappa*), the immensely long period of time measurement that the Vedic scriptures reckon as 4,320 million solar years. One *jataka* tells of the distant past, long before Prince Siddhartha's birth and enlightenment, even before his earlier lifetime as Prince Vessantara—when he lived on Earth as a hermit known as *Sumedha*. During that *kalpa*, Dipankara, the Buddha of Fixed Light, lived and taught the Dharma. When the two met, Dipankara was so favorably impressed by Sumedha's devotion to the pursuit of spiritual perfections that he predicted Sumedha would one day in a future lifetime become a Buddha. Sumedha fulfilled that prediction when he took birth as Prince Siddhartha, attained enlightenment and became the Buddha of our current *kalpa*. In Nepal, Dipankara Buddha usually appears as a standing image wearing an elaborate jeweled crown and colorful flowing robes, his right hand raised in *abhaya mudra* and the left in *varada mudra* (fig. 84).

Another deity widely worshiped in Nepal is Prajnaparamita, Goddess of Transcendent Wisdom, an embodiment of the Prajnaparamita Sutras, a series of Mahayana texts on the subject of *prajna* (wisdom). These sutras are so revered in the Mahayana tradition that the goddess Prajnaparamita is sometimes called the "Mother of all Buddhas." A rare sixteenth-century bronze repousse statue from Nepal represents this deity seated on a double lotus throne (fig. 85). Two of her hands are posed together in the *dharmachakra* mudra; her two other hands are raised in the *vitarka mudra*.

Amitabha Buddha, venerated across East Asia, is worshiped by some Tantric schools in his alternate form

as Amitayus, the Buddha of Infinite Life (Tibetan, *Che-dpag-med*). Amitayus may be considered the *sambhogakaya* ("enjoyment body") emanation of Amitabha Buddha.[70] A gilt copper statue from the fourteenth century characterizes Amitayus in his hieratic posture, seated in meditation with a flask containing the magical elixir *amrita* held in his joined hands (fig. 86). The modeling of this statue is exquisitely detailed with bracelets, necklaces, armbands, and a crown, all elegantly inlaid with colored gemstones.

Buddhism's view of the endless cycle of birth, death, and rebirth is graphically revealed in the "Wheel of Life" or "Wheel of Existence" (Sanskrit, *bhava-chakra*; Tibetan, *sipay khorlo*), a diagram of Buddhist cosmology popular in Tibet and Nepal (fig. 87).[71] The Wheel comprises four concentric circles:

1. Starting at the hub, or innermost circle, we see a pig (symbolizing ignorance), a snake (hatred or anger), and a rooster (desire or greed), each biting the next one's tail to represent the stimuli which cause rebirth and power the Wheel.
2. Looking outward, the second circle is divided into two halves. On the left side, three fortunate beings who have performed meritorious actions and acquired good karma are rising up toward the Buddha and the heavenly realms. On the right side, three beings who have performed bad actions are tumbling down toward an attendant of the Lord of Death and the hell realms.
3. The third circle, the largest area of the Wheel, consists of six sectors representing the six *gati*, or realms of existence. Beginning at top-center and viewing clockwise, we see: (1) *deva* (gods) in their heavenly realms; (2) *asura* (lower gods), who are constantly engaged in conflict; (3) *tir-yagyoni* (animals); (4) *naraka* (hell-beings); (5) *preta* (hungry ghosts), spirits whose past lives were dominated by greed and envy, and accordingly now suffer the torture of hunger, as indicated by their huge bellies and tiny mouths;

Fig. 83. *Cover of a Sutra Picturing Five Transcendent Buddhas. Left to right: Akshobhya, Ratnasambhava, Vairochana, Amitabha, and Amoghasiddhi*. Painted wood, H: 3¼ x 15¾ in. (8.3 x 40 cm). Nepal, 19th century.

Fig. 84. (Right) *Dipankara Buddha*. Bronze with gilt and paint, H: 28 in. (71 cm). Nepal, 17th–18th centuries.

Fig. 85. (Opposite) *Goddess Prajnaparamita*. Bronze repousse inlaid with semiprecious stones, H: 16½ in. (42 cm). Nepal, 16th century.

Fig. 86. *Amitayus Buddha*. Copper, gilded and inlaid with gemstones, H: 15¾ in. (40 cm). Nepal, 14th century.

Fig. 87. (Opposite) *Wheel of Life*. Tempera on cloth, 15¾ x 11¾ in. (40 x 29.8 cm). Nepal, 20th century.

and (6) *manusya* (humans). In this depiction of the Wheel of Life, Avalokitesvara stands in every realm, teaching all beings the path to liberation from *samsara*. To the *devas* he brings a lute whose music rouses them from complacency; to the *asuras*, a sword of wisdom; to the animals, knowledge, represented by a book; to the hell-beings, a purifying flame; to the *pretas*, spiritual sustenance; to the humans, an alms bowl and staff.

4. The fourth and outermost circle has twelve scenes symbolizing the twelve links in the chain of interdependent arising. This Buddhist concept shows how one phenomenon gives rise to another, to hold all beings in *samsara*, the endless cycle of birth, death, and rebirth. Starting at top-right and viewing clockwise, we see: (1) a blind man guided by a stick (symbolizing ignorance); (2) a potter creating a pot (formation); (3) a monkey (consciousness); (4) two men in a boat (name and form); (5) a house with six windows (the six senses: sight, hearing, smell, touch, taste, and mind); (6) a couple embracing (sense contact); (7) a man struck in the eye by an arrow (sensation or feeling); (8) a man drinking (craving or thirst); (9) a man picking fruit (grasping or attachment); (10) a young woman (the process of becoming); (11) a woman giving birth (birth); and lastly at top-left (12) a man carrying a corpse to the funeral pyre (old age and death).

The entire wheel is clutched by the fangs and claws and feet of Yama, wrathful Lord of Death. He wears a headpiece of skulls and gold bands on his arms and legs, has three bulging eyes and flaming eyebrows—and can swallow up the Wheel at any moment, a reminder of the impermanence of all things. In the picture's top-right corner is a standing image of the Buddha. Having freed himself from the endless cycle of birth, death, and rebirth, he stands outside the wheel, pointing the way to liberation. At the top-left corner stands Avalokitesvara, aiding beings on that path.

An often-seen design variation of the Wheel of Life configures the six realms of existence in just five sectors by grouping *devas* and *asuras* together in the same sector. Their areas are separated by a magical wish-granting tree (Sanskrit, *kalpavrksa*) that grows on the *asuras'* side but bears fruit on branches reaching across the *devas'* side—an effective allusion to the conflicts that can beset neighbors in any realm.

TIBET

Tibet, the Land of Snows, abounds in Buddhist legends. A creation myth tells that in the distant past, the Bodhisattva Avalokitesvara took birth as an ape and the Bodhisattva Tara appeared as a female demon. The couple mated and had offspring who in turn gave birth to the native people of the Yarlung Valley in what is now central Tibet. Tradition also says that Buddhism first came to Tibet in A.D. 173 and was gradually assimilated into the national culture. A major dissemination did begin in A.D. 632 during the reign of King Songtsen Gampo, when he took as his brides two princesses—one from China, one from Nepal. Both were devout Buddhists who carried sacred texts and images from their homelands to the palace in Lhasa, which later became Tibet's capital city. The king established two temples in Lhasa: the Jokhang Temple, to house an image of Akshobhya Buddha belonging to his Nepali consort; and the Ramoche Temple, to house an image of Sakyamuni Buddha belonging to his Chinese consort.[72] The king brought monks from India to teach and spread the faith, and sent his minister, Thonmi Sambhota, to India to study Sanskrit. As a result, a Tibetan alphabet was created, patterned after Sanskrit, and a program was initiated to translate Buddhist scriptures into the Tibetan language.

On through the eighth century more Indian Buddhists arrived to help propagate the teachings, including Padmasambhava (Tibetan, *Guru Rinpoche*: "Precious Guru"), a highly accomplished monk and mystic from the kingdom of Oddiyana. When Padmasambhava arrived in Tibet, its principal native religion was an ancient form of Shamanism called *Bon*, which gives reverence to spirits embodying the forces of Nature. Rather than challenge the Bon faith and its priests, Padmasambhava accepted the deities they worshiped into Tibet's Buddhist pantheon. This accommodation led to the evolution of Tibet's distinctive form of Vajrayana Buddhism. Padmasambhava's students and disciples included Tibet's ruler at that time, King Trisong Detsen (755–797), and the *Nyingmapa* school that originated with Padmasambhava continues today as one of Tibet's major religious orders. Padmasambhava was immortalized as a saintly founding father of Tibetan Buddhism and deified as the "Second Buddha"—as articulated in this Tibetan verse: "As Dharmakaya, there is Amitabha / As Sambhogakaya, there is Avalokitesvara / And as Nirmanakaya, there is Guru Padmasambhava."[73]

The Tibetan word *pa* ("person of" or "follower of") is commonly suffixed to the names of religious orders. Thus, the *Nyingma* ("Ancient") school and its followers are also referred to as *Nyingmapa*—both words expressing the phonetic spelling. The formal spelling of *Nyingmapa* by the Wylie system for transliterating Tibetan words is *rNying ma pa*. Tibet's five major Buddhist schools are:

- Nyingma / Nyingmapa / rNying ma pa
- Kadam / Kadampa / bKa' gdams pa
- Kagyu / Kagyupa / bKa' brgyud pa
- Sakya / Sakyapa / Sa skya pa
- Gelug / Gelugpa / dGe lugs pa.[74]

One of Tibet's most famed artistic traditions is *thanka*—paintings, usually on cloth, that can be rolled up like scrolls for easy transport. The raw fabric that will become the artist's canvas is first stretched across a wooden frame using lengths of string, then treated on both sides with a glue made from animal hides. After the surfaces have been dried and polished, the artist will sketch an outline conforming to traditional iconographic specifications, then use a palette of mineral or vegetable pigments to paint the actual picture. The finished canvas is usually fitted with a silk border and a front cover flap that is raised for viewing during worship, meditation, and other rites.[75]

Fig. 88. *Padmasambhava* (*Main Form*). Ground mineral pigments on cotton, 27¼ x 18⅞ in. (69 x 48 cm). Nyingma Lineage, Tibet, 1800–1899.

The thanka in fig. 88 portrays Padmasambhava's main form, attired in robes of different colors and encircled by a rainbow sphere. He is seated atop a sun and moon disc above a multi-colored lotus blossom rising from the blue waters of Dhanakosha Lake in Oddiyana—an illustration of the legend of his birth. He wears gold earrings and a necklace; his head is covered with a lotus hat, a gift of the King of Zahor, made from silk brocade topped with a half-*vajra* and a vulture feather. His right hand holds an upright gold *vajra*. His left hand, placed in his lap, holds a white skull cup filled with nectar, jewels, and a long-life vase. The ornate *katvanga* staff of a Vajrayana mendicant festooned with white streamers rests against his left shoulder. Seated to the left is Princess Mandarava, Padmasambhava's Indian consort; to the right is Yeshe Tsogyel, his Tibetan consort. At top center of the painting is the primordial Buddha Samantabhadra (dark blue in color), naked, his two hands placed in his lap and seated in the *vajrasana* posture. To the left is Amitabha Buddha (red), attended by two bodhisattvas. To the right is Padmapani Avalokitesvara (white), attended by two bodhisattvas. At the bottom left is Shantirakshita, a distinguished Indian scholar (Sanskrit, *pandita*; Hindi, *pandit*; English, *pundit*), wearing monastic robes and a red *pandita* hat, and attended by two monks. To the right is King Trisong Detsen, performing the Dharma teaching *mudra*. The Queen sits to the lower right while two laymen in front present offerings. In between, the ground is strewn with piles of wish-fulfilling jewels, precious objects, and a golden Dharma wheel (*dharmachakra*).[76]

The "First Propagation" period of Buddhism in Tibet ended in the middle of the ninth century when the Bonpo shamans regained power and launched a violent persecution of the Buddhists. Monks were harassed or banished and their temples were destroyed. But Buddhism had by then taken root and survived, especially in western Tibet, which continued receiving Vajrayana devotional art and teachings from neighboring

Kashmir and northeastern India. A vigorous revival of Buddhism known as the "Second Propagation" began in the mid-eleventh century—some say commencing in the year 1040 with the arrival in Tibet of an eminent Indian monk known as Atisha (982–1054), famed as a holy man, teacher, and artist. Under his direction, existing monasteries in poor condition were renovated and many new ones were constructed. The order founded by Atisha and his disciples became the reformed *Kadampa* school, noted for its programs of mental training to cultivate *bodhichitta*, an enlightened mind.

A famous Tibetan yogi and translator named Marpa (1012–1096) studied Tantric practices for sixteen years in Bihar, India under the tutelage of Naropa, a prominent *mahasiddha* (Sanskrit: "great master of perfect abilities"—a master of Tantric teachings). Marpa returned to Tibet, where he and his chief disciple, Milarepa, became acknowledged as Tantric masters and founded the *Kagyupa* school, especially known for its *mahamudra* (Sanskrit: "great seal") teachings centered on comprehending *sunyata* and achieving liberation from *samsara*. One particularly influential lineage of the Kagyupa is its Karmapa sub-school, founded in the late twelfth century and sometimes referred to as the "Black Hats" (Tibetan, *Sha-nak*) for the black ceremonial headdress worn by their leader, the Karmapa. The Karmapa lineage "appears to have introduced the idea of succession through reincarnation. It is said that when the second Black Hat Karmapa, head of the Black Hat lineage, died in 1283 a child was recognized as his reincarnation and trained to occupy once more his religious and administrative position."[77]

In the thirteenth century, Tibet's northern neighbors the Mongols created an immense empire that ruled China through their Yuan dynasty (1279–1368) and exerted power all the way to eastern Europe. The *Sakyapa*, a Tantric school founded in Tibet in 1073, had close links to the Mongols, and as a result enjoyed a period of political ascendancy beginning in 1244 when the Mongol Khan, Kodan, appointed the

Sakyapa's chief lama to be regent of Tibet. This continued a pattern of Tibet's sectarianism being rooted more in the diverse origins of the respective monastic hierarchies and their secular support, rather than in their spiritual traditions, which mostly followed similar Tantric Buddhist principles and practices inherited from India.[78]

Newari artists from Nepal also figured significantly in the development of Tibet's Buddhist culture. Not only did the Newaris work in Tibet creating paintings and statuary, they trained Tibetan artists to produce works replicating classical Pala designs from India.[79]

Stylistic inspiration from Newari artists of Nepal is apparent in a copper statuette of the Bodhisattva Maitreya produced in Tibet around the eleventh to twelfth centuries (fig. 89)—for example, the lozenge pattern on his *dhoti*, a skirt-like garment worn wrapped around the waist.[80] Likenesses of Maitreya often include a miniature *stupa* emblem at the front of his headdress, as seen here. This symbolizes a legendary *stupa* reputed to exist atop *Kukkutapadagiri* ("Cock's foot Mountain") in north-central India, which is said to hold the remains of Mahakasyapa, senior monk during Sakyamuni Buddha's lifetime. Just prior to his *parinirvana*, Sakyamuni entrusted a golden monastic robe to Mahakasyapa, to safeguard and eventually deliver to the Bodhisattva Maitreya. When Maitreya descends from the Tushita Heaven to become the next Buddha, he will visit that *stupa* and through superhuman means receive the robe from Mahakasyapa, who will then attain *parinirvana*.[81]

Another of Maitreya's primary attributes seen on this statuette is the *kalasa* bottle of *amrita* elixir held in his left hand. He also wears jeweled accessories such as a crown, necklace, earrings, and armbands that identify a bodhisattva, along with an antelope skin over his left shoulder. The sacred thread (Sanskrit, *upavita*) draped over his left shoulder, down the chest and looped inside the low sash around his waist, originated in Hinduism as an insignia of Brahmin priests, and was adopted by Buddhism as part of a bodhisattva's attire.

Fig. 89. *Bodhisattva Maitreya*. Copper with traces of pigment, H: 14⅝ in. (37 cm). Tibet, circa 11th–12th centuries.

Fig. 90. *Akshobhya Buddha*. Gilt copper, H: 22⅞ in. (58 cm). Central Tibet, late 12th or early 13th century.

Some intriguing hypotheses have suggested that legends about Maitreya may have developed under influences from religions in the Middle East. For example, as the bodhisattva destined to appear in the future and become the next Buddha, his name *Maitreya* might be related to *mashiah*, the Hebrew root of messiah, or to the name *Mithras*, the Persian god of light.

Akshobhya, the Immovable Buddha said to reside in his eastern paradise of Abhirati, is not commonly worshiped as an individual, but is seen mainly in the Vajrayana pentad with four other transcendent Buddhas: Amitabha, Amoghasiddhi, Ratnasambhava, and Vairochana. A gilt copper Tibetan statue appears to be a rare image of Akshobhya Buddha as it bears his hieratic traits (fig. 90).[82] The pose is *bhumisparsha mudra*, with the right hand touching the ground and the left hand resting upon the lap with thumb and one finger pressed together as if holding an object (now lost) such as a *vajra*, Akshobhya's ritual symbol. If this statue had been created as a likeness of Sakyamuni Buddha, its left hand would likely rest flat open in its lap, the thumb not touching any fingers (see as examples the statues of Sakyamuni in figs. 12, 13, and 14). This statue of Akshobhya Buddha has the hair painted blue, a Tibetan tradition conforming to the *lakshana* characteristics of a great man as described in the *Lalitavistara Sutra*.[83] The legs are pulled in tightly together in the *vajrasana* posture, each foot resting atop the opposite thigh, the bottom sides of both feet visible. This statue was probably created in Tibet in the late twelfth or early thirteenth century, following late Gupta and early Pala traditions of northeastern India, as reflected in the rendering of the upper portion of the monastic robe smooth and sheer and marked by an undulating line down the chest.

A Tibetan thanka painting from about the same period depicts Sakyamuni Buddha with scenes from his life (fig. 91). This thanka is a rare example of an early Tibetan painting tradition that was patterned after Pala art—which was obliterated from its homeland

Fig. 91. *The Buddha with Scenes from his Life*. Colors on cotton cloth, 31½ x 23½ in. (80 x 59.7 cm). Central Tibet, 12th century.

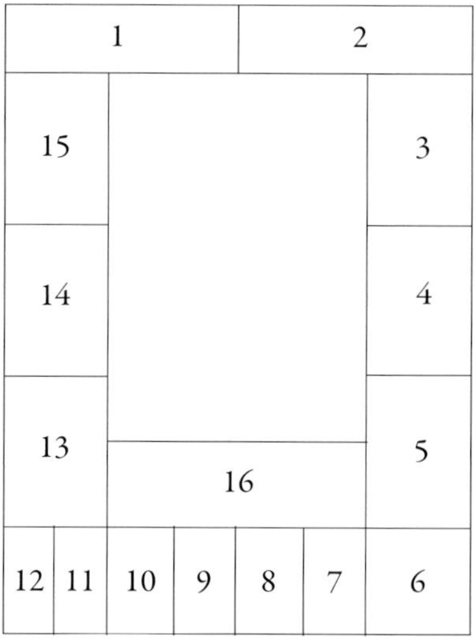

(1) Preaching in the Tushita Heaven before his birth as Prince Siddhartha.
(2) Passing away and attaining *parinirvana*.
(3) Descending from the Trayastrimsa Heaven.
(4) Preaching his first sermon in the Deer Park.
(5) His birth as Prince Siddhartha, son of Queen Maya.
(6) As the infant Siddhartha being presented to Asita.
(7) His horse Kanthaka returns to the palace with his clothes and diadem.
(8) His Great Departure from the palace.
(9) Cutting off his hair as his Great Renunciation.
(10) Sitting in meditation, he is tempted by Mara's daughters.
(11) Sujata offering him rice-milk.
(12) Preaching.
(13) The Miracle of the Monkeys.
(14) The Miracles at Sravasti.
(15) Taming the elephant Nalagiri.
(16) Mara's daughters tempting and Mara attacking the Buddha.

in eastern India in the twelfth century when Buddhism virtually disappeared from that country. In this thanka, "the smooth tubular bodies of the central Buddha, his attendants, and the deities in the peripheral scenes, the stylized forms of headdresses, crowns, thrones and rock shrines, and the expressive line and red and gold color scheme are all hallmarks of this Pala style in Tibet."[84] The central portion of this thanka has Sakyamuni Buddha seated before a large, ornate shrine, touching the ground to signify his enlightenment. Two bodhisattvas stand at his sides. Other key events in his life unfold in a series of smaller pictures positioned around the central image. They are diagramed above. Scene 16, for example, directly below the main likeness, reveals Mara's daughters tempting and Mara attacking the Buddha in their unsuccessful efforts to prevent him from attaining enlightenment.[85]

Another genre of Tibetan art that often takes form as thanka paintings is the *mandala* (Sanskrit: "circle"; Tibetan, *dkyil khor*)—a symbolic diagram or cosmogram of the celestial realm of a Buddha, bodhisattva, or deity that provides a visual frame of reference for

Fig. 92. (Left) *Mandala of Tara*. Ground mineral pigments on cotton, 14¼ x 11½ in. (36 x 29 cm). Sakya Lineage, Tibet, 1400–1499.

Fig. 93. (Above) Detail of fig. 92.

worship or meditation. A typical mandala looks like the overhead view or architect's plan of a celestial palace, with four entrance gates, one at each cardinal direction. The tutelary deity dwells at the realm's center, attended by sacred icons and guardian figures arrayed in symmetrical patterns on all sides. Concentric bands illustrating retinue figures and other Buddhist themes are usually included, circling inside and outside the central square enclosure. Buddhist mandalas are oriented with East at the bottom of the picture, West at the top, North at the right, and South at the left.

Since early times, Tibetans have created two-dimensional mandalas from colored pebbles, sand, and gemstones, composing the designs on the ground for ceremonial use.[86] When the ritual ends, the mandala is scattered or erased as a reminder of the impermanence of all things. Interestingly, some Native American tribes have similar traditions of making ritual sand pictures for their religious practices.[87] Mandalas can also be constructed in three-dimensional form, as scale models of temples and other sacred places.

Most mandalas are paintings on fabric, such as fig. 92, which visualizes the celestial realm of the Bodhisattva Tara and includes the families of the five transcendent Buddhas. Its center section is enlarged in fig. 93. The presiding deity, Tara (dark green in color), sits at the center, gazing forward peacefully, wearing a tiara of gold and jewels, red ribbons, large earrings, bracelets, and anklets. She is embracing her consort, Amoghasiddhi Buddha (light green), their arms and legs entwined in the *yab-yum* position. *Yab-yum* (Tibetan: "father-mother"; Sanskrit, *yuganaddha*) is a visualization of sexual union between two deities that expresses a spiritual communion of the male principle of compassion with the female principle of wisdom.

The next surrounding circle comprises eight individual portraits of the four other Buddhas of the Vajrayana pentad and each one's *sakti* (female counterpart or consort), all seated in the *vajrasana* or full lotus posture. Viewing this circle of eight figures clockwise, beginning directly above Tara and Amoghasiddhi, we see Amitabha Buddha (red) and his consort Pandara Vasini (white); Akshobhya Buddha and his consort Mamaki (both blue); Vairochana Buddha and his consort Vajradhatvisvari (both white); and Ratnasambhava Buddha and his consort Locana (both yellow). Beyond their circle but still within the main square enclosure are four female attendants, one at each corner: Mukunda (yellow), Muraja (red), Vamsha (green), and Vina (white). Positioned at each of that enclosure's four T-shaped gateways is a female guardian deity: at the left, Varamukha (yellow) with a pig's face; above, Shvanamukha (red) with a dog's face; at the right, Simhamukha (white) with a lion's face; below, Hayamukha (white) with a horse's face. This square enclosure represents the walls of the celestial palace, its roof levels rising symbolically above each T-shaped gateway and topped with a Dharma wheel (*dharmachakra*) flanked by two kneeling deer—a symbol of the first sermon given by the Buddha.

Various celestials occupy the next band, which has a bright red background. Beyond it is another, narrower band composed of the five colored flames of pristine awareness. Outside of that colored band, in the upper left corner are the deity Chakrasamvara with a *mahasiddha* and a monk. In the upper right corner are Amitayus Buddha and his consort with two monks. In the lower right corner are Vajravarahi with two monks. In the lower left corner is Rakta Yamari with two monks. At the top of the mandala is a row of nine figures, starting from the left: Sakyamuni Buddha, the Green Tara, and seven teachers of the lineage, alternating in light and dark colors. At the bottom is another row of nine figures, starting from the left: three monks, Padmapani Avalokitesvara (white), the wrathful Vajrapani (blue), the wealth deity Jambhala (yellow), the wrathful Mahakala (black), the Shri Devi (light blue) riding a mule, and an unidentified monk, likely the patron of the painting.[88]

We have seen examples of the *lokapala* ("world protector") and *dvarapala* ("gate protector"), subsidiary gods whose fierce demeanor helps them fulfill their guardian tasks. Tantric Buddhist tradition also applies another Sanskrit term, *dharmapala* ("Dharma protector"), to describe generically all such guardian figures. Some normally appear in "mild" form, but may also assume alternative "wrathful" identities (Sanskrit, *krodha*) to better defend the Dharma and destroy obstacles hindering the spiritual progress of those on the path to enlightenment. The mandala of Tara includes a number of such "wrathful deities," many of whom are occasionally pictured in individual portraits.

Fig. 94. *Bhurkumkuta*. Gilt-copper with pigments, H: 5⅝ in. (14.2 cm). Tibet, circa 15th–16th centuries.

One example is Vajrapani, noted earlier as a bodhisattva who served as a companion and guardian of the Buddha. A fierce statuette of Bhurkumkuta, a wrathful emanation of Vajrapani (fig. 94), is similar to his icon in the bottom row of the Tara mandala. Created from gilt copper with pigments, this masterpiece of sculpture depicts Bhurkumkuta with his six arms raised menacingly. The mouths of his three faces rage through teeth, fangs, and tongues; his hair is drawn up into a mound of fire. His intricately detailed royal attire includes a crown, jewelry on the torso and every limb, and a tiger skin covering his lower body.[89] Such embellishments fill an important function in Tibetan spiritual beliefs: "Precious substances, for Tibetans, are concrete analogies of spiritual value (just as despised substances are synonymous with what is repellent in this world). It is for this reason that statues are encrusted with jewels, and paint pigments mixed with crushed gems and rare medicines."[90]

As in other Buddhist societies, sacred texts hold an esteemed place in Tibet's religious traditions. Their artists apply their remarkable skills to create superbly detailed illustrations on the pages and covers of *sutras* and other books. "The Tibetans were particularly fond of carved book covers, a practice that was virtually unknown in either India or Nepal. The carved images and decorations were often embellished further with gilding and pigments, so that the total effect was quite sumptuous."[91] Fig. 95 is a thirteenth-century gilded wood book cover sculpted with five seated images—from left to right: Sakyamuni Buddha posed in *bhumisparsha mudra*; Sadaksari Lokesvara (an emanation of Avalokitesvara); Prajnaparamita; Vajrananga Manjusri (a Tantric form of Manjusri); and Syamatara (Green Tara).

Tsongkhapa (1357–1419), a renowned Tibetan monk and scholar from the country's northeast, studied in the Kadampa and Sakyapa orders. He then founded the reformed *Gelugpa* school that stresses observance of the *vinaya* code of monastic discipline and

Fig. 95. *Manuscript Cover.* Gilded polychromed wood, carved with figures of five deities. Left to right: Sakyamuni Buddha, Sadaksari Lokesvara, Prajnaparamita, Manjusri, and Syamatara (Green Tara), H: 10⅝ in. (27 cm). Tibet, 13th century.

study of classic Buddhist teachings by Nagarjuna and other Mahayana masters. With time, this school gained such extensive appeal that it effectively absorbed the Kadampa order founded by Atisha and his disciples. Today the Gelugpa is largest of Tibet's Buddhist schools, and is known colloquially in the West as the "Yellow Hats" (Tibetan, *Sha-ser*), for the conical, yellow headdresses worn by their lamas. Like other Tibetan schools, the Gelugpa adopted a system of recognizing *tulkus*—persons identified as the incarnations of deceased revered monks and in certain cases the emanations of deities as well. By the end of the fifteenth century this tradition of ecclesiastical succession through reincarnation had evolved into the selection of a Grand Lama as a spiritual and secular leader.

In 1578, a Mongol prince known as Altan Khan conferred on Sonam Gyatso, the third Grand Lama of the Gelugpa lineage, a new title: *Dalai Lama* (Tibetan and Mongolian: "Ocean Lama"—a supreme lama possessing wisdom as vast as the ocean). Relations between the Mongols and the Tibetans—especially the Gelugpa school—grew even stronger when a Mongolian great-grandson of Altan Khan was named the fourth Dalai Lama. Ongoing support from the powerful Mongol court aided the fifth Dalai Lama to be recognized as supreme religious and secular leader of all Tibetans. This tradition has continued into modern times, with each Dalai Lama revered as both the *tulku* of his predecessor and the earthly manifestation of the Bodhisattva Avalokitesvara.

The fifth Dalai Lama created and bestowed on his teacher (the abbot of Tashi Lhunpo monastery) the title *Panchen Lama* ("Great Scholar Lama"). Every subsequent Panchen Lama has been selected based on being the reincarnated *tulku* of his predecessor. The Panchen Lama would often serve as a religious preceptor to a young Dalai Lama, and vice versa.

> When one of the incarnate Lamas dies, his "spiritual being" or, as we should say, his soul, goes first to a celestial abode, then, at the end of a period varying from forty-six days to four years, is reborn in the body of a child, who from birth gives signs of his supernatural character. When public report or the inquiries of the Lamas have pointed out the locality where the child in question is to be found, the chapter of the monastery, or (if it is the matter of the Dalai-Lama) the sacred college of the *Qambo* (counsellors), holds an inquiry into the authenticity of the facts alleged, and goes to the spot to subject the child to a series of tests, the chief of which consists in making him recognize among several similar objects (cups, books, rosaries, &c.) those which the dead Qubilghan [Mongolian: the incarnation of a deity or saint] or Dalai-Lama habitually used. After due trial, the child is proclaimed a rebirth and is brought to the convent or the palace of Potala, if it is a question of succession to the Dalai-Lama.[92]

In some cases, before a senior lama passes away, he may prophesize the vicinity or circumstances in which he will be reborn, or leave other clues about his future rebirth. After his death, the clergy designated to locate his new incarnation can follow those indicators.

Nearly all Buddhists venerate the *Triratna* ("Triple Gem"): the Buddha, the Dharma, and the Sangha. However, in Vajrayana Buddhism's esoteric traditions the religious teacher's role is crucially important: he interprets

Fig. 96. *The Abbot Yongzin Ngawang Zangpo*. Gilt bronze with turquoise and silver inlay, H: 7¼ in. (18.5 cm). Tibet, 1600 or earlier.

the sacred texts, explains their mysteries, and guides his students through the initiations and secret rites that lead to spiritual liberation. The personage of the lama-teacher and his activities are then so sacrosanct that, in Western literature, the doctrine itself is commonly called *Lamaism*. Esteemed lamas are frequently remembered in paintings and sculptures kept in places of honor in monastery halls and monks' quarters. Such portraits can depict venerable masters seated upon elegantly stylized lotus and lion pedestals similar to those that traditionally enthrone images of Buddhas, bodhisattvas, and divinities. Some are likenesses of distinguished lamas in postures customarily associated only with Buddhas. Fig. 96, for example, is a gilt bronze image of a lama touching the ground with his right hand (*bhumisparsha mudra*), suggesting a revered monk who had attained enlightenment or had demonstrated the determination and dedication needed to do so. Inlaid with turquoise and silver, this image is inscribed on the back of its pedestal to identify the subject as Yongzin Ngawang Zangpo, a scholar, historian, teacher, and practitioner of the Nyingmapa school who lived from 1546–1615.[93]

When performing initiation rites and other ceremonies, the presiding lama often wears a ritual headdress such as the elegantly embroidered satin and silk crown in fig. 97. Its five connected panels are shaped like

Fig. 97. *Lama's Crown*. Embroidered in satin stitch with five transcendent Buddhas, l–r: Amitabha, Akshobhya, Vairochana, Ratnasambhava, and Amoghasiddhi; trimmed with gold-wrapped silk thread, H (each section): 7⅞ in. (20 cm). Tibet, late 16th century.

1. Thunderbolt or Diamond scepter
Sanskrit, *vajra*
Tibetan, *dorje*

2. Bell
Sanskrit, *ghanta*
Tibetan, *drilbu*

3. Prayer wheel
Tibetan, *mani chos-khor*

4. Dagger
Sanskrit, *kila*
Tibetan, *phurpa*

5. Axe
Sanskrit, *parasu*
Tibetan, *dgra sta*

6. Chopper
Sanskrit, *karttrika*
Tibetan, *trigug*

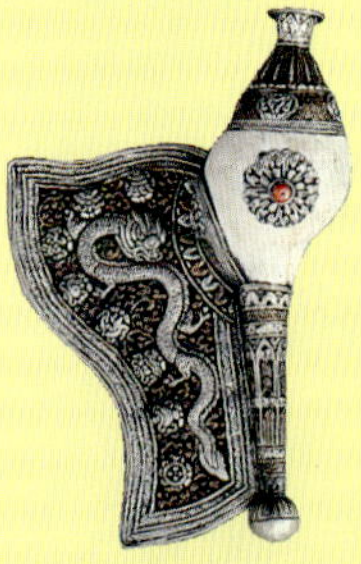

7. Conch shell
Sanskrit, *shankha*
Tibetan, *dung*

8. Skull cup
Sanskrit, *kapala*
Tibetan, *thod pa*

9. Libation jug
Sanskrit, *kamandalu*
Tibetan, *las bum*

Fig. 98. *Tantric Buddhism Ritual Objects*. Tibet and Nepal.

lotus petals, each panel depicting one of the five transcendent Buddhas of the Vajrayana pentad seated on a lotus throne and displaying his traditional attributes—from left to right: Amitabha Buddha (red) posed in *dhyana mudra*; Akshobhya Buddha (blue) in *bhumisparsha mudra*; Vairochana Buddha (white) in *dharmachakra mudra*; Ratnasambhava Buddha (yellow) in *varada mudra*; and Amoghasiddhi Buddha (green) in *abhaya mudra*.[94]

Tantric practices employ sundry ritual objects that often take form as works of art. Fig. 98 shows:

1. A "thunderbolt" or "diamond" scepter (Sanskrit, *vajra*; Tibetan, *dorje*), the masculine symbol of skillful means, is held in the right hand in conjunction with
2. A bell (Sanskrit, *ghanta*; Tibetan, *drilbu*), the feminine symbol of wisdom that is held in the left hand.
3. A prayer wheel (Tibetan, *mani chos-khor*), whose round metal cylinder has *mantras* or prayers engraved on its outside and contained as written form on its inside, can be rotated around its handle to radiate the *mantras* and gain religious merit. Most hold the *mantra* of Avalokitesvara: *Om Mani Padme Hum* (Sanskrit: "Om, jewel in the lotus, hum").
4. A ceremonial dagger (Sanskrit, *kila*; Tibetan, *phurpa*) of the kind used by Padmasambhava to destroy forces that threatened Buddhism, now protects against evil.
5. The axe (Sanskrit, *parasu*; Tibetan, *dgra sta*) is another instrument for symbolically destroying ignorance.
6. A chopper (Sanskrit, *karttrika*; Tibetan, *trigug*) represents the cutting away of bonds of ignorance.
7. A conch shell (Sanskrit, *shankha*; Tibetan, *dung*) suggests the melodious sounds of the Buddha's voice and his teachings.
8. The skull cup (Sanskrit, *kapala*; Tibetan, *thod pa*), fabricated from human skulls or made from materials

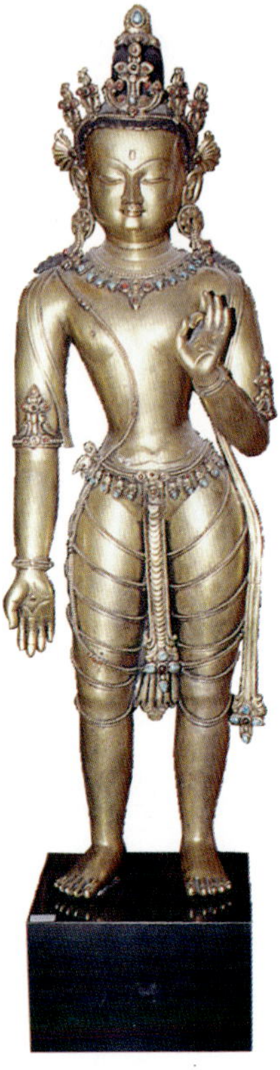

Fig. 99. *Padmapani* (*Avalokitesvara*). Gilt bronze with inlaid gemstones, H: 30¾ in. (78.1 cm). Tibet, 19th century.

shaped to look like one, holds blood or other liquids during certain Tantric rituals.

9. The libation jug (Sanskrit, *kamandalu*; Tibetan, *las bum*) carries consecrated water for purification rites.

Tibetan Buddhism's pantheon embraces innumerable Buddhas, bodhisattvas, male and female divinities, protector gods, and deified saints. Among all of these, the most adored by worshipers is Avalokitesvara, a bodhisattva who appears in many forms. One popular form is *Padmapani* (Sanskrit: "Lotus Bearer"), a bodhisattva attired with a five-leafed crown and the jeweled regalia of an Indian prince. He usually appears standing, his right hand lowered in *varada mudra* (bestowing a blessing), his left hand raised in *vitarka mudra* (teaching or discussion)—such as the gilt-bronze statue in fig. 99. The lotus flower is one of his primary symbols, and is often held in his hand or placed on his shoulder. As with other manifestations of Avalokitesvara, Padmapani is associated with Amitabha Buddha, and sometimes has a small seated emblem of Amitabha at the face of his crown.

Another form of Avalokitesvara encountered extensively in Tibet is Chenrezig. Stories say the Bodhisattva *Chenrezig* had vowed to his spiritual father, Amitabha Buddha, that he would save all humankind from suffering. But when he comprehended the vast extent of evil and ignorance in our world and the near impossibility of saving all beings, he was so struck with grief that his head burst into ten pieces. Amitabha came to his aid, transforming each piece into an individual head and assembling them upon Chenrezig's body in three levels of three, with the tenth head on top fashioned in a wrathful countenance. Amitabha then replicated an image of his own face and positioned it as the eleventh, topmost head. He also gave Chenrezig one thousand arms, with a wisdom eye in the palm of every hand to endow omniscient vision. Chenrezig thenceforth was able to survey the world in every direction, to locate and rescue beings in distress.

Fig. 100. *Chenrezig* (*Avalokitesvara*). Gilt copper, H: 15 in. (38.1 cm). Tibet or Nepal, 19th century.

The gilt copper statue of Chenrezig in fig. 100 has eight principal hands: the top pair are pressed together grasping a wish-fulfilling gem; one right hand is lowered in *varada mudra*; the other five principal hands hold a lotus, vase, rosary, wheel, bow and arrow. Thirty-eight smaller hands fan out from the torso to symbolize his thousand arms. He stands on a double-lotus throne and displays additional attributes such as an antelope skin over his left shoulder, large earrings and other princely jewelry, and a crown with five leafed sections adorning each of his nine principal faces. In another popular form he has four arms and sits upon a lotus. Chenrezig is venerated as a bodhisattva and as a *yidam* (Tibetan: "firm mind"), a type of personal deity and, in this instance, a divine protector of the Tibetan people, perpetually incarnating among them in the holy personage of the Dalai Lama.

SRI LANKA

King Asoka the Great of India is famed for propagating the Buddha's teachings across much of the subcontinent and many neighboring countries. He sent his own son, a missionary monk known as Mahinda, to introduce the Dharma into Sri Lanka. Before Mahinda's arrival, the island kingdom may have been familiar with the Buddhist faith, along with Jainism, Brahminism, and aboriginal cults worshiping various kinds of spirits. But historical chronicles of Sri Lanka tell that when the monk Mahinda arrived there in 250 B.C., he explained the Buddha's teachings to the country's ruler, King Devanampiya Tissa, in such an effective and impressive manner that the king and some forty thousand members of his court immediately embraced the faith.

Mahinda's efforts were so successful that King Asoka sent a second mission to the island, this one led by his daughter, a *bhikshuni* (Buddhist nun) named Sanghamitta. She brought with her a golden urn containing a sapling transplanted by King Asoka from the Bodhi Tree under which the Buddha had attained enlightenment. The king of Sri Lanka planted the branch in a garden in his capital city, Anuradhapura, and enthusiastically constructed monasteries, residence halls for monks, stupas, and other monuments to the Buddha's teachings. Sanghamitta established a local community of *bhikshunis* to ordain Sinhalese women who wished to take the monastic vows. She and her brother Mahinda spent their remaining years in Sri Lanka. Their missionary zeal and the royal patronage given by King Devanampiya Tissa quickly gave the faith roots across the island.

In some locations, caves were developed as temples and dwelling places for monks. The largest and most eminent complex of caves is Dambulla Viharaya—"Cave temple of Infinite Buddhas," situated near Sri Lanka's geographical center. Dambulla houses hundreds of

Fig. 101. *Dambulla Viharaya Cave Temple.* Sri Lanka, Buddhist artworks installed circa 1st century B.C. on through the 18th century A.D.

Buddhist sculptures and paintings, installed over a long span of time that began with its founding in the first century B.C. and continued into the late eighteenth century A.D. (fig. 101).

It was in Sri Lanka, around 83 B.C., that the Buddhist Canon was first recorded in written form, as Pali language texts inscribed on palm leaves. They are believed to convey the original scriptures compiled orally at the First Council in India shortly after the Buddha's death. The Pali texts sustain the core precepts of Theravada Buddhism, the conservative doctrine which preserves the Buddha's words and teachings and the activities of the Sangha as practiced during his lifetime. Sri Lanka became a bastion of the Theravada doctrine, transmitting those teachings to other countries, most notably in mainland Southeast Asia.

Buddha images first appeared in Sri Lanka during the Anuradhapura period (third century B.C.–tenth century A.D.), likely brought from India in the second or third century A.D. Scholars are still debating whether the first likenesses of the Buddha made by Sri Lanka's native artists were produced through their own independent creative powers, or were patterned after imported Indian prototypes. A beautiful standing bronze statue of the Buddha, presumably made at Anuradhapura, is now in a museum in Vietnam, no doubt carried or shipped to that country by Sri Lankan missionaries (fig. 102). The influence of southeast Indian art from Amaravati during the Later Andhra dynasty is apparent in the robe's design, its folds indicated by a series of engraved lines and raised ridges. Additionally, we notice here one uniform hallmark of Sinhalese Buddha images—a torso suggesting immense physical strength, with broad powerful shoulders tapering to a small waist—a characteristic possibly inspired by early statues made at Mathura, India.

Fig. 102. *Sakyamuni Buddha.* Bronze, H: 42½ in. (1.08 m). Sri Lanka, late Anuradhapura period, circa 3rd–7th centuries.

Although Theravada Buddhism has been the dominant religion of Sri Lanka since its introduction there in the third century B.C., Mahayana beliefs reached the island as well via southern India and evidently achieved substantial followings during the late Anuradhapura period. One unique masterpiece of metalwork from Sri Lanka is a standing, gilded bronze statue of Tara, a Mahayana female bodhisattva, discovered near the city of Trincomalee on the island's east coast (fig. 103). Her right hand extends forward in the *varada mudra* gesture of bestowing a blessing or charity; her raised left hand may once have held a lotus or other attribute.

Fig. 103. *Bodhisattva Tara.* Gilt bronze, H: 57⅛ in. (1.45 m). Sri Lanka, late Anuradhapura period, 8th century.

The empty niche in her towering headdress would originally have contained a small Buddha image, probably a miniature likeness of Amitabha Buddha. Many Sinhalese believed this stunning statue depicted *Pattini Devi*, a Hindu divinity, until art historians determined it actually represents the Bodhisattva Tara of Mahayana Buddhism. This confusion apparently began around the end of the Polonnaruva period (993–1235), when the Mahayana faith virtually disappeared from Sri Lanka and some of its icons were given Hindu identities.[95]

The later part of the Anuradhapura period was marked by political unrest and invasions from India, with Sri Lanka coming under the rule of the Chola Empire of South India in 1017. Vijayabahu I defeated the Cholas and became king of Sri Lanka in 1070. He established a new capital at Polonnaruva and launched a revival of Buddhism on the island kingdom—revitalizing the ordination of monks, repairing temples and stupas damaged during years of war, and sponsoring related cultural programs.

Fig. 104. *Pair of Colossal Statues Carved from Stone.* (left) Standing image of the monk Ananda, H: 23 ft. (7 m). (right) Reclining image of Sakyamuni Buddha's Parinirvana, Length: 46 ft. (14 m). Gal Vihara, Polonnaruva, Sri Lanka, 12th century.

An impressive example of monumental sculpture produced during the Polonnaruva period (993–1235) comprises a pair of colossal images cut from stone at Gal Vihara (fig. 104). The larger statue is of the Buddha reclining, at the moment of his passing away into *parinirvana*. Its highly idealized style of depicting the *parinirvana*—which hints the statue could almost have been created standing upright and then lowered into the reclining pose—can be traced back to early Indian sculptures of this event (see fig. 32), and is also seen in other similar monuments throughout Asia. Here, too, are styling resemblances to the Sri Lankan bronze statue in fig. 102—broad, well-rounded shoulders with a slim waist; the series of narrow folds in the robe marked by incised lines and raised ridges. Poised near the head of this *parinirvana* image is the second rock-cut statue, a standing portrait believed to represent the monk Ananda, the Buddha's chief attendant.

Seated Buddha images from Sri Lanka are remarkably consistent in design and convention, perhaps to some degree a reflection of the conservative nature of

Fig. 105. *Life-Size Diorama of Seated and Standing Images of Sakyamuni Buddha.* Stucco and wood. Nagavimanas Kandy Vihara, South wall, Kandy, Sri Lanka, 18th century.

the Theravada school. Nearly all Sinhalese seated statues of the Buddha show him in the pose of meditation, hands resting together in his lap in *dhyana mudra,* legs folded right atop left in *virasana* posture. Another feature of most Buddha images from Sri Lanka is the stylized flame emanating from the *ushnisha* atop his head, an embellishment evidently invented by craftsmen of Nagapattinam, in southeastern India, and adopted by the Sinhalese. These design elements appear in a statue of the Buddha seated in meditation, the central subject of a life-size diorama of sculptures and wall paintings from the Kandy period (1592–1815), known for its bright and lively mural pictures of events in the Buddha's life and *jataka* stories of his previous births (fig. 105). This Sri Lankan tradition of creating colorful devotional paintings with Buddhist themes has continued to the present time, as shown by fig. 31.

BURMA (MYANMAR)

The earliest known inhabitants of Burma (today officially called *Myanmar*) came mainly from two ethnic groups: the *Mon* people, also called *Talaing*, whose settlements reached from lower Burma to what is now central Thailand, and who spoke a language of the Mon-Khmer linguistic group; and the *Pyu* people, who came from Central Asia, spoke a Tibeto-Burmese language and began settling in the valleys of the Irrawaddy River in central Burma sometime early in the first millenium A.D.

Like a number of Asian civilizations, Burma's early tribal cultures practiced animism, worshiping nature deities they call *nats,* thought to dwell in elements such as trees and rivers, and in some instances being associated with the spirits of their deceased.[96] Gradually their animistic practices merged with the Theravada Buddhist beliefs they learned through missionaries from India and Sri Lanka. Burma and eastern India share a long land border as well as coastal access to the Bay of Bengal's sea lanes. Since ancient times—the first millenium B.C. or earlier—Burma had been absorbing cultural influences from India's traveling merchants, colonists, and missionaries. While India's Hindu faith never acquired massive congregations in Burma, its Buddhist beliefs certainly did.

The *Mahavamsa*, a historical chronicle compiled during the fifth century A.D. in Sri Lanka by a Buddhist monk named *Mahanama,* tells of the third century B.C. when King Asoka of India dispatched missionaries to spread the Buddha's teachings—and that two of those missionaries, *Sona* and *Uttara*, visited a Southeast Asian state called *Suvarnabhumi* ("Golden Land"). It is generally believed that Suvarnabhumi was an ancient civilization located in what now constitutes lower Burma, around or near the Mon city of *Thaton*, giving a possible historical basis to the Burmese fondness for referring to their country as the Golden Land.

Fig. 106. *Votive Tablet illustrating Eight Great Events in the Buddha's Life and his Seven Stations of Enlightenment.* Terracotta, H: 7¾ in. (19.7 cm). Pagan, Burma (Myanmar), 7th–10th centuries.

One of the oldest forms of Buddhist devotional art is the votive tablet—small plaques molded from clay and then fired or sun-baked. This art form originated in ancient India to produce sacred icons that pilgrims could carry away as remembrances of their visits to holy places and use in spiritual practices such as meditation. Crafting each tablet was moreover believed to generate merit for its creator. Images impressed upon the tablets usually depicted episodes in the Buddha's life, sometimes with inscriptions about the object's maker or sponsor.

The "Eight Great Events" in the Buddha's life and his "Seven Stations of Enlightenment" at Bodhgaya unfold in the rare Burmese votive tablet in fig. 106. The tablet's top four horizontal rows of figures exhibit the "Eight Great Miracles" in a format reminiscent of Pala-Sena sculpture from India, much like the stone stele of fig. 44. This Burmese tablet shows: (top row) the Buddha reclining, passing into *parinirvana*; (2nd row, left) calming the elephant, Nalagiri; (2nd row, right) descending from heaven after visiting his mother; (3rd row, left) preaching his first sermon; (3rd row, right) performing the Miracle of Sravasti; (4th row, left) receiving honey from the monkey; (4th row, right) being born as Prince Siddhartha, son of Queen Maya, shown here giving birth while supported by her sister Prajapati; and (4th row, center) the Buddha seated in front of a shrine, touching the earth to confirm his enlightenment. Flanking that central image of the Enlightenment are two small figures in profile, kneeling with their hands clasped in a gesture of adoration. Artworks often include two monks at the Buddha's sides, customarily his two chief disciples, Sariputra and Maudgalyayana (Pali, *Sariputta* and *Moggallana*). However, on this votive tablet the two kneeling figures could portray the merchants Tapussa and Bhallika, the Buddha's first two converts, who came from an area that became part of Burma. When Tapussa and Bhallika presented offerings of food to the Buddha in the seventh week after his enlightenment at Bodhgaya, he gave the two men several strands of his hair that they carried home and enshrined in a golden stupa which became known as Shwedagon Pagoda in Rangoon.

The seven seated and standing figures in the tablet's bottom row picture the "Seven Stations," starting with that row's center image of the Buddha touching the earth to mark his enlightenment in the first week. Events of the ensuing six weeks are represented by the other six Buddha images in that bottom row: (2nd week) gazing at the Bodhi Tree while standing in meditation; (3rd week) walking in meditation along a golden path;

(4th week) sitting in meditation in a jeweled chamber; (5th week) sitting in meditation under a banyan tree; (6th week) sitting in meditation during a rainstorm while shielded by the *naga raja*; and (7th week) receiving an offering of food from Tapussa and Bhallika.

Stylistically related to the votive tablets just discussed are a variety of carved stone plaques known as *andagu*—Burmese for the yellow-beige pyrophyllite rock from which they are usually sculpted. Most *andagu* plaques illustrate the "Eight Great Miracles" together with the "Seven Stations of Enlightenment." While the bulk of *andagu* pieces have been retrieved in Burma and are thought to have been produced there, some may have been created by ateliers in eastern India, since a number of unquestionably Indian images have been found that were sculpted from the same type of stone.[97]

In 1056 a Burmese king named Anawrahta, who ruled the Pyu kingdom from their capital at Pagan, captured the Mon city of Thaton and unified the country under a new dynasty. Theravada Buddhism was recognized as the state religion, although Mahayana and Vajrayana continued to be practiced as well. Plenty of Mon artists and craftsmen from Thaton were taken to Pagan, where they were employed to build temples and other structures, bringing Mon aesthetics and Theravadin Buddhist beliefs that greatly enriched Pagan's cultural milieu. Anawrahta's reign launched a golden age of Burmese art and architecture that continued until 1287, when Pagan was invaded and sacked by the Mongol armies of Kublai Khan.

Most famous of the thousands of monasteries and monuments that rose at Pagan is the Ananda Temple, an enormous white structure topped with a series of golden pinnacles. Ananda Temple has served worshipers since its construction early in the twelfth century under the auspices of King Kyanzittha (1084–1111). Forming its core is a solid mass of brick and stone extending upward to support an intricately sculpted central stupa. The interior walls are covered by more than a thousand ceramic panels illustrating the Buddha's life story and *jataka* tales of his previous existences. Each of the central core's four sides is shaped into a tall pointed niche displaying a colossal standing Buddha statue. These statues represent the four most recent *manushi* (human) Buddhas, said to have lived and taught the Dharma in our *kalpa*, or world cycle: Sakyamuni, the historical Buddha of our age (whose statue stands in the west niche); his predecessor, Kasyapa Buddha (south niche); his predecessor, Kanakamuni Buddha (east niche); and his predecessor, Krakucchanda Buddha (north niche).[98]

Especially interesting is the gilded wood statue of Kanakamuni Buddha (fig. 107), standing with his arms lowered to his sides, both hands palm-open in a variation of *varada mudra*. This unique pose is not commonly found in any other country and has therefore become a signature of Burmese Buddhist art now replicated in countless sizes of wood and lacquer images for devotees, pilgrims, and collectors—although virtually all these reproductions are likely considered to represent Sakyamuni Buddha, not Kanakamuni.

Burmese art covers the gamut of Buddhist artistic expression. As in other countries, Burma's artisans created manuscripts recording Pali canonical texts, the Buddha's life story, and the *jataka* tales of his previous existences. "There are two main types of [Burmese] manuscripts: those written on oblong strips of palm leaves (called *pe-za* in Burmese), and those on long sheets of paper, folded concertina fashion, to make a folding book (called *parabaik* in Burmese)."[99] A number of them are miniature masterpieces of narrative painting, brightly colored and trimmed with gold—such as the *parabaik* book whose folding leaves recount Prince Siddhartha's Great Departure (see fig. 6).

In early Buddhist societies the prevailing manner of representing the Buddha was in traditional mendicant robes, posed in any of the customary postures. But artists of India's Pala-Sena period brought into vogue a style of creating sculptures of him wearing an opulent crown and lavish jewelry, presumably to reflect his royal

Fig. 108. *Crowned Buddha in Royal Attire.* Gilt wood and lacquer with inlaid gemstones and glass. Shan States, Burma (Myanmar), circa 19th century.

ancestry and the Mahayanist concept of him as a supramundane being. In Burma, picturing the Buddha "in royal attire" is immensely favored—as with the extravagantly ornamented, gilt wood statue in fig. 108. This long-standing trend might be explained, at least in part, by a legendary affair during the Buddha's life in India that has vast circulation in Burma. This story tells that an Indian king named Jambupati was plotting to depose and take over the lands of a neighboring monarch. The Buddha intervened by appearing before King Jambupati wearing royal robes, jewels and crown and sitting atop a magnificent throne. Jambupati was so humbled by the Buddha's demonstration of the insignificance of regal trappings that he

Fig. 107. (Opposite) *Standing Buddha Statue.* Lacquered and gilded wood, H: 31 ft., 5 in. (9.59 m). Ananda Temple, Pagan, Burma (Myanmar), circa 12th century.

Fig. 109. *Reclining Buddha.* White marble with gilt and paint, Length: 101 in. (2.56 m). Burma (Myanmar), circa 19th–20th centuries.

abandoned his scheme of aggression, quit his own throne and joined the Buddha's following. The relevance of this legend is evident in that the Burmese refer to all crowned Buddha images as "Jambupati."

Besides the ubiquitous pose of the Buddha standing with both hands extending down in *varada mudra*, another design that is also a hallmark of Burmese art is their visualization of his reclining image. Similar statues made in other countries typically picture him in a rigidly stylized reclining position (see figs. 32 and 104). But the Burmese usually show him in a relaxed pose, such as the gilded marble statue in fig. 109. Here the Buddha reclines on his right side, as always, with his right hand supporting his head. However, in contrast to conventional imagery, his left arm lies loosely atop his left side, and his robes drape down naturally across his upper body and legs. Some Buddhists believe this shows the Buddha's *parinirvana*; some believe it shows him at rest.

Artisans who create Buddhist imagery normally shun originality and innovation. The majority adhere

Fig. 110. *The Buddha Shielded by Muchalinda the Serpent King.* Gilt wood, H: 46 in. (1.17 m). Shan States, Burma (Myanmar), circa 18th century.

scrupulously to traditional poses, designs, and templates recorded in scriptures and other respected texts—especially among the conservative Theravada cultures of Southeast Asia. Occasionally, though, stylistic surprises do appear. From Burma, one instance is a carved and gilded wood statue of the Buddha seated atop the coils of Muchalinda, the Serpent King (fig. 110). Customarily this pose has the Buddha seated in meditation, hands together in *dhyana mudra*, under protective cover of the *naga's* raised head and hood, recalling the sixth week at Bodhgaya. But this Burmese statue has the

Fig. 111. *Five Buddhist Monks.* Gilt and black lacquer on teakwood, H: 20 in. (50.8 cm). Burma (Myanmar), 18th century.

Buddha's right hand reaching toward the ground, as at his enlightenment. Most uniquely, each of the *naga's* four additional heads rises up independently to display a small image much like the famed standing Buddha in the Ananda Temple at Pagan.[100]

In Burma, as in most Buddhist cultures, monks fill a central role in religious practices as well as other aspects of daily life. They are therefore portrayed with realistic features in sculptures and paintings in assorted poses. Fig. 111 is a set of woodcarvings depicting five Burmese monks seated in various postures that might be observed in a monastery or other settings.

From the golden age of Pagan down to the present day, Theravada Buddhism has been Burma's dominant religion. Even so, branches of the Mahayana have drawn followings there as well. The copper-alloy statue in fig. 112 has been identified as Bhaisajyaguru Buddha by the medicine bowl in his left hand and the health-giving myrobalan fruit grasped in the fingers of his right hand. He is adorned with elaborate jewelry and a tall, pointed crown that extends on two sides into large, distinctively Burmese openwork ribbons that spread above and around the ears, reaching down to matching shoulder epaulets. Bhaisajyaguru Buddha is usually considered Mahayanist, yet many Burmese Buddha statues in Theravada temples also hold the myrobalan fruit, so the identification of this image is tentative.

Fig. 112. *Bhaisajyaguru Buddha.* Copper alloy, H: 10½ in. (26.7 cm). Shan States, Burma (Myanmar), 18th century.

Fig. 113. *Buddha's Footprint.* Carved stone, engraved with auspicious emblems and gilded, 67⅜ x 39⅜ in. (1.71 x 1.00 m). Burma (Myanmar), 19th century.

We know from biographies of the Buddha that he never traveled outside his homeland in southern Nepal and the northeastern Indian states where he attained enlightenment and taught the Dharma. Still, there exist in Burma, Sri Lanka, Thailand, and other regions folk beliefs saying he visited those places. A number of such legends relate to "footprints" found in those countries and believed made by him. These are larger than life-size, stylized impressions in stone slabs and metal plates that share conceptual origins with ancient symbolic footprints that were fashioned by artisans in India to represent the Buddha during those early times before figural images of his human form were created. As time went by, it came to be believed that some of these footprints had been made by the Buddha himself. Most are engraved with good-omen symbols totaling 108—an auspicious number according to astrologers in ancient India. One example from Burma is the carved stone footprint in fig. 113.

Buddhist beliefs and folklore include a proliferation of regional variations. In some parts of South and Southeast Asia, the thirty-two *lakshana*, bodily characteristics identifying a great man or a Buddha, are thought to specify that his fingers are of equal length, as are his toes. This stylistic convention, often followed in Burma and Sri Lanka, sometimes in Thailand, too, is incorporated in the footprint of fig. 113 and some of the other likenesses printed here.

INDONESIA

Sanskrit inscriptions discovered on the western reaches of Java tell of immigrants from India settling on that island in the fourth century A.D. Seafaring traders and explorers from India had no doubt been visiting Java and Sumatra since even earlier times, bringing with them the beliefs and artistic impulses of Hinduism and Buddhism. Such cultural influences from India were so far-reaching and significant that the eminent scholar George Coedes popularized the expression "Indianized states of Southeast Asia" for the lands that became Indonesia, Malaysia, Burma, Thailand, Laos, Cambodia, and Vietnam. Coedes and other Western historians in the nineteenth and twentieth centuries also referred to Southeast Asia as "Farther India."[101]

A substantial number of small, independent states were scattered about the Malay Peninsula and the islands of the archipelago that now make up the Republic of Indonesia. Many were absorbed into the Indianized empire known as Srivijaya, a maritime kingdom that dominated the Straits of Malacca and much of its surrounding regions from the seventh to thirteenth centuries, ruling from a capital city at Palembang, on the southern end of Sumatra. The most significant and acclaimed product of Indian cultural influences in the archipelago is Borobudur, an enormous Buddhist stupa and temple complex erected in the Kedu Plain of Central Java (fig. 114). An immense, three-dimensional mandala, Borobudur is the largest Buddhist monument in the world and an acknowledged global wonder, yet its construction and history are steeped in mystery. Even the meaning of its name is uncertain: "The most convincing translation perhaps is 'many Buddhas,' deriving from the local usage of *Para Buddha* (Barabudur, which is also sometimes used), or *Vara Buddha* (Buddha the adored one)."[102]

Information about Borobudur's creation is scarce, but the consensus is that it was designed and built by

Fig. 114. (Opposite above) *Borobudur*. Constructed from stone, H: 115 ft., 9 in. (35.29 m), Width: 393 ft., 9 in. (120 m). Central Java, Indonesia, 8th–9th centuries.

Fig. 115. (Opposite below) *Borobudur*. One of 72 Buddha statues on the upper three levels, with its covering stupa partially removed.

the Sailendra dynasty of Central Java in the eighth to ninth centuries. It has the appearance of a man-made mountain of shrines, carved rock walls, and a large central stupa as its peak. Its configuration seems patterned after the Indian concept of Mount Meru, the "World Mountain" said to be positioned at the center of the universe. This begins with the lowest level representing the hell states and the realm of desire. Above it are a series of five terraces and stone wall corridors sculpted with bas-relief narrations of the Buddha's biography (see, for example, fig. 7, The Great Renunciation); *jataka* tales of his prior lifetimes; and *avadana* ("great deed") stories of Buddhist heroes that extol the merits of good behavior. The outsides of these walls are fitted with alcoves holding 432 seated Buddha statues.

The top-most portion comprises three circular terraces supporting seventy-two small stupas that surround a large central stupa. Each small stupa was built as a latticework grille of stone with a consistent series of perforations so viewers can glimpse the Buddha image contained inside. Fig. 115 shows one of these stupas, which has parts of its stone grille removed.

The design and placement of Borobudur's Buddha statues conform to Vajrayana configurations. Those on the lower four balustrades depict four of the transcendent Buddhas: the statues on the east wall represent Akshobhya in the pose of touching the earth (*bhumisparsha mudra*); south wall, Ratnasambhava bestowing a blessing (*varada mudra*); west wall, Amitabha meditating (*dhyana mudra*); and the north wall, Amoghasiddhi granting protection (*abhaya mudra*). Each of the seventy-two small stupas on the top terraces contained a seated Buddha in the gesture of turning the wheel of the law (*dharmachakra mudra*), the characteristic pose of Vairochana Buddha, said to reside in the center of the cosmos.

There is some uncertainty about the iconography of the statues on all four sides of the fifth level's outer walls, because they are all portrayed with the right hand raised, index finger and thumb touching in the pose of

teaching (*vitarka mudra*). These statues may represent the supreme Buddha of the Vajrayana faith, known as Vajradhara or Samantabhadra. However, they might be intended as additional likenesses of Vairochana, or possibly represent Sakyamuni, the historical Buddha. Front and side view pictures of a seated stone statue of Ratnasambhava Buddha give a fuller appreciation of the Borobudur style of sculpture (figs. 116 and 117).

Fig. 116. (Left) *Ratnasambhava Buddha seated in Varada Mudra.* Andesite volcanic stone, H: 52½ in. (1.33 m). Style of Borobudur, Central Java, Indonesia, 8th–9th centuries.

Fig. 117. (Right) Side view of fig. 116.

> The style of the Buddha images of Borobudur, as may be seen even in single detached heads, is derived directly from the Gupta style of Sarnath. These Buddhas are made with great mathematical nicety of measurement from one of the systems of proportion for sacred images followed throughout the Indian world. The finest of them represent such a beautiful realization of plastic mass and volume, such breathing life and transcendent spiritual clarity of expression that they may rank among the greatest examples of sculptural genius in the entire world.[103]

Fig. 118. *Buddha seated European fashion, in the pose of Dharmachakra Mudra.* Stone, H: 9 ft., 10 in. (2.99 m). Chandi Mendut, Java, Indonesia, 8th–10th centuries.

The mystique surrounding Borobudur continues with its apparently abrupt abandonment as a place of worship after the demise of Java's royal court around A.D. 928. Little is known about the monument's history from that time until it was mentioned again in local accounts early in the eighteenth century.

Chandi Mendut is another Central Javanese Buddhist monument. Located at nearby Magelang, it is smaller than Borobudur yet significant in its own right. *Chandi*, or *Tjandi*, a Javanese word probably derived from the Sanskrit *chaitya*, means "ancient temple" when used in the names of Buddhist and Hindu structures in Indonesia. The temple building at Chandi Mendut contains a trinity comprising sculpted stone figures of

Fig. 119. *Kubera.* Copper alloy, H: 4¾ in. (12.1 cm). Central Java, Indonesia, early 9th century.

the Bodhisattvas Vajrapani and Avalokitesvara flanking a large stone Buddha seated in "European" fashion, his hands positioned in the *dharmachakra mudra* (fig. 118).

Almost all of Indonesia's ancient monumental artworks were created from stone, but their craftsmen had metalworking expertise as well. A rare copper-alloy image from the early-ninth century portrays *Kubera* (also called *Kuvera*), a God of Wealth in the Hindu pantheon responsible for guarding and dispensing Earth's riches (fig. 119). He is identified by his contentedly obese body studded with precious stones. Arrayed conspicuously at the front base of his throne are seven pots of jewelry and other riches. In Mahayana

Fig. 120. *The Buddhist Deities Avalokitesvara and Vasundhara.* Silver and bronze, 4¾ x 5⅛ in. (12.1 x 13.1 cm). Java, Indonesia, approx. 850–950.

Buddhism, Kubera is also revered as a manifestation of the Lokapala Vaisravana, Guardian of the North.[104]

An unusual Central Javanese silver and bronze statuette from approximately A.D. 850–950 pictures Avalokitesvara seated with Vasundhara, Goddess of Abundance, on matching lotus thrones and posed in identical postures, each with the right hand extended in *varada mudra* (fig. 120). This is a unique composition, since there is no known textual or epigraphic evidence linking these two deities. In fact, Vasundhara (also called *Vasudhara*) is often paired with Kubera, God of Wealth, as his consort, although there is no connection between this object and the image of Kubera in fig. 119. These two silver likenesses of Avalokitesvara and Vasundhara may have been created as separate components of a mandala or other assembly of figures, and brought together on this pedestal at some later date.[105]

CAMBODIA

One of Southeast Asia's earliest Indianized kingdoms was *Funan*, a prosperous trading state centered on the lower reaches of the Mekong River in what is now Cambodia. Little is known of Funan's beginnings, which Chinese chronicles date to the first century A.D., but by the fifth century its dominion probably extended downriver as far as the Mekong delta and west to the Malay Peninsula. Funan went into decline during the sixth century and was absorbed into the realm of its northern neighbors, the Khmers, whose homeland included areas that would eventually become northeastern Thailand and southern Laos. The Khmer Empire came to be known by its Sanskrit name, *Kambuja* (Khmer, *Kampuchea*), and later by the westernized spelling, *Cambodia*.

As in many of the ancient states in Southeast Asia, the Indian culture that reached the Khmers included the teachings and artistic expressions of both Hinduism and Buddhism. Among the oldest surviving religious artworks from Cambodia is a seventh-century sandstone statue of the Buddha found at Preah Theat (fig. 121). He stands with both arms raised, but only the right hand remains intact, its thumb and index finger touching in *vitarka mudra*. This type of pre-Angkorian sculpture calls to mind the abstract stylings of Gupta statuary from northern India. The body is formed with smooth, simplified contours; the robe spreads down broadly from the arms and waist but is rendered so sheer that the upper torso almost appears uncovered; and the serene gaze of the Master's half-closed eyes suggests meditation. Also keeping with Gupta patterns, a number of *lakshana* specifications are emphasized—the fingers are noticeably webbed and the curls of hair are shaped dramatically like snail shells that rise into a rounded *ushnisha* atop the head. However, the *urna*, the small protuberance usually seen on the Buddha's forehead, is absent.

Fig. 121. *Standing Buddha.* Sandstone, H: 35½ in. (90 cm). From Preah Theat, Cambodia, 7th century.

During the reign of Jayavarman II (circa 802–850), the close relationship between Khmer royalty and their Brahmin priests gave rise to a theocratic cult of the king as a *devaraja*—an omnipotent "god-king" wielding spiritual and temporal power integral with his absolute mastery of the realm. This brought forth a tradition of creating and worshiping images of Hindu and Buddhist deities that physically resembled and were named after the monarch and members of his royal court.

At the height of its power in the twelfth century, the Khmer realm included much of what is now central and northeastern Thailand, as evidenced by the

Fig. 122. *Angkor Wat.* Cambodia, 12th century.

ruins of Khmer temples and shrines scattered across the Korat Plateau. Khmer hegemony reached parts of Vietnam, Burma, and the Malay Peninsula. The grandest monument to Khmer glory is their architectural masterpiece, Angkor Wat, erected by Suryavarman II (1113–1150) along the southern edge of Angkor City, which stretches across the northern environs of Tonle Sap, Cambodia's great lake. Angkor Wat is an enormous temple-city surrounded by a broad moat and covers roughly two square kilometers (fig. 122).

The surfaces of its stone walls, galleries, and towers are carved in relief depictions of classical themes such as the Indian legendary epics, *Ramayana* and *Mahabharata*, and scenes memorializing the exploits of Khmer kings and their armies. Designed as a terrestrial microcosm of the Hindu universe, Angkor Wat perpetuated the cult of the *Devaraja* through the deification of Suryavarman II as an incarnation of the god Vishnu. A stone block from Angkor Wat carved in deep

Fig. 123. *Queen Maya Giving Birth to Prince Siddhartha, the Future Buddha.* Stone, 29⅜ x 24¼ in. (74.6 x 61.6 cm). From Angkor Wat, Cambodia, 12th century.

relief pictures Queen Maya standing beneath a *sala* tree in the wooded grove of Lumbini at the moment she gave birth to Prince Siddhartha, the Future Buddha (fig. 123). The queen is supported by her sister, Prajapati. The newborn prince is atop a small throne held by the kneeling god Brahma while attendants look on. The figures are depicted in Khmer court costumes and jewelry, Queen Maya and Prajapati wearing the distinctive national style of long, pleated sarongs wrapped by ornate belts with pendants.

Fig. 124 shows a seated Buddha image of twelfth-century Angkor Wat style. Cast in bronze that now bears an olive-green patina, this image sits with his right

hand touching the ground in *bhumisparsha mudra*. His left hand holds a small round object resembling a medicine pot, suggesting a portrayal of Bhaisajyaguru Buddha. He wears the elaborate crown, necklace, and armbands associated with images in royal attire, but the upper torso is otherwise bare—a Khmer styling

Fig. 124. *Seated Buddha*. Bronze, H: 13 in. (33 cm). Angkor Wat style, Cambodia, 12th century.

Fig. 125. *Goddess Prajnaparamita.* Bronze, H: 8⅝ in. (22 cm). Angkor Wat style, Cambodia, 12th century.

convention unlike Burmese and Thai likenesses in this genre that usually cover the entire body with jewelry and golden robes.[106]

Another creation from the Angkor Wat period is a gracefully modeled bronze statuette of the Mahayana goddess Prajnaparamita standing on a rectangular base (fig. 125). She is identified by the blue lotus in her right hand and the *pustaka* book of scriptures in her left hand. She wears a conical diadem decorated with a band of stylized lotus patterns and a small seated Buddha image. Additional adornments include earrings, necklaces, bracelets, and a Khmer-style pleated skirt folded over a belt fastened with pendants. Her facial

Fig. 126. *Hevajra.* Bronze, H: 9½ in. (24 cm). Khmer-Lopburi art, 12th century.

characteristics have typical Angkor Wat stylings: eyebrows connected in a single long line; eyes rendered large and wide open; full lips forming a serene smile.

The esoteric mysticism of Vajrayana Buddhism evidently had a robust cult following among the Khmers from the eleventh to thirteenth centuries. A favored deity was *Hevajra*, a Tantric personification of enlightenment. Hevajra is said to have eight heads, sixteen arms and four legs, and is characteristically pictured in a ritual dancing pose that symbolizes the dynamic process of enlightenment (fig. 126). His three lower heads represent the *nirmanakaya* forms of the Buddha, Lokesvara, and Vajrapani as they appear in our world.

Fig. 127. *Ritual conch with an image of Hevajra flanked by attendant figures and naga guardians.* Bronze, H: 8¾ in. (22.2 cm). Angkor Wat style, Cambodia, circa 12th century.

His middle tier of four heads represents four transcendent Buddhas of the Vajrayana pentad: Amitabha, Akshobhya, Ratnasambhava, and Amoghasiddhi. His single topmost head is that of Vairochana, the fifth transcendent Buddha who traditionally appears at the center of the cosmos. At first glance, images of Hevajra such as this one seem to have only two legs. But a close inspection reveals that the sculptors engraved shallow grooves in the outer edges of both legs, thus symbolically contouring each one as a joined pair and fulfilling the prescribed configuration of four legs.[107]

Our section on Tibet mentioned that Tantric ceremonies involve a variety of sacred paraphernalia. Some conch shells, for example, function as musical instruments; others hold consecrated water. Fig. 127 is the second type, a Khmer conch fabricated from bronze and shaped with a likeness of Hevajra in his traditional dance pose, flanked by attendants and *naga* guardians. The finely wrought metalwork shows another of Hevajra's attributes: as he dances to enlightenment, he tramples a recumbent Mara figure.

As discussed and illustrated earlier, many Vajrayana congregations worship the pentad of five transcendent Buddhas, and may include a sixth, such as *Vajrasattva* ("Thunderbolt" or "Diamond" Being), an embodiment of purity often identified as the Adi-Buddha, the supreme Buddha of the Vajrayana school. Representations of Vajrasattva depict him wearing a crown and royal attire, his right hand holding a *vajra* scepter, his left hand holding a *ghanta* bell, as in the Khmer statue of fig. 128.

Jayavarman VII (1181–1220) was the last of the great Khmer kings. He expanded the empire to its farthest reaches, stabilized it politically and launched a massive construction program that built roads, hospitals, temples, and monuments. He was a devout follower of Mahayana Buddhism, and many structures erected under his auspices included stone towers carved with four large, serenely smiling human faces aligned with the four cardinal points to symbolize the all-seeing

gaze of Lokesvara, an emanation of Avalokitesvara, Bodhisattva of Compassion. Each face is also thought to be a likeness of Jayavarman VII that confirms his deification as a *Buddharaja*—an earthly embodiment of Lokesvara and the successor to previous *Devarajas* who practiced the Hindu faith. Most famous of the

Fig. 128. *Vajrasattva*. Bronze, H: 9 in. (23 cm). Khmer-Lopburi art, circa 12th century.

Fig. 129. *The Bayon*. Angkor Thom, Cambodia, constructed circa 1190.

Fig. 130. *Asuras Pulling a Naga*. Sandstone. Angkor Thom, Cambodia, circa 1190.

Four Faces are those carved on the Buddhist shrine of Bayon and its surrounding towers, which Jayavarman VII installed as part of his construction of the Angkor Thom temple complex around 1190 (fig. 129). He created Angkor Thom, his royal city, on the site of an older temple from a century earlier, directly north of Angkor Wat.

Angkor Thom is surrounded by a broad moat. Figure 130 shows the carved stone balustrade of fifty-four *asura* statues pulling the body of a *naga* serpent atop the right edge of the causeway leading to the city's south gate. A matching array of fifty-four *deva* statues lines the left edge. Both rows begin at the causeway's entrance, where the *nagas* raise their enormous seven-headed hoods. This iconography is believed to illustrate the "Churning of the Sea" legend in Hindu mythology.[108] But the likely main purpose of these *nagas* is to protect the city. *Nagas*, deities that have the appearance of snakes or serpents, are ubiquitous in Cambodian mythology. Their theme is almost commonplace among the religions of South and Southeast Asia.[109] Hindus regularly portray their god Vishnu reclining on the body of *Ananta*, a multi-headed cosmic serpent; and the goddess *Manasa* is usually seen with her seven-headed snake's hood rising up prominently from her shoulders. A popular icon in the Jain faith in India shows the saint *Parsvanartha* protected beneath the outstretched hood of a *naga,* a pose reminiscent of the Buddha being shielded by the *naga raja* known as Muchalinda (see fig. 15). "The serpent, from the annual renewal of its skin, is a symbol of immortality, and when represented with its tail in its mouth, forming a circle, symbolizes the Yoga principle of Union, or the Circle of Regeneration."[110]

Buddhist lore tells of one *naga* so devoted to the Dharma that he transformed himself into a young human man so he could join the Buddha's monastic order. He was ordained as a *bhikshu*, a Buddhist monk, but when he fell asleep his body metamorphosed back to his snake form and he had to be expelled from the monkhood. The Buddha explained to him that only humans are accepted for ordination, but did grant his request to establish a tradition that is still observed in Theravada ordinations: Each applicant is referred to as *"Naga"* up to the moment he receives his monk's robes. Later in the ceremony each applicant is asked, "Are you a human being?" to ensure that non-humans do not get ordained.

Naga likenesses also appear repeatedly in Southeast Asian architecture as guardians of temples and palaces. Stylized *nagas* stretch down the side edges of each triangular frame on the building's gable roof, rearing their heads protectively at the bottom corners. Protector *nagas* also appear on railings atop stairways, and on doorways and frames around windows. In many of Asia's early animist societies the *naga raja* (Sanskrit: "serpent king") were worshiped as benevolent deities who ruled over rivers, lakes, and oceans. Interesting how their name acquires a far more fearsome connotation when translated into Western languages to describe that species of snake as "king cobra."

By the twelfth century, a Khmer stronghold that probably functioned as a provincial capital was in place at Lavo, now the Thai city Lopburi, 153 kilometers north of Bangkok. The styles of Khmer art and architecture found in that region (today's central and northeastern Thailand) are therefore often designated "Lopburi" or "Khmer-Lopburi."

Fig. 131. *Radiating Avalokitesvara.* Sandstone, H: 62¼ in. (1.58 m). From Prasat Muang Singh, Kanchanaburi Province, Thailand; Lopburi art, influenced by Khmer Bayon style, 13th century.

In addition to the distinctive Four Faces carved on the stone towers of Angkor Thom, another unique type of Lokesvara likeness created by Khmer sculptors is the "Radiating Avalokitesvara." The Bayon style Khmer-Lopburi example in fig. 131 portrays Lokesvara standing with eight arms that are raised to his sides. The hands, now lost, would have held attributes such as a lotus and a flask. His upper torso is uncovered and sculpted with hundreds of tiny Buddhas seated in *dhyana mudra* like the larger effigy of Amitabha Buddha at the front of his headdress. Another seated icon with arms outstretched is carved at the center of the chest, and may represent the goddess Prajnaparamita, since many Mahayanists at the Khmer court worshiped a trinity comprising the Buddha, Avalokitesvara, and Prajnaparamita. A similar style of seated effigy is repeated in a series that encircles the statue at its waist. Additional small Buddha images are fitted to rings on the toes and bands around both ankles. The statue wears a short *sampot* (traditional Cambodian wrapped skirt) with a fishtail flap in front, held to the waist by a thick belt.

Fig. 132. *Apsaras*. Sandstone. The Bayon, Angkor Thom, Cambodia, circa 1190.

His hair is pulled up in a tall chignon; the third eye popular in Tantric imagery is marked on the center of the forehead. Other characteristics of Khmer stone sculpture seen here are the circular incisions outlining the knees, and the massive size given the legs and feet.

A favorite subject of Khmer sculptors was the *apsaras*—beautiful celestial maidens whose origins can be traced to the Vedas, India's oldest sacred literature. Hundreds of *apsara* images in various sizes and poses are carved across the temple walls of Angkor. Many

Fig. 133. *Apsaras*. Sandstone. Angkor Wat, Cambodia, 12th century.

are captured in exuberant dance movements (fig. 132). Although they appear in a great proportion of Hindu and Buddhist paradise scenes, *apsaras* are not usually worshiped, but serve as celestial dancers and attendants to the presiding deities. A number of their images at Angkor are elaborately detailed portraits sculpted in deep relief to represent contemporary ideals of feminine grace and beauty among the ladies of the Khmer court, thus providing a visual record of the hairstyles, clothing, and jewelry of the time (fig. 133).

The decline of the Khmer Empire began at the death of King Jayavarman VII in 1220 and was hastened by the concurrent rise to power of the Thai kingdoms to the west. The fourteenth and fifteenth centuries saw

Fig. 134. *Cambodian scripture cabinet illustrating the "Five Buddhas of this Auspicious Age."*

nearly continual warfare between the Khmers and the Thais. In 1431 the city of Angkor fell to attacking Thai armies and was later abandoned by the Khmers, who moved their capital southeast to Phnom Penh.

While the Mahayana and Vajrayana faiths enjoyed the patronage of Khmer royalty and the highborn, starting in about the thirteenth century Theravada Buddhism took root among Cambodia's masses and—as in Sri Lanka, Thailand, Laos, and Burma—became the country's most popular religion. Theravada orthodoxy does not recognize the transcendent Buddhas and bodhisattvas of Mahayana and Vajrayana. But Theravada tradition does acknowledge a number of past Buddhas. In the section on Burmese art, which is predominantly Theravadin, we spoke of the Ananda Temple in Pagan with its statues of Sakyamuni and three previous Buddhas who are believed to have been his predecessors and taught the Dharma in our world. Adding the Bodhisattva Maitreya, the Future Buddha, completes the series known as the "Five Buddhas of this Auspicious Age." They are illustrated on a Cambodian scripture cabinet (fig. 134), with each Buddha seated on a lotus throne above a roundel picturing his symbol. Clockwise, beginning from top center, their names in Sanskrit / Pali are:

- Maitreya / Metteyya, with his symbol, a lion
- Kanakamuni / Konagamana, with his symbol, a serpent
- Sakyamuni (Gautama) / Gotama, with his symbol, a cow
- Kasyapa / Kassapa, with his symbol, a turtle
- Krakucchanda / Kakusandha, with his symbol, a rooster.

Arrayed across the top of the design are six celestial musicians. At the lower corners are two ceremonial emblems.

Fig. 135. *Wheel of the Law and a Deer*. Black stone, H: 82¾ in. (2.10 m). From Nakhon Pathom Province, Thailand, Dvaravati period, 6th–8th centuries.

THAILAND

There is still some scholarly debate on the origins of the Thai people, but one of their early homelands was in southern China, where they acquired the name *Tai*, from a Chinese word meaning "glorious" or "great." From southern China, especially Yunnan province, where a sizeable ethnic Thai population (Chinese, *Dai*) still lives today, large groups of Thais migrated farther south. By the end of the first millenium A.D. they were settling in parts of what are now northern Burma, Laos, northern Vietnam, and most significantly the territories that became the Thai kingdom of *Siam*—later renamed *Prathet Thai*, or Thailand.

Before the arrival of the Thais, much of modern-day central Thailand was populated by the Mons, who also inhabited parts of Burma and since early times practiced a blend of animism and Theravada Buddhism. Architectural remains and artifacts from Mon settlements have been found at U-Thong and Lopburi, as far south as Songkhla near the present border with Malaysia, and in the north at Haripunjaya, today's Lamphun. The largest Mon state, *Dvaravati*, was centered at present-day Nakhon Pathom, a city fifty kilometers west of Bangkok. Nakhon Pathom is an ancient site which may have been settled as early as the time of Suvarnabhumi ("Golden Land"), the legendary Southeast Asian kingdom that was either inhabited by the Mons or predated them. Nakhon Pathom is famed for its *Phra Pathom Chedi*, a colossal stupa 417 feet (127 meters) high, the world's tallest Buddhist monument, built over a very old core stupa that local people believe contains relics of the Buddha given by King Asoka's missionaries.[111]

The most ancient Buddhist artifacts surviving from the Mon period in Thailand are statues in the Amaravati style of India, likely brought from there by Indian traders and missionaries. Some of the oldest examples of indigenous Mon art emulate the early Indian tradition

Fig. 136. *The Buddha Shielded by Muchalinda the Serpent King*. Black stone, H: 30 in. (76.2 cm). Prachinburi Province, Thailand, Dvaravati period, 8th–10th centuries.

of representing the Buddha through aniconic tokens of prominent events in his life. Fig. 135 shows a Wheel of the Law and a kneeling deer cut from stone in Dvaravati. Both symbolize the Buddha preaching his first sermon in the Deer Park near Sarnath.

By about the eighth century Mon artists were also creating human likenesses of the Buddha. One theme they preferred was to show him sitting in meditation, shielded by Muchalinda, the Serpent King, such as the stone stele in fig. 136, which incorporates a number of characteristics of Dvaravati statues: The Buddha's hands and feet are large in proportion to his body; the eyebrows are long, emanating from a common point above the nose and sweeping over the eyes in a continuous line. The lips are full and natural, the nose rather flat. His face is wide with a low forehead emphasizing the unusually large, closely bunched curls of hair—a design apparently patterned after prototypes from Gupta India.

Fig. 137. *Bodhisattva Padmapani* (*Avalokitesvara*). Bronze, H: 24⅞ in. (63 cm). Surat Thani Province, Thailand, Srivijiya period, 8th century.

The long peninsula stretching down through today's southern Thailand, western Malaysia, and Singapore served in ancient times as a series of meeting points and transit zones for travelers from India, China, and countless Southeast Asian cultures. As noted earlier in regard to Indonesia, *Srivijaya* was a maritime kingdom with its capital near Palembang in Sumatra and held political control over much of the peninsula from about the seventh to thirteenth centuries. Theravada Buddhism, Mahayana Buddhism, Vajrayana Buddhism, and Hinduism were all practiced at various times and places in Srivijaya. *Chaiya*, today a town in Thailand's southern province of Surat Thani, was a regional center of Srivijaya's realm.

Fig. 137 is a masterpiece of Mahayanist devotional art found at Chaiya, now on display in Bangkok's National Museum: the torso of an eighth-century statue of Bodhisattva Padmapani, an emanation of Avalokitesvara. Cast from bronze with silver inlay, this image was modeled fully in the round in a graceful swaying pose. The figure wears the traditional regal jewelry of a bodhisattva, including an elaborate necklace and armbands. Its elegant headdress would have included a small emblem of Amitabha Buddha atop its front section, now lost. Another mark of Avalokitesvara is the miniature antelope skin, its head draping over the left shoulder together with the *upavita*, or sacred thread that reaches down to the right side of the waist.

From about the tenth to twelfth centuries, the Khmer Empire of Cambodia encompassed parts of what now constitute central and northeastern Thailand. Lopburi, 153 kilometers north of Bangkok, was a major Khmer city then, probably a provincial capital, so the art and architecture of that time and vicinity are often categorized as "Lopburi" or "Khmer-Lopburi" style. Many Khmer-Lopburi antiquities are similar in style and iconography to products of that era from Cambodia, but some have features suggesting kinship with Mon or Thai art. The Mon and Khmer languages are related, and by about the tenth century most of the Mon communities had been absorbed into the Khmer Empire.

Fig. 138 is a gilt bronze statue of the Buddha crowned and wearing royal attire, a favorite theme of the Khmers. It was found in Thailand's Ratchburi Province, southwest of Nakhon Pathom, and dates to the twelfth to thirteenth centuries. The pose signifies the Buddha's return to our world after visiting his mother, Queen Maya, in the Trayastrimsa Heaven. Paintings usually interpret this event by picturing the Buddha descending from heaven down a triple staircase, accompanied by the gods Brahma and Indra (see fig. 27). But in sculptures such as this Khmer example, the Buddha stands with his arms raised symmetrically, both hands having the index finger touching the thumb to symbolize him creating an opening between the heavenly realm and Earth—as a person might grasp the edges of two sections of a closed curtain and draw them open.

This pose is also seen in Mon sculpture.

One of the first major settlements of the Thais in what would become the kingdom bearing their name was *Chiang Saen*, a town near the Mekong River's south bank. Questions remain about chronologies of the northern Thai kingdoms, but it is estimated that Chiang Saen was flourishing by the twelfth century. It was probably around that time, in that area, that the first Thai Buddhist art appeared.

Fig. 138. *The Buddha Descending from Heaven*. Gilt bronze, H: 49¾ in. (1.26 m). Ratchburi Province, Thailand, 12th–13th centuries.

The gilt bronze seated statue of the Buddha touching the earth to mark his enlightenment, shown at the center on the front cover and in fig. 12, is patterned after Chiang Saen art. This style is part of a broader category called "Lanna art," spanning the eleventh to eighteenth centuries and named after the Lanna kingdom of the Thais that once ruled the northern provinces and founded the city of Chiang Mai in 1296. The majority of Chiang Saen Buddha statues were cast from bronze and depict his enlightenment, or "Subduing Mara." The face is rounded; the hair is formed into traditional curling spirals; the eyebrows are long and curved, arching above half-closed eyes; a thin ridge of the monastic garment extends over the left shoulder, down the center of the prominent chest and under the right arm. Other marks of Chiang Saen imagery are the lotus-like bulb atop the *ushnisha*; the narrow strap of cloth representing the folded outer robe (*sanghati*) that ends just below the left shoulder; and the full lotus posture of the legs, tucked tightly together with the bottoms of both feet visible. These characteristics recall and are apparently derived from the Pala statuary of India, likely transmitted via Burma.

Southward migration of the Thais continued and by the thirteenth century they had a flourishing kingdom at *Sukhothai*, nearly halfway from Chiang Saen to the Gulf of Thailand, that gave rise to a golden age of Thai culture. This steady expansion of the Thai realm also pushed back the Khmers into their homeland in present-day Cambodia. Early Buddhist artworks from Sukhothai resemble those of the Lanna styles. However, cultural exchanges with Sri Lanka brought fresh artistic impulses that contributed to the birth in the fourteenth century of a unique, high classic style of Sukhothai Buddhist art. Moreover, Sukhothai sculptors developed a new type of Buddha statue—a "walking" image in the round, a likeness theretofore seen only occasionally in paintings and relief carvings. The Walking Buddha is believed to represent the time immediately after his return to Earth following his visit with his mother, Queen Maya, in the Trayastrimsa Heaven.[112]

The graceful, fourteenth-century gilt bronze statue in fig. 139 exemplifies the Sukhothai high classic Walking Buddha. Its overall impression is soft and supple, almost feminine except for the broad, well-rounded shoulders. The face is oval, with sharply curved eyebrows springing from a common point above the long, idealized nose. A small crescent-shaped indentation marks the chin; the mouth has a natural appearance; the long, distended earlobes curve gracefully from the neck. The hair is formed as spirals following the lines of the eyebrows into a peak at the center of the forehead. The robe is sheer, almost diaphanous to the point

Fig. 139. *The Buddha Walking*. Gilt bronze, H: 21 in. (53.3 cm). Thailand, Sukhothai period, 14th century.

Fig. 140. *The Enlightenment of Sakyamuni Buddha*. Bronze, H: 40⅛ in. (1.02 m). Thailand, Sukhothai period, 2nd half of 14th century.

of suggesting an absence of sexuality. Two more characteristics of Sukhothai Buddha images are seen here: the strap of cloth crossing the left shoulder reaches down nearly to the waist, and a stylized flame finial is placed atop the *ushnisha*.[113]

> There was Sinhalese influence in the flame finial which became a hallmark of the Sukhothai style. The flame, called a *ketumala* or a *rashmi*, signifies the spiritual power and fiery energy of the Buddha, and is equivalent to a halo. A flame finial shaped like a lotus bud appeared on the Pala images of Northeast India and in turn influenced the art of North Thailand. . . . In South India, the flame can be seen on the eleventh-to thirteenth-century images produced at Nagapattinam. Such a finial was known in Sri Lanka as early as the eighth century and became very popular during the Polonnaruva (1070–1235) and Gampola (1341–1415) periods, the latter being the dynasty that was contemporary with the classic period of Sukhothai art and which exercised considerable influence over the architectural decoration of Sukhothai.[114]

A bronze image of the Enlightenment illustrates how Sukhothai artists blended traditional, idealized features of the Buddha with a fresh vision of grace and elegance to create a high classic style of Thai art (fig. 140).

During their migration south, the Thais encountered and evidently shared cultural and religious ideas with the Khmers and the Mons. One result was a transitional Thai school of art spanning the twelfth to fifteenth centuries that is referred to as "U-Thong," after the ancient city of that name, southwest of Lopburi. The classical Sukhothai seated Buddha in fig. 140 offers an interesting comparison with one from U-Thong (fig. 141). Both touch the ground with the right hand in *bhumisparsha mudra*. But the U-Thong statue bears a Khmer flavor through its masculine modeling, with its major planes formed as straight lines running parallel or perpendicular to each other. Also adapted from

Fig. 141. *The Enlightenment of Sakyamuni Buddha*. Bronze, H: 40⅝ in. (1.03 m). Thailand, U-Thong period, 13th–14th centuries.

Khmer styling is the thin band or ridge bordering the hairline at the forehead. The treatment of its hair is a distinctive U-Thong trademark, being formed from unusually small, peg-like curls that are also seen on some Mon and Burmese statues. The vigorous, Khmer-inspired treatment continues with more vertical and horizontal strokes forming the eyes, eyebrows, nose, and mouth. The top of the head is fashioned with a Khmer-style, conical *ushnisha*, although many other U-Thong Buddhas were crowned with a Sukhothai-style flame finial. Still, despite some Khmer influences, the Thai essence in U-Thong art asserts itself in the slender body and naturally modeled, oval face. Also inherited from Sukhothai prototypes are the long, slender fold of cloth reaching over the left shoulder and down to the navel, and the *virasana*, or half-lotus seated posture with the right leg resting directly atop the left.

In the fourteenth century the city of U-Thong was beset by a cholera epidemic that forced an exodus by the bulk of its Thai inhabitants. A prince of U-Thong therefore moved the capital toward the east and founded a new Thai kingdom at Ayutthaya in 1350, becoming its first king. Endowed with an abundance of fertile farmland and surrounded by three rivers, which provided an unlimited water supply while protecting the city, Ayutthaya grew into a powerful realm that conquered and absorbed neighboring cities and territories in every direction. At the height of its glory, Ayutthaya's rule reached north to Luang Prabang in today's Laos, west to the Shan States of Burma, south down the entire Malay Peninsula, and east across Cambodia.[115]

Ayutthaya became more prosperous and influential than any previous Thai state and legendary among its trading partners in Europe and Asia as a colorful, cosmopolitan city of impressive palaces and temples. But this era is not noted for significant innovations in the visual arts. During the fourteenth and fifteenth centuries, Ayutthaya's artists generally replicated the designs of Sukhothai, Lopburi, and U-Thong. Their religious sculpture in later years consisted largely of bronze Buddha statues richly crowned and adorned in regal attire, where the basic figure served mainly as a foundation for dazzling necklaces, diadems, rings, and gold filigree (see fig. 23). This penchant for ornamentation was, however, splendidly applied to the decorative arts: as gold paintings on black lacquer and mother-of-pearl inlay for cabinets and chests to hold religious texts, and delicately carved gilt wood doors, windows, and gables to beautify temple buildings.

In 1767, after four centuries as the capital of one of Southeast Asia's richest and most powerful kingdoms, the city of Ayutthaya was attacked and destroyed by Burmese armies. The Thais who survived that assault regrouped under leadership of the governor of their northwestern city of Tak. He became known as King Taksin the Great after successfully driving the Burmese

Fig. 142. *Crowned Buddha Dispelling Fear*. Gilt bronze, H: 96½ in. (2.45 m). Bangkok, Thailand, Ratanakosin period, 19th–20th centuries.

out of the Thai realm. He also established a new capital downriver from Ayutthaya at *Thonburi*, on the west bank of the Chao Phraya River near the Gulf of Thailand. His successor Rama I, the first king of the Chakri dynasty, relocated the capital to the east bank of the river in 1782. He named the city *Krung Thep* (City of Angels), though it continues to this day to be known internationally by its older name, Bangkok.

Devotional art of the early Bangkok, or *Ratanakosin* era, largely continued the styles of Ayutthaya. Statues of the Buddha were usually "in royal attire," extravagantly gilded and adorned with headpieces and jewelry. The statue of the Buddha in fig. 142, for instance, could be the work of a master goldsmith or lapidary: the tall, spired crown and ornate earrings extend down to the shoulder epaulets. Engraved jewelry inlaid with glass chips covers the torso. Every toe, finger, and thumb wears a delicately shaped ring. The figure stands on a round lotus base atop a four-tiered pedestal, and the entire ensemble is lavishly gilded.

One notable enterprise early in the Ratanakosin era was that approximately twelve hundred abandoned Buddha images were retrieved from various sites in the central and northern provinces and brought to Bangkok where they were restored, then placed in temple *viharas* and galleries. As a result, Buddhist statuary from virtually every period in the kingdom's history, along with samples from other countries, can be seen in Bangkok temples such as *Wat Phra Chetuphon* (also called *Wat Pho*), *Wat Benchamabopit* (the Marble Temple), *Wat Bovoranives*, and the National Museum, once the palace of the *Upparat* (Viceroy).

Among the most impressive accomplishments in the visual arts of the Bangkok or Ratanakosin period to date are its mural paintings, for the most part finely detailed illustrations of episodes from the Buddha's life and the *jataka* stories of his previous births. For example, the mural scene in fig. 27—*Buddha Descending from Heaven*—exemplifies a skilled mix of brushwork conventions: distinctively Thai stylization, meticulous

draftsmanship, a palette of bright colors, and the ideal measure of gold leaf accents. These traditional techniques and stylings are still practiced today. Although created with modern acrylic pigments, the contemporary painting of Prince Siddhartha's birth in fig. 143 follows a classical formula: the foreground shows the newborn Siddhartha standing atop a miniature pedestal held by the green-hued god Indra while shielded by a parasol of the god Brahma. Queen Maya stands at the picture's center, still grasping the tree branch as at the moment of her son's birth. Two other lovely young women attend her; one would be her sister, Prajapati. Five celestials watch from above, together with a number of onlookers and royal attendants in Thai palace dress.

Another Thai religious format is the *phra bot* (Buddhist painting on a long cloth panel). First popularized during the Sukhothai era, these colorful paintings are typically suspended as banners on temple walls. Devotees often create or sponsor them as a means of accruing merit for themselves or family members. The illustrations usually tell of the Buddha's life and *jataka* tales of his previous births. The example in fig. 1 comprises two sections: The top scene has the Buddha standing at center with his two chief disciples, the monks Sariputra and Maudgalyayana. The lower section pictures a famous shipwreck scene from the *Mahajanaka Jataka*, the story of the Buddha's earlier birth as Prince Mahajanaka, whose ship was destroyed during a storm. Mahajanaka survived by swimming courageously for seven days, demonstrating the virtues of perseverance, self-reliance, and dedication to the path of righteousness.[116]

About 95 percent of Thailand's 62 million people are Buddhist, and a substantial number have Buddha images in a shrine room or other sacred space in their homes. Most also possess one or more small Buddhist amulets (Thai, *phra khreung*), often wearing them on gold or silver chains. Some amulets and votive figures

Fig. 143. (Opposite) *Queen Maya Giving Birth to Prince Siddhartha, the Future Buddha.* By Sangduen Rawijan. Acrylics on canvas, 46 x 31 in. (117 x 79 cm). Thailand, 2001.

1. *Three Buddha images* (bronze)

2. *Buddha and the Bodhi Tree* (bronze)

3. *Buddha Reclining beneath a Tree* (bronze)

4. *Dharmachakra,Wheel of the Law* (molded powder)

5. *Buddha Standing* (bronze, in a gilt bronze case)

6. *Seated Buddha: Luang Pho Sai* (gilt bronze)

7. *Buddha shielded by the Naga Raja* (silver)

8. *Somdet Phra Nyana Samvara* (bronze)

9. *Buddha Seated in Meditation* (bronze with blue enamel)

10. *Buddha Seated on a Throne* (terracotta)

11. *Buddha Seated in Meditation* (bronze)

12. *Amitabha Buddha Standing* (bronze)

are issued to commemorate religious observances; many are distributed or traded through shops and markets.

> Because an amulet is believed to possess a specific quality such as reinforcing good virtue, avoiding catastrophe, bringing general prosperity, or providing supernatural powers, Thais typically wear many amulets to ensure complete protection. In choosing a piece, it is important to amulet collectors that it is made and blessed by a revered teacher or monk. A valuable amulet must come from a person who is thought to have special power. Unsacralized amulets, like Buddha images, are somehow considered incomplete. Since an amulet is chosen by its qualities, the more stories of efficacy that can be attributed to an amulet, the more it will attract potential buyers. At one time amulets were popular only among men, but at present they are worn strung on a necklace under the clothing, and only in odd numbers, by most Thais of both sexes.[117]

Fig. 144 is a selection of typical Thai amulets. Since most Thais observe Theravada beliefs, a majority of their amulets bear likenesses of Sakyamuni, the historical Buddha, and a number of these replicate revered, large-size statues. Number 6, for instance, is a miniature likeness of a seated Buddha figure known as *Luang Poh Sai*. Other Thai amulets, such as number 8, honor venerated Buddhist monks.

Fig. 144. (Opposite) *Buddhist Amulets and Miniature Figures*. From Thailand, various styles, subjects, materials, and eras.

VIETNAM

Spanning the long eastern coastline of mainland Southeast Asia, Vietnam received cultural influences from both China and India. The country's northern region was under the political control of China for much of the period from 111 B.C. to A.D. 938—ten centuries that instilled in Vietnamese art and architecture an indelible range of Chinese influences, and brought to Vietnam the Chinese concept of the "Unity of the Three Religions," which blended aspects of Buddhism, Confucianism, and Daoism with native forms of animism.

Directly south of the Vietnamese homeland in the northern region was the kingdom of Champa, which was inhabited by the Cham people and at its zenith covered much of today's central Vietnam. The Cham had little in common with the Vietnamese, their neighbors and frequent adversaries to the north. The Cham had closer ethnic, linguistic, and cultural links with similarly Indianized states in Malaya and Indonesia and the Khmer empire—all of them having learned the Sanskrit language and kingship traditions of India, along with Hinduism and Buddhism.

Buddhist missionaries from India and Sri Lanka were active in Champa by the sixth century A.D. or earlier. One of the finest specimens of Buddhist art unearthed in the territories of Champa is the bronze standing image of the Buddha shown in fig. 102. Because it was recovered from the ruins of Dong Duong, a monastery complex of vast dimensions near the coast of central Vietnam that flourished in the ninth to tenth centuries, some historians initially labeled it Cham art. But its styling and iconography point to creators at Anuradhapura in Sri Lanka between the third to seventh centuries.[118]

A large bronze standing statue of the Bodhisattva Tara was also found at Dong Duong (fig. 145). This superb product of Cham metalsmiths was cast by the

Fig. 145. (Opposite) *Bodhisattva Tara*. Bronze, H: 47¼ in. (1.20 m). Dong Duong, Vietnam, 9th–10th centuries.

lost-wax method and appears to draw characteristics from Indian, Southeast Asian, and East Asian prototypes. The broad, sternly modeled face, full lips, and flat nose resemble features seen on many other Cham artworks, but are accented by a unique set of inlays at the eyes and eyebrows. Braided rows of hair rise into a headdress whose front bears the Mahayanist's traditional little image of Amitabha Buddha seated in meditation. Her bare upper torso is powerfully shaped with thick arms, ample breasts, and a very narrow waist, suggesting ancestry shared with the Tara statue from Sri Lanka in fig. 103. Her hands are posed symmetrically in what may be a variation of the double *vitarka mudra* popular in Mon and Khmer imagery (see fig. 138), though in this instance likely expressing a teaching activity. Two layers of dress are wrapped around the midsection to the ankles, formed as contrasting series of fine and broad pleats and tucked in at the waist.[119]

> Cham art is distinguished in general both by its profound and vigorous originality, and by its openness to outside influences. . . . Cham art borrowed but did not copy. Its originality is always clearly visible, not only in the attire and jewellery of the personages, which naturally reflect local custom, but above all from a purely aesthetic viewpoint. Champa appears to have developed a very specific vision of the human and divine worlds, real or imagined. This vision can vary widely according to the scene depicted, and occasionally shifts radically in a short space of time, e.g. the contrast between the sculptures of Dong Duong and those of My Son or Tra Kieu. But it is always highly individualistic and can occasionally produce an indisputable masterpiece.[120]

Another smaller but similarly rare Cham bronze depicts the Mahayana Bodhisattva Vajrapani (fig. 146). His slender body stands in the supple *tribhanga* triple bending pose atop a bell-shaped base. He is identified by the miniature *vajra* thunderbolt held in his right hand.

Fig. 146. *Bodhisattva Vajrapani*. Bronze, H: 13 in. (33 cm). Cham art, Vietnam, 8th century.

Fig. 147. *Amitabha Buddha*. Gilt lacquer with paint on wood, H: 33 in. (83.8 cm). Vietnam, circa 19th century.

Beginning around 980 the Vietnamese embarked on an aggressive southward expansion and by the mid-fifteenth century had gained dominion over virtually all of the former territories of Champa. Vietnamese emperor Gia Long consolidated the north and the south into a unified kingdom in 1802. In 1832, his son and successor, Minh Mang, defeated the last of the Cham forces and brought an end to the kingdom of Champa. Vietnam reached its present size in the mid-1800's after annexing the lands surrounding the Mekong delta that were once ruled by the Khmers.

The Vietnamese dynasty of Ly (1009–1224) saw growing popularity of Amitabha Buddha (Vietnamese, *A-Di-Da*) among devotees hopeful of being reborn in their next life in his celestial Pure Land (Vietnamese, *Tinh Do*). As in many other Mahayanist societies, Amitabha continues to the present time as the pre-eminent deity in Vietnam, worshiped through likenesses such as the nineteenth-century gilt-lacquer-on-wood statue in fig. 147. This image incorporates the uncommon variation of having Amitabha hold a small round object in his left hand, conceivably the wish-fulfilling jewel usually carried by the Bodhisattva Ksitigarbha.

Ksitigarbha is worshiped in Vietnam and East Asia as a compassionate bodhisattva dedicated to rescuing souls from the torments of hell. He is believed to have vowed "not to rest until every corner of the hell-states is empty." A gilt wood Vietnamese statue shows Ksitigarbha holding his two primary attributes: in his left hand, a *chintamani*, the wish-fulfilling jewel; in his right hand, a *khakkara*, or monk's staff, fitted with metal rings on its end—his magical key that unlocks the gates of hell (fig. 148). He sits on a lotus throne atop a protector lion, another of his symbols.

A common technique for gilding a religious icon—whether metal, wood, or stone—begins by coating it with black lacquer that acts as an adhesive with the gold paint or leaf that is applied next. Vietnamese and Chinese artisans routinely add another step—brushing a coat of clear lacquer over the gilding to seal and preserve the gold finish. When the glossy surface ages, it acquires a distinctive, orange-hued "old gold" luster, as examples the images of Amitabha (fig. 147) and Ksitigarbha (fig. 148).

Fig. 148. *Bodhisattva Ksitigarbha Seated Atop a Lion*. Gilt wood, H: 22½ in. (57.2 cm). Vietnam, circa 18th–19th centuries.

Fig. 149. *Bodhisattva Avalokitesvara*. Gilded and lacquered wood, H: 34½ in. (87.6 cm). Vietnam, circa 1750.

The Bodhisattva Avalokitesvara, or Guanyin (Vietnamese, *Quan Am*), is associated with Amitabha Buddha but is also worshiped independently, often through representations as a goddess with multiple arms, as popularized in China. A gilded and lacquered wood statue from Vietnam shows Avalokitesvara with twelve arms: the main pair of hands are joined in prayer; another pair extend from the edges of the robe to rest upon the legs; and the remaining hands are in ritual poses (fig. 149).

A unique seated image of Sakyamuni Buddha touching the ground to mark his enlightenment was

Fig. 150. *The Enlightenment of Sakyamuni Buddha*. Gilded and painted wood with inlaid gemstones. Vietnam, 19th century.

found in Vietnam but blends a number of Southeast Asian stylings (fig. 150). Here the Buddha wears the kind of globular crown and sumptuously jeweled robes popular in the "royal attire" theme, with the distinctively Burmese touch of two *naga* heads rising from the base beneath the legs.

Budai, the legendary Chinese monk known universally as the "Laughing Buddha," is revered in Mahayanist cultures as an incarnation of the Bodhisattva Maitreya. He is also one of the many Chinese figures that have been adopted into Vietnamese Buddhist traditions. A nineteenth-century gilt bronze image from

Fig. 151. *The Monk Budai*. Gilt bronze, H: 18¼ in. (46.4 cm). Vietnam, 19th century.

Vietnam retains his traditional huge belly, perpetually smiling face, and the hemp sack that held his worldly possessions as he roamed China's countryside (fig. 151).

The altars inside Theravada temples can display an abundance of statues, but most are likenesses of Sakyamuni, the historical Buddha, posed in the numerous *asana* and *mudra* configurations that recall the principal events in his life. Mahayana temples, on the other hand, can contain statues and paintings of a dozen or more different Buddhas, bodhisattvas, deities, and venerable monks. Fig. 152 is the main altar of a Mahayana temple in southern Vietnam. The largest and principal figure is Amitabha Buddha, positioned atop the center of the rear row. In front of him is a popular trinity known as the "Buddhas of the Three Ages," consisting of Kasyapa, "Buddha of the Past"; Sakyamuni, "Buddha of the Present"; and Maitreya, "Buddha of the Future." Attending them are standing statuettes of the monks Ananda and Mahakasyapa.

Fig. 152. *Main Altar of a Mahayana Temple*. Giac Vien Temple, Ho Chi Minh City, Vietnam.

We also see images of the Chinese monk Budai and the newborn Prince Siddhartha pointing to the heavens, and several guardian deities. Subsidiary altars toward the sides of the room hold images of the Bodhisattvas Avalokitesvara and Mahasthamaprapta, and the eighteen *arhat*s (Chinese, *luohan*; Vietnamese, *lahan*).

Like many of its neighbors, Vietnam has absorbed and harmonized a remarkable assortment of religious and aesthetic influences, yet the core teachings of Buddhism continue to flourish in the country's spiritual beliefs and artistic expression. Fig. 153 is a modern Vietnamese mother-of-pearl, lacquer-on-wood portrait of the Buddha seated in meditation that employs a blend of traditional styling elements to faithfully evoke the moments leading to his enlightenment under the Bodhi Tree some twenty-five centuries ago.

Fig. 153. *Sakyamuni Buddha Seated in Meditation beneath the Bodhi Tree*. Mother of pearl inlay with pigments and lacquer on wood, 23 x 15½ in. (58.4 x 39.4 cm). Vietnam, 20th century.

APPENDIX 1:
MUDRA, ASANA, AND BHANGA TERMINOLOGY

Three Sanskrit words—*mudra*, *asana*, and *bhanga*—form the core of a visual vocabulary of terms that describe and classify key attributes of Asian artworks. The word *mudra* ("seal" or "sign") is associated with symbolic gestures or poses of the hands and fingers. Fig. 154 shows those commonly seen in Buddhist imagery:

1. *Abhaya mudra* (granting protection or dispelling fear) is indicated by raising one or both hands, palm facing outward in front of the chest.
2. *Anjali mudra* (respectful greeting or offering reverence) has the two hands clasped together in front of the chest. This gesture is also known as *namaskara mudra*.
3. *Varada mudra* (bestowing a blessing or charity) can be performed by having either hand extended down, palm facing outward.
4. *Vitarka mudra* (teaching or discussion) has the right hand raised, index finger and thumb touching, in front of the chest.
5. *Dharmachakra mudra* (turning the Wheel of the Law) shows both hands with index finger and thumb touching, raised together in front of the chest to represent the Buddha preaching his first sermon in the Deer Park near Sarnath, India.
6. Bodhyangi mudra (fist of wisdom) has the erect index finger of one hand held in the closed fist of the other hand. This gesture is also known as *bodhyagiri mudra* (supreme wisdom).
7. *Dhyana mudra* (meditation) shows the two hands resting together in the lap, usually right atop left.
8. *Bhumisparsha mudra* (earth touching), the distinctive principal emblem of Buddhism, shows the seated

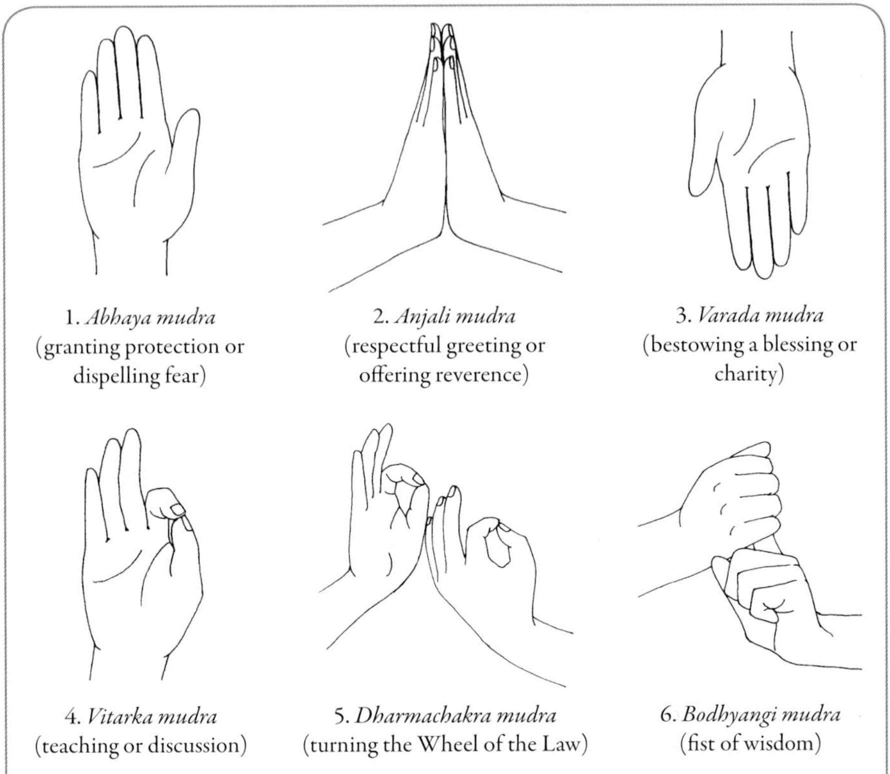

Fig. 154. Mudra gestures often seen in Buddhist art.

Buddha's right hand touching the ground to call the Earth Goddess to witness his victory over Mara, and therefore symbolizes his achieving enlightenment.

Dhyana mudra and *bhumisparsha mudra* are normally found only among seated figures. The other gestures mentioned here are seen in seated and standing forms. *Abhaya mudra* is sometimes shown by the right hand in combination with the left hand posed in *varada mudra*.

The Sanskrit word *asana* originally categorized yoga poses and was extended to describe other positions of the lower body and legs. Some samples are pictured in fig. 155:

1. *Padmasana* (lotus posture) denotes the seated yoga position where the legs are tucked in tightly together and crossed at the ankles, usually right atop left, with the bottoms of both feet visible facing upward and resting on opposite thighs. This term is a typical combination of *asana* with a prefix, in this case *padma* (lotus). *Padmasana* is sometimes defined more specifically as "full lotus posture." This pose is also known as *vajrasana*. The word *vajra* has two interpretations. Its original meaning comes from Hinduism, where *vajra* is the divine "thunderbolt" weapon of the god Indra. In the Buddhist context, *vajra* can also symbolize the indestructible and is thus translated as "diamond" or "adamantine." *Vajrasana* then means "diamond posture." Additionally, this pose can be called *dhyanasana* (meditation posture).
2. *Ardhapadmasana* (half-lotus posture) is a more relaxed seated meditation position where the right leg rests squarely atop the left. The bottom of the right foot is visible, facing upward, but the left foot is mostly covered beneath the right lower leg. This pose is also known as *virasana* (hero posture).
3. *Lalitasana* (relaxation posture) means sitting at rest upon a pedestal, one leg bent horizontally atop the

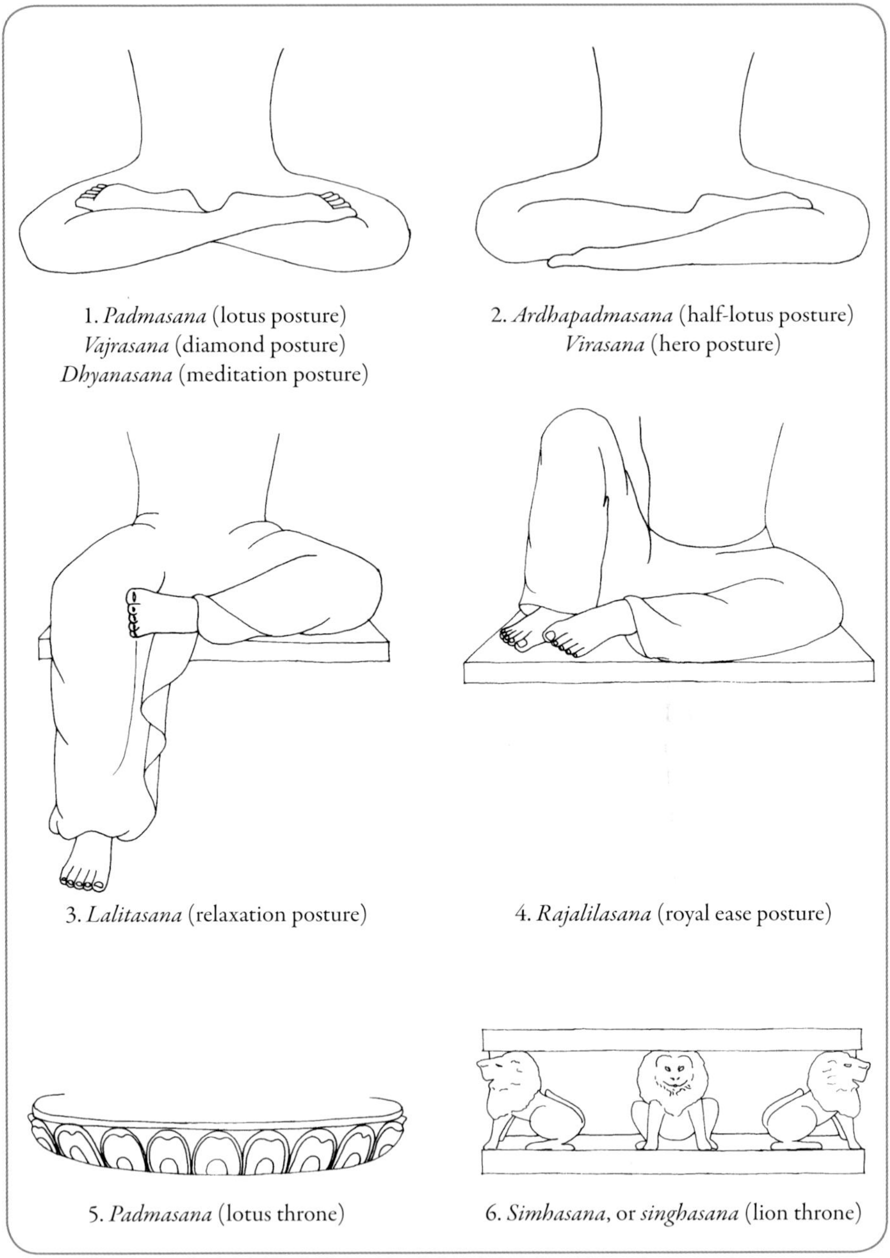

Fig. 155. Asana terms in Buddhist art.

pedestal, the other leg extending down toward the floor.

4. *Rajalilasana* (royal ease posture) is a variation of the *lalitasana* pose but with one leg resting horizontally and the other raised vertically, its knee up near to chest level, with both feet together atop the pedestal. This posture is reserved for images of royalty and eminent deities such as Avalokitesvara.

The word *asana* has a second meaning, employed to describe the seat or throne beneath a figure:

5. *Padmasana* then takes the interpretation "lotus throne," a seat or throne fashioned with one or more rows of stylized lotus petals, probably the most favored pedestal design in Buddhist art.
6. *Simhasana*, or *singhasana* (lion throne) is also seen frequently, a pedestal base supported by one or more lions, a symbol of the Buddha's royal ancestry and the great strength of his teachings.
7. *Vajrasana* has another meaning in this context, for the "Diamond Throne"—a monument installed by King Asoka in the third century B.C. marking the spot under the Bodhi Tree where the Buddha attained enlightenment.

Another set of terms used to describe artwork poses stems from the Sanskrit word *bhanga* ("posture"). *Samabhanga* indicates a body standing or sitting perfectly straight; nearly all seated and standing Buddha images display this posture. *Dvibhanga* means bending at two points—usually neck and hips—for example the Padmapani statue in fig. 99. *Tribhanga* describes a body bending at three points—usually neck, hips, and knees—such as the image of Queen Maya in fig. 4 and the bronze Vajrapani in fig. 146.

APPENDIX 2:

THE FIVE TRANSCENDENT BUDDHAS OF THE MAHAYANA AND VAJRAYANA FAITHS

The Mahayana movement and its branches encompass a vast pantheon of Buddhas, bodhisattvas, and deities. The Vajrayana branch especially venerates a pentad of five specific transcendent Buddhas.

	Akshobhya Immovable Buddha	**Ratnasambhava** Jewel Born Buddha
LOCATION IN THE COSMOS	east	south
MUDRA POSE	*bhumisparsha* (touching the earth)	*varada* (bestowing a blessing)
SYMBOL	*vajra* (thunderbolt)	*chintamani* (wish-fulfilling jewel)
COLOR	blue	yellow
ASSOCIATED BODHISATTVA	Vajrapani	Ratnapani
SAKTI (female counterpart)	Locana or Mamaki	Mamaki or Locana
VAHANA (mount or vehicle)	elephant	horse
ELEMENT	air	fire

The chart below lists their prime characteristics, many of which can be seen in the Nepali sutra cover of fig. 83, the Tibetan mandala of fig. 92, and the Tibetan lama's crown of fig. 97.

Vairochana Resplendent Buddha	**Amitabha** Infinite Light Buddha	**Amoghasiddhi** Infallible Buddha
center	west	north
dharmachakra (turning the wheel of the law)	*dhyana* (meditating)	*abhaya* (granting protection)
chakra (wheel)	*patra* (alms bowl)	*visva-vajra* (double thunderbolt)
white	red	green
Samantabhadra	Avalokitesvara	Visvapani
Vajradhatvisvari	Pandara	Tara
lion	peacock	garuda
ether	water	earth

GLOSSARY

Abbreviations:
B. Burmese
Ch. Chinese
J. Japanese
K. Korean
Kh. Khmer (Cambodian)
N. Nepali
P. Pali
S. Sanskrit
Tb. Tibetan
Th. Thai
Vt. Vietnamese

Adi-Buddha (S.) primordial, supreme Buddha of the Vajrayana doctrine; sometimes called Samantabhadra, Svayambhu, Vajradhara, or Vajrasattva; usually represented wearing a crown and royal robes.

Akshobhya (S.), **Achu** (Ch.), **Ashuku Nyorai** (J.), **Mibskyod-pa** (Tb.) the Immovable Buddha, one of the pentad of five transcendent Buddhas of the Mahayana and Vajrayana doctrines; resides in Abhirati, the eastern paradise; usually represented seated in the pose of touching the earth (*bhumisparsha mudra*).

Amitabha (S.), **Amituofo** (Ch.), **Amita-bul** (K.), **Amida** (J.), **Hod-dpag-med** (Tb.), **A-Di-Da** (Vt.) the Buddha of Infinite Light, one of the pentad of five transcendent Buddhas of the Mahayana and Vajrayana doctrines; resides in Sukhavati, the western paradise; usually represented seated in the pose of meditation (*dhyana mudra*).

Amitayus (S.), **Chang Shengfo** (Ch.), **Muryoju** (J.), **Chedpag-med** (Tb.) the Buddha of Infinite Life, an alternate form of Amitabha Buddha.

Amoghasiddhi (S.), **Fukujoju Nyorai** (J.), **Don-grub** (Tb.) the Infallible Buddha, one of the pentad of five transcendent Buddhas of the Mahayana and Vajrayana doctrines; usually represented in the northern sector of the cosmos in the pose of granting protection (*abhaya mudra*).

amrita (S.), ***amata*** (P.) deathless or immortal; also a magical beverage of the gods, said to give eternal life.

Ananda (S. and P.) a senior monk during Sakyamuni Buddha's lifetime; was also his cousin and personal attendant.

Anathapindada (S.), **Anathapindika** (P.) a wealthy merchant and devoted follower of the Buddha who donated the Jetavana park at Sravasti as a *vihara*.

Angulimala (S. and P.) "Garland of Fingers": a vicious thief and murderer who hacked a finger off the hand of each of his victims and wore them on a string around his neck.

apsara (S.), ***acchara*** (P.), ***tian-nu*** (Ch.), ***hiten*** (J.), ***lha'i-bu-mo*** (Tb.) celestial maiden; often pictured as a voluptuous dancer or attendant.

arhat (S.), ***arahant*** (P.), ***luohan*** (Ch.), ***rakan*** (J.), ***gnas-brtan*** (Tb.), ***lahan*** (Vt.) "venerable one" who has attained enlightenment.

asana (S. and P.) (1) Symbolic poses or positions of the lower body and limbs of a figure. (2) Styles of seat or throne beneath a figure. See appendix 1 for a review and illustrations.

Asoka the Great King of Magadha and surrounding lands (c. 273–232 B.C.); converted to Buddhism, which he spread across India, Sri Lanka, and other places by constructing temples and sending missionaries to teach the Dharma.

Avalokitesvara (S.), **Lokesvara** (S.), **Padmapani** (S.), **Guanyin**, or **Guan Shih Yin** (Ch.), **Kwanseum Posal** (K.), **Kannon** (J.), **Chenrezig** (Tb.), **Guan Im** (Th.), **Quan Am** (Vt.) Bodhisattva of Compassion, the most widely worshiped bodhisattva in the Mahayana faith; often associated with Amitabha Buddha.

Bhaisajyaguru (S.), **Yaoshi Fo** (Ch.), **Yaksayorae** (K.), **Yakushi** (J.), **Sangs-rgyas** (Tb.) "Medicine Teacher": a Mahayana Buddha embodying the healing powers of the Dharma.

bhanga (S.) the posture or pose of a figure. See appendix 1 for a review.

bhava-chakra (S.), ***sipay khorlo*** (Tb.) "Wheel of Life" or "Wheel of Existence": a diagram of Buddhist cosmology depicting the reasons for the endless cycle of birth, death, and rebirth.

bhikshu (S.), ***bhikkhu*** (P.) a Buddhist monk.

bhikshuni (S.), ***bhikkhuni*** (P.) a Buddhist nun.

Bodhgaya the place in northeastern India where Prince Siddhartha attained enlightenment and became the Buddha.

bodhi (S. and P.) "enlightenment" or "awakening": the highest spiritual state of a fully awakened mind, pure and free from all craving and attachment—nirvana in this world.

Bodhi Tree the fig tree at Bodhgaya, beneath which Prince Siddhartha attained enlightenment and became the Buddha.

bodhichitta (S.) "enlightened" or "awakened" mind.

bodhisattva (S.), ***bodhisatta*** (P.), ***pusa*** (Ch.), ***posal*** (K.), ***bosatsu*** (J.), ***byang chub sems-dpa*** (Tb.), ***phra photisat*** (Th.) "enlightenment being": in Theravada Buddhism, an individual who has accrued boundless wisdom and merit during many lifetimes with the aim of becoming a Buddha. Mahayana Buddhism focuses more on transcendent bodhisattvas, benevolent celestials who have attained enlightenment but postpone entering final nirvana to assist other beings on the path to liberation.

Buddha (S. and P.), **Fotuo** (Ch.), **Yo-Rae**, or **Bul-ta** (K.), **Butsu**, or **Hotoke** (J.), **Bat** (B.), **Preah Put** (Kh.), **Phra Phutthachao** (Th.) (1) "Enlightened" or "Awakened" One who has attained and taught the highest level of insight and compassion. (2) Prince Siddhartha Gautama of the Sakyas, who renounced his royal life, attained enlightenment, and became known as the Buddha. He is also called the "Historical Buddha" and *Sakyamuni* ("Sage of the Sakya people") and *Gautama Buddha*. (3) Other Buddhas, usually identified by their full names, for example *Amitabha Buddha* and *Vairochana Buddha*.

chaitya (S.), ***cetiya*** (P.) originally a burial mound; evolved into a monument commemorating the Buddha's final passing into *parinirvana*. Synonymous with stupa.

Chan Buddhism (Ch.) see Zen.

deva (S. and P.), ***tianshen*** (Ch.), ***ten*** (J.), ***lha Yi-dam*** (Tb.) celestial being or god. *Deva* is usually the male form and *devi* is the female.

Devadatta (S. and P.) cousin and jealous would-be rival of Sakyamuni Buddha.

Dharma (S.), **Dhamma** (P.) the teachings of the Buddha.

dharmachakra (S.), ***dhammacakka*** (P.) "Wheel of the Law": a symbol of the Buddhist Dharma.

dharmapala (S.) "Dharma protector": a generic term for guardian figures such as *lokapalas*, *dvarapalas*, and other deities who defend the Dharma and destroy obstacles impeding the spiritual progress of devotees.

dhyana (S.), ***jhana*** (P.) meditation; concentration absorptions experienced in meditation.

Dipankara (S. and P.) a Buddha said to have lived and taught the Dharma in a *kalpa* of the distant past.

duhkha (S.), ***dukkha*** (P.) suffering and other unsatisfactory aspects of existence.

dvarapala (S.) "gate protector": fierce warrior guardians of the entrances to temples and other sacred places; usually shown in pairs.

Enlightenment see *bodhi*.

Five Ascetics companions of Sakyamuni Buddha during his years as an ascetic; were ordained by him as the first five *bhikshu*, or monks of the Sangha. Their names in Sanskrit / Pali are: Kaundinya / Kondanna, Vaspa / Vappa, Bhadrika / Bhaddiya, Mahanaman / Mahanama, and Asvajit / Assaji.

Four Noble Truths the basic truths of existence as taught by the Buddha: (1) There is suffering; (2) Craving is the cause of suffering; (3) The elimination of craving leads to the end of suffering; (4) The elimination of craving is achieved by the Noble Eightfold Path.

gati (S. and P.) realms of existence in which rebirth can occur: hell-beings (*naraka*), hungry ghosts (*preta*), animals (*tiryagyoni*), humans (*manusya*), lower gods (*asura*), and gods (*deva*).

Gautama (S.), **Gotama** (P.) family or clan name of Prince Siddhartha / Sakyamuni Buddha.

Guanyin (Ch.) see Avalokitesvara.

Hevajra (S.) a Tantric deity worshiped as the personification of enlightenment, especially in Cambodia and Tibet.

Hinayana (S.), **Xiaocheng** (Ch.), **Shojo Bukkyo** (J.) "Lesser Vehicle": Mahayanist disparaging term for earlier, orthodox schools of Buddhism such as Theravada.

jataka (S. and P.) "birth tale": biographical stories about the Buddha's previous lives.

kalpa (S.), *kappa* (P.) "world cycle": the immensely long period of time measurement that the Vedic scriptures reckon as 4,320 million solar years.

Kapilavastu (S.), **Kapilavatthu** (P.) capital city of the Sakyas; home of Prince Siddhartha until his renunciation.

karma (S.), *kamma* (P.) physical, verbal, and mental actions; in Buddhism, the rule of cause and effect by which a being's actions have bearing on his or her present and future circumstances.

Kaundinya (S.), **Kondanna** (P.) a Brahmin priest who attended the name-giving ceremony of the infant Prince Siddhartha and predicted he would choose the religious life; later he became the first ordained disciple of Sakyamuni Buddha.

Ksitigarbha (S.), **Dizang** (Ch.), **Chijang Posal** (K.), **Jizo** (J.), **Sahi-sning-po** (Tb.) a bodhisattva of the Mahayana faith venerated as a savior able to rescue souls from the torments of hell.

Kusinara town in northern India where the Buddha passed away into *parinirvana*.

lakshana (S.), *lakkhana* (P.) mark or sign; the 32 major auspicious bodily marks of perfection identifying a great man.

lama (Tb.) senior monk.

lokapala (S. and P.), *lishi*, or *tien-wang* (Ch.), *shi-tenno* (J.), *rgyal-chen-bzhi* (Tb.) "world protector": four fierce warrior gods who guard the four sides of Mount Meru and protect the Buddhist teachings. Their individual names in Sanskrit / Chinese / Japanese are:
Guardian of the North: Vaisravana / Duowen / Bisha-monten, or Tamonten.
Guardian of the South: Virudhaka / Zengzhang / Zochoten.
Guardian of the East: Dhritarashtra / Chiguo / Jikokuten.
Guardian of the West: Virupaksha / Guangmu / Komokuten.

Lokesvara (S.) "Lord of the World": a form of Avalokitesvara worshiped in some Tantric sects.

Lumbini birthplace of Prince Siddhartha, who attained enlightenment and became the Buddha.

luohan (Ch.) see "arhat."

Magadha an ancient kingdom in northeastern India where some of the Buddha's travels and teachings occurred.

Magadhi a northeastern Indian dialect believed to be the principal language spoken by the Buddha and his followers; it is closely related to the Pali language.

maha (S. and P.) "great," as in *maharaja*, "great king."

Mahakasyapa (S.), **Mahakassapa** (P.) senior monk at the time of the Buddha's *parinirvana*.

Mahasthamaprapta (S.), **Dashizhi** (Ch.), **Taesaji Posal** (K.), **Seishi**, or **Daiseishi** (J.) a bodhisattva of the Mahayana faith who often appears as an attendant of Amitabha Buddha, usually in a trinity with Avalokitesvara.

Mahayana (S.), **Dacheng** (Ch.), **Daijo** (J.) "Great Vehicle": schools of Buddhism practiced mainly in Nepal, Tibet, China, Mongolia, Korea, Japan, and Vietnam.

Maitreya (S.), **Metteyya** (P.), **Miluo Fo** (Ch.), **Miruk** (K.), **Miroku** (J.), **Champa** (Tb.), **Phra Si An** (Th.) the Buddha of the Future, a bodhisattva currently dwelling in the Tushita Heaven, preparing to appear on Earth as the next Buddha.

mandala (S.), ***mantuoluo*** (Ch.), ***mandara*** (J.), ***dkyil-khor*** (Tb.) a diagram of divinities and symbols used to guide worship and meditation.

Manjusri (S.), **Wenshu** (Ch.), **Moonsoo Posal** (K.), **Monju** (J.), **Jam-pai** (Tb.) Bodhisattva of Wisdom in the Mahayana faith.

mantra (S.) a prayer or chant.

Mantrayana see Vajrayana.

Mara (S. and P.) lord of the realm of desire and, traditionally, a personification of evil.

Maudgalyayana (S.), **Moggallana** (P.) one of Sakyamuni Buddha's two chief disciples (with Sariputra).

Maya, Queen, also **Mahamaya** (S. and P.) mother of Prince Siddhartha and wife of King Suddhodana.

Muchalinda (S. and P.) a *naga raja*, a king of the *nagas*, a serpent king.

mudra (S. and P.) symbolic gestures or poses of the hands and fingers. See appendix 1 for a review.

naga (S. and P.) snake or serpent; a deity that has the appearance of a snake or serpent.

naga raja (S. and P.) a king of the *nagas*, a serpent king.

nirvana (S.), ***nibbana*** (P.), ***nihan*** (Ch.), ***nehan*** (J.), ***mya ngan las hdas pa*** (Tb.), ***niphan*** (Th.) liberation from the cycle of birth, death, and rebirth.

Noble Eightfold Path the spiritual formula taught by the Buddha for the elimination of craving and suffering: (1) right view, (2) right thought, (3) right speech, (4) right action, (5) right livelihood, (6) right effort, (7) right mindfulness, (8) right concentration.

Pali an ancient Indian language related to the Magadhi dialect; was given lettered form in Sri Lanka during the first century B.C. and used to record the first written transcripts of the Buddhist scriptures; the sacred language of the Theravada doctrines.

parinirvana (S.), ***parinibbana*** (P.) complete and final nirvana; attained by an enlightened being after death, never to be reborn again.

Prabhutaratna (S.) in the Mahayana faith, a Buddha of eons ago who traveled through time and space to join Sakyamuni Buddha when he preached the Lotus Sutra at Vulture Peak Mountain in India.

Prajapati, also **Mahaprajapati** (S.), **Pajapati**, also **Mahapajapati** (P.) Sakyamuni Buddha's maternal aunt and stepmother; was ordained as the first Buddhist nun.

Prajnaparamita a goddess worshiped by many Mahayana and Vajrayana sects as the embodiment of the Prajnaparamita Sutra.

Rahula (S. and P.) son and only child of Prince Siddhartha and his wife Yasodhara.

Ratnasambhava (S.), **Baocheng Fo** (Ch.), **Hosho Nyorai** (J.), **Rin-byung** (Tb.) the Jewel Born Buddha, one of the pentad of five transcendent Buddhas of the Mahayana and Vajrayana doctrines; usually represented in the southern sector of the cosmos in the pose of bestowing a blessing (*varada mudra*).

sakti (S.) female counterpart or consort.

Sakya (S. and P.) clan to which Prince Siddhartha was born.

Sakyamuni, also **Shakyamuni** (S. and P.), **Shijia Fo** (Ch.), **Sokamonibul** (K.), **Shaka Nyorai** (J.), **Sha-kya Thub-pa** (Tb.) "Sage of the Sakya people"; an epithet for the historical Buddha.

Samantabhadra (S.), **Puxian** (Ch.), **Pohyun Posal** (K.), **Fugen** (J.), **Kun-tu bzang-po** (Tb.) a bodhisattva of the Mahayana faith often associated with Vairochana Buddha; also worshiped as a form of the Adi-Buddha in some Vajrayana sects.

samsara (S. and P.) "wandering": the endless cycle of birth, death, and rebirth.

Sangha (S. and P.) the community of ordained monks, nuns, and novices established by the Buddha. A wider definition also includes lay followers.

Sanskrit the classical language of ancient India.

Sariputra (S.), **Sariputta** (P.) one of Sakyamuni Buddha's two chief disciples (with Maudgalyayana).

Sarnath location of the Deer Park where Sakyamuni Buddha preached his first sermon.

Shinto (J.) an indigenous religion of Japan; a form of animism that worships Nature divinities called *kami*.

Siddhartha (S.), **Siddhattha** (P.) given name of the Sakya prince who became the Buddha: Siddhartha Gautama (S.) / Siddhattha Gotama (P.).

Six Realms of Existence see *gati*

stupa (S.), ***thupa*** (P.), ***ta lin*** (Ch.), ***tap*** (K.), ***sotoba*** (J.), ***mchodrten*** (Tb.), ***dagon*** (B.) originally a burial mound; evolved into a monument commemorating the Buddha's final passing into *parinirvana*. Synonymous with *chaitya*.

Suddhodana, King (S. and P.) father of Prince Siddhartha and King of the Sakyas.

sunyata (S.), ***sunnata*** (P.) "emptiness" or "absolute void": the ultimate reality that makes possible all existence and the expression of the Buddha-nature; the total encompassment and unity of all creation, often emblemized by a simple black circle having no beginning and no end.

sutra (S.), ***sutta*** (P.) narrative or discourse, usually on religious or philosophical subjects. In Buddhism, a sermon or discourse attributed to the Buddha.

tantra (S.) sacred Hindu and Buddhist illustrated texts which aid prayers, chants, and meditation.

Tantrayana (S.) see Vajrayana.

Tara (S.), **Tuoluo** (Ch.), **Tara Bosatsu** (J.), **Dolma** (Tb.) a female bodhisattva widely worshiped in Mahayana Buddhism.

tathagata (S. and P.), ***nyorai*** (J.) roughly "Thus gone (to nirvana)": an epithet for one who has attained enlightenment; used often by the Buddha when speaking of himself, and by devotees when referring to him.

thanka (Tb.) illustrated scroll created by painting, wood-block printing, weaving, or embroidery.

Theravada (P.) "Teachings of the Elders": schools of Buddhism which closely adhere to the original Canon formulated at the first Buddhist Council; today widely practiced in Sri Lanka and mainland Southeast Asia.

transcendent Buddha any of the celestial Buddhas of the Mahayana and Vajrayana doctrines; an omniscient celestial who transcends all aspects of time, space, and form.

Trayastrimsa (S.), **Tavatimsa** (P.) Heaven of the 33 Gods; paradise abode of the god Indra and other celestials such as Queen Maya.

Tripitaka (S.), **Tipitaka** (P.) "Three Baskets" comprising the canon of Buddhist scriptures: *Vinaya Pitaka* ("Rules of Discipline Basket"), *Sutra Pitaka* ("Sutras Basket"), and *Abhidharma Pitaka* ("Higher Dharma Basket").

Triratna (S.), **Tiratna** (P.) "Triple Gem" or "Three Jewels": the Buddha, the Dharma, and the Sangha.

Tushita (S. and P.) paradise abode of bodhisattvas such as Maitreya who are preparing for a final incarnation in our mortal world.

urna (S.) tuft of hair or small, pearl-like mole on the forehead of a Buddha or bodhisattva.

ushnisha (S.) the protuberance atop the head of a Buddha representing his supreme wisdom.

vahana (S.) mount or vehicle of a Buddha, bodhisattva, or deity.

Vairochana (S.), **Palushena** (Ch.), **Pirochanabul** (K.), **Birushana**, or **Rushana**, or **Dainichi Nyorai** (J.), **Rnam-par-snan-mdsad** (Tb.) the Resplendent Buddha, one of the pentad of five transcendent Buddhas of the Mahayana and Vajrayana doctrines; usually represented at the center of the cosmos in the pose of turning the Wheel of the Law (*dharmachakra mudra*).

vajra (S.), ***jingangchu*** (Ch.), ***kongo-sho*** (J.), ***dorje*** (Tb.) (1) Original meaning from Hinduism is "thunderbolt," the divine weapon of the god Indra. (2) In Buddhism, can also symbolize the indestructible and is then translated as "diamond" or "adamantine."

Vajrasattva see Adi-Buddha.

Vajrayana (S.), **Mizong** (Ch.), **Mikkyo** (J.) "Diamond Vehicle": a branch of Mahayana Buddhism employing meditation, *tantras*, *mantras*, and esoteric rituals to achieve spiritual salvation and supernatural powers. Also known as Tantra-yana, or Mantrayana.

vihara (S. and P.) original meaning was "dwelling place"; in South and Southeast Asia it now usually indicates a monastic dwelling or Buddhist monastery.

Wheel of Life / Wheel of Existence see *bhava-chakra.*

yaksha (S.) supernatural (male) beings in Hindu and Buddhist mythology representing forces of nature. The female form is *yakshi.*

Yasodhara wife of Prince Siddhartha.

Zen (J.), **Chan** (Ch.), **Son** (K.), **Thien** (Vt.) school of Buddhism founded in China during the sixth century A.D. and now universally known by its Japanese name, *Zen*; emphasizes spiritual development through a disciplined practice of meditation, harmony with Nature, and detachment from worldly comforts. The name derives from a Sanskrit word for meditation, *dhyana.*

NOTES

1. For an interesting early guide to transliterating English, Sanskrit, Zend (writings of the Zoroastrian religion), Pehlevi (Pahlavi), Persian, Arabic, Hebrew, and Chinese, see: "Transliteration of Oriental Alphabets Adopted for the Translations of the Sacred Books of the East" in Cowell, Max Muller, and Takakusu, eds. and trans., 1969, pp. 204–207.

2. Bays, trans., 1983, pp. 156–157.

3. Different sources sometimes vary on details of Siddhartha's biography. Instead of *Yasodhara*, some name his wife *Bhaddakacca* or *Subhaddaka*; one refers to her as *Rahulamata*, "mother of Rahula"; still other works call her *Bimba* or *Gopa*: Thomas, 1997, pp. 48–50. For a genealogical chart of their families, see: Thomas, 1997, p. 26.

4. There are many interpretations of *nirvana* and *parinirvana*. See for example: Williams, 1989, pp. 52–54, 67–69 and 181–184; Thomas, 1997, pp. 187–191; and Humphreys, 1990, pp. 127–129.

5. Different sources offer varying accounts of the Buddha's activities during these seven weeks. See for example: Bays, trans., 1983, pp. 559–589; and Herbert, 1993, pp. 40–43.

6. The law of interdependent arising (Sanskrit, *pratityasamutpada*; Pali, *paticcasamuppada*), also called "conditioned arising," is a key Buddhist teaching that explains how one phenomenon gives rise to another, to hold all beings in samsara, the endless cycle of birth, death, and rebirth.

7. E. Lamotte, in Bechert and Gombrich, eds., 1984, pp. 47–53; and Rahula, 1967, pp. 16–50.

8. Rahula, 1959, pp. 17–27.

9. A wider definition of the Sangha also includes lay followers.

10. Thomas, 1997, pp. 98–99.

11. Weldon and Singer, 1999, p. 106.

12. Brewster, 1956, pp. 212–214.

13. This chant or prayer can be interpreted in several ways. "'*Namo Buddhaya, namo Dharmaya, namo Sanghaya*': 'I worship Buddha, I worship the Doctrine, I worship the Community'—such is the formula which represents the quintessence of the Buddhist religion." J. Deniker in Getty, 1962, p. xix. The Pali version is *Buddham saranam gacchami, Dhammam saranam gacchami, Sangham saranam gacchami.*

14. In ancient India 84,000 was an auspicious number sometimes used as a synonym for "an immense amount." Indian folklore tells, for example, that the Buddha spoke of 84,000 mental ailments that afflict humankind, and that there are 84,000 paths to enlightenment.

15. "The term aniconic was popularized by Foucher in his writing of the 1920s. It is a depiction of a narrative in a relief in which the Buddha's presence is indicated by symbols or emblems as an 'absent signifier' and in which the anthropomorphic (human) form of the Buddha is absent." Ghose, with Ho and Yeung, 1998, p. 12.

16. "The Mahayana sutras were clearly the product of monks, albeit monks whose vision of the Dharma embraced the aspirations of the laity, and who used lay figures in the sutras to embody a critique of other monks seen as elitist or perhaps ultra-conservative." Williams, 1989, p. 23.

17. Williams, 1989, pp. 175–179; and Schuhmacher and Woerner, eds., 1991, p. 229.

18. Williams, 1989, p. 170.

19. Williams, 1989, pp. 29–31.

20. An English translation of the two Sukhavativyuha Sutras is given in Cowell, Max Muller, and Takakusu, eds. and trans., 1969, Part II, pp. 1–107.

21. For a description of Avalokitesvara's many forms, see: Getty, 1962, pp. 55–100.

22. For a description of Tara's many forms, see: Getty, 1962, pp. 119–127.

23. Webb, 2000, pp. 34–37.

24. Seckel, 1964, p. 156.

25. A. Foucher wrote persuasively that the earliest images of the Buddha "must have been created under the industrious fingers of some *Graeculus* of more or less mixed descent—and perhaps, also, who knows? at the command of a Greek or an Eurasian convert to Buddhism . . ." in "The Greek Origins of the Image of Buddha" in Foucher, 1917, p. 128. A. K. Coomaraswamy responded

equally persuasively that "The evidence is not sufficiently precise to warrant us in forming a theory as to the priority of either [Gandhara or Mathura] school. I am inclined to presume on general grounds a priority for Mathura . . ." and "In view of the considerations and facts brought forward [in his essay], it becomes impossible to treat the phrase 'Greek origin of the Buddha image' as representing anything more than a rhetorical misuse of language . . ." in Coomaraswamy, 1972b, pp. 37–38. And B. Rowland wrote that: "Actually, the Gandhara sculptures have little to do with Greek art either in its Hellenic or Hellenistic phase, and are much more closely related to Roman art" in Rowland, 1981, p. 125. For more discussions, see: Rowland, 1963, pp. 9–12; Pal, ed., 1984, pp. 146–149; and Krishan, 1988/1989, pp. 255–275.

26. For an illustrated description of the monastic robes, see: Bowie with Diskul and Griswold, 1972, pp. 15–25.

27. Rowland, 1981, p. 154.

28. Errington and Cribb with Claringbull, eds., 1992, p. 199.

29. Coomaraswamy, 1972b, p. 23.

30. Rowland, 1981, p. 251.

31. Published in Pal, ed., 1984, p. 201.

32. Dehejia, 1997b, p. 118.

33. *Si-Yi-Ki: Buddhist Records of the Western World*, translated from the Chinese of Hiuen Tsiang (A.D.: 629) by Samuel Beal. Delhi: Motilal Banarsidass, 1981. First published 1884.

34. E. Zurcher, in Bechert and Gombrich, eds., 1984, p. 196.

35. Dunhuang Institute for Cultural Relics, 1981, p. 1.

36. Bechert and Gombrich, eds., 1984, pp. 208–209; and Brinker, 1987, pp. 12–18. For an introduction to Daoism (Taoism), see: Paul Wildish, *Principles of Taoism*; London: Thorsons, an imprint of Harper Collins Publishers, 2000, especially "Chapter 8: The Buddhist, Confucian and Taoist Synthesis," pp. 108–118. For an illustrated overview of Buddhism, Daoism, Confucianism, Hinduism, Jainism, Shinto, and other religions, see: Chris Richards, ed., *The Illustrated Encyclopedia of World Religions*; New York: Barnes & Noble Books, 1997.

37. Fisher, 1993, p. 91.

38. G. Kuwayama, in Pal, ed., 1984, p. 296.

39. Barnet and Burto, 1982, p. 42.

40. Brinker, 1987, pp. 85–92.

41. H. Brinker, in Ghose, with Ho and Yeung, 1998, p. 123.

42. Pal, ed., 1984, p. 213.

43. Ghose, with Ho and Yeung, 1998, pp. 337–338.

44. Pal, ed., 1984, pp. 310–311.

45. Brinker, 1987, pp. 67–70.

46. Wood, 1985, pp. 8–11. For an English translation of the sutra, see: "The Vagrakkhedika or Diamond Cutter," in Cowell, Max Muller, and Takakusu, eds. and trans., 1969, Part II, pp. 109–144.

47. For an illustrated study of early Chinese artworks of Guanyin, see: D. P. Leidy, "Avalokiteshvara in Sixth-Century China," in Baker, 1998, pp. 88–103.

48. Williams, 1989, pp. 234–235; and Getty, 1962, pp. 79–80.

49. Frederic, 1995, pp. 96–100.

50. Stevens, 2001, pp. 74-89.

51. National Museum of Korea, 1991, p. 40.

52. Kim and Lee, 1974, pp. 69–70.

53. Fisher, 1993, pp. 137–138.

54. Snelling, 1997, pp. 174–175.

55. For a study of Shinto, see: Sokyo Ono, with W. P. Woodward, *Shinto: The Kami Way*. Tokyo: Charles E. Tuttle Company, 1983. First published 1962.

56. R. Heinemann, in Bechert and Gombrich, eds., 1984, p. 214.

57. A comprehensive list of corresponding Buddhist terms in Sanskrit and Japanese is given in Frederic, 1995, pp. 289–300.

58. Mason, 1993, p. 59.

59. Kobayashi, 1975, pp. 14–86.

60. Mason, 1993, pp. 33–34.

61. Mason, 1993, pp. 109–121.

62. Quoted in Suzuki, 1996, p. 61. Also described in Brinker, 1987, pp. 4–5.

63. Along with the word "emptiness," another, perhaps more applicable translation of *sunyata* is "absolute void"—the total encompassment and unity of all creation, perfectly emblemized by the black circle having no starting point and no end.

64. Brinker, 1987, pp. 36–39 and 117–137.

65. Batchelor, 2000, pp. 31–41; Brinker, 1987, pp. 103–111; Barnet and Burto, 1982, pp. 82–86; and Korean Buddhist Chogye Order, 1996, pp. 116–117.

66. A. G. Poster, in Pal, ed., 1984, pp. 96–99.

67. Brinker, 1987, pp. 86–87.

68. Okazaki, 1977, p. 29.

69. Kramrisch, 1964, p. 23.

70. Doboom Tulku and Mullin, n.d., p. 6.

71. An interesting Chinese version of the Wheel is published in Howard, 2001, pp. 6–10.

72. Reynolds, Heller, and Gyatso, 1986, p. 16.

73. Doboom Tulku and Mullin, n.d., p. 13.

74. "Table of Phoneticized and Transliterated Sanskrit and Tibetan Words." Reynolds, Heller, and Gyatso, 1986, pp. 206–208.

75. Reynolds, Heller, and Gyatso, 1986, pp. 129–130; and Doboom Tulku and Mullin, n.d., p. 4.

76. J. Watt, www.himalayanart.org (Padmasambhava; Main Form; Item no. 188)

77. Williams, 1989, p. 191.

78. Gethin, 1998, pp. 266–271.

79. Huntington and Huntington, 1989, p. 40.

80. Weldon and Singer, 1999, pp. 92–93.

81. Hiuen Tsiang, and Beal, trans., 1981, pp. 142–144.

82. Eskenazi, et al, 1995, pp. 26–27.

83. Bays, trans., 1983, pp. 156–157.

84. V. Reynolds, in Pal, ed., 1986, p. 176.

85. Pal, ed., 1984, pp. 24 and 63.

86. Illustrated in Bechert and Gombrich, eds., 1984, p. 237.

87. Bryner, 1956, p. 13.

88. J. Watt, www.himalayanart.org (Tara; General; Item no. 779)

89. Weldon and Singer, 1999, pp. 116–117.

90. Reynolds, Heller, and Gyatso, 1986, pp. 30–32.

91. Pal and Meech-Pekarik, 1988, pp. 168–170.

92. J. Deniker, in Getty, 1914, pp. xxxviii–xxxix.

93. T. T. Bartholomew, in Castile, et al, n.d., p. 158.

94. For illustrations of two similar diadems and descriptive data, see: Lee, 1995, pp. 70–76.

95. von Schroeder, 1999, p.74.

96. For a study of Nat worship and its relationship to Buddhism and Hinduism, see: Vossion, Louis, *Nat Worship among the Burmese* (Reprinted from the Journal of American Folklore, April-June 1891). Cambridge, Mass., USA: The Riverside Press, 1891.

97. Bautze-Picron, 1999, pp. 37–52; and Dehejia, 1997a, pp. 246–254.

98. Strachan, 1989, pp. 65–71; and Getty, 1962, p. 10.

99. Herbert, 1993, pp. 10–11.

100. For an illustrated study of other unusual and rare Burmese images, see: Singer, N., "The Jeyasura and Detkhina-tharkhar Buddhas of Myanmar." *Arts of Asia*, March-April 1996, pp. 132–141.

101. Coedes, 1968, pp. xv–xxi and 14–35.

102. Tranchini, 1991, p. 80.

103. Rowland, 1963, p. 20.

104. Getty, 1962, pp. 156–160 and Plate XLVIII.

105. N. Hock, in Castile, et al., n.d., pp. 158–159; and Getty, 1962, p. 130.

106. Tucker, et al., 1998, pp. 16–17.

107. Lobo, 1994, pp. 113–127.

108. In Hindu mythology the "Churning of the Sea" tells of a great flood that swept away many valued objects. To retrieve them, Vishnu appeared in the form of a tortoise and swam to the bottom of the sea. His back supported Mount Mandara, around which the *devas* and *asuras* wrapped a giant naga serpent. The *devas* and *asuras* then pulled on opposite ends of the *naga*, churning the sea to send all the valuables up to the surface where they could be recovered—including the magical *amrita* elixir, said to give eternal life.

109. For a detailed study, see: Jumsai, Sumet, with R. Buckminster Fuller, *Naga: Cultural Origins in Siam and the West Pacific*. Bangkok: Chalermnit Press & DD Books, 1997.

110. Getty, 1962, p. 172.

111. M.C. Subhadradis Diskul, in *The Excursion to Nakorn Pathom and Phra Pathom Chedi.* Bangkok: The Siam Society, 1976, pp. 5–10; and Frederic, n.d., pp. 37–38. "Nakhon Pathom" and "Nakorn Pathom" are anglicized spellings of the modern Thai pronunciation of the Sanskrit name, *Nagara Pathama*.

112. Phra Phimontharm Rachabandit, 1990, pp. 157–164.

113. Tucker, et al., 1998, pp. 26–29.

114. Fickle, 1989, p.61.

115. Manich Jumsai, M. L., *Popular History of Thailand.* Bangkok: Chalermnit, 1972, pp. 110–112.

116. Incherdchai, et al, 2002, pp. 6–14 and 64.

117. Chirapravati, 1997, pp. 71–72.

118. Rowland, 1981, pp. 364–365.

119. Guillon, 2001, pp. 102–104.

120. Guillon, 2001, p. 29.

BIBLIOGRAPHY

GENERAL STUDIES

Asvaghosha. *The Awakening of Faith in the Mahayana.* Translated by the editors of The Shrine of Wisdom. Surrey: The Shrine of Wisdom, 1964.

Bautze–Picron, C. "Between India and Burma: The 'Andagu' Stelae." *Marg*, June 1999, pp. 37–52.

Bays, G., trans. *The Voice of the Buddha: The Lalitavistara Sutra*. 2 vols. Berkeley, California: Dharma Publishing, 1983.

Bechert, H., and R. Gombrich, eds. *The World of Buddhism.* London: Thames and Hudson Ltd., 1984.

Bercholz, S. and S. C. Kohn, eds. *An Introduction to the Buddha and His Teachings.* New York: Barnes & Noble, 1997.

Bhattacharya, D. C. *Studies in Buddhist Iconography.* Delhi: Manohar Publishers, 1978.

Bidyalankarana, H.H. Prince. "The Buddha's Footprints." *The Journal of the Siam Society*, vol. 28, part 1, 1935, pp. 1–14.

Boisselier, J. *The Wisdom of the Buddha*. C. Lovelace, trans. London: Thames and Hudson Ltd., 1994.

Brewster, E. H. *The Life of Gotama The Buddha, Compiled exclusively from the Pali Canon*. London: Routledge and Kegan Paul Ltd., 1926. Reprinted 1956.

Buddhadatta Mahathera, A. P. *Concise Pali-English Dictionary*. Columbo: U. Chandradasa DeSilva, 1968.

Bunce, F. W. *An Encyclopaedia of Buddhist Deities, Demigods, Godlings, Saints & Demons.* 2 vols. New Delhi: D. K. Printworld (P) Ltd., 1994.

———. *A Dictionary of Buddhist and Hindu Iconography—Illustrated*. New Delhi: D. K. Printworld (P) Ltd., 1997.

Castile, R., et al. *Asian Art Museum: Selected Articles from Orientations*. San Francisco: Asian Art Museum, n.d.

Chandaburinarunath, Kromphra, H.R.H. Prince Kitiyakara. *Pali-Thai-English-Sanskrit Dictionary*. Bangkok: King Maha Makuta's Academy, 1970.

Coedes, G. *The Indianized States of Southeast Asia*. W. F. Vella, ed.; S. B. Cowing, trans. Kuala Lumpur: University of Malaya Press, 1968.

Conze, E. *The Prajnaparamita Literature.* Tokyo: The Reiyukai, 1978.

———, et al, trans. and eds. *Buddhist Texts Through the Ages*. Oxford: Oneworld Publications, 1995.

Coomaraswamy, A. K. *Elements of Buddhist Iconography*. New Delhi: Munshiram Manoharlal Pub., 1972a.

———. *The Origin of the Buddha Image*. New Delhi: Munshiram Manoharlal Pub., reprinted 1972b.

Cowell, E., ed. *The Jataka, or Stories of the Buddha's Former Births*. 6 vols. Delhi: Cosmo Publications, 1978.

Cowell, E., F. Max Muller, and J. Takakusu, trans. and eds. *Buddhist Mahayana Texts.* New York: Dover Publications Inc., 1969. First published 1894.

Cummings, M. *The Lives of the Buddha in the Art and Literature of Asia.* Ann Arbor, Michigan: University of Michigan, 1982.

Dhanit Yupho. *Dharmacakra or the Wheel of the Law.* Bangkok: The Fine Arts Department, 1990.

Edgerton, F. *Buddhist Hybrid Sanskrit Grammar and Dictionary.* 2 vols. Delhi: Motilal Banarsidass, 1970.

Eskenazi, J., et al. *Images of Faith* (exh. cat.). London: John Eskenazi Ltd., 1995.

Fa-Hien. *A Record of Buddhistic Kingdoms, being an account of the Chinese Monk Fa-Hien of his travels in India and Ceylon (A.D. 399–414) in search of the Buddhist Books of Discipline.* J. Legge, trans. New York: Paragon Book Reprint Corp., 1964. First published 1886.

Felten, W., and M. Lerner. *Thai and Cambodian Sculpture from the 6th to the 14th centuries.* Stuttgart: Ernst Klett Verlage GmbH and Co., 1988.

Fisher, R.E. *Buddhist Art and Architecture.* London: Thames and Hudson Ltd., 1993.

Foucher, A. *The Beginnings of Buddhist Art and Other Essays in Indian and Central-Asian Archaeology.* L.A. Thomas and

F. W. Thomas, trans. Paris: Paul Geunthner, 1917.
Frederic, L. *Encyclopaedia of Asian Civilizations*. 10 vols. Villecresnes, France: Louis Frederic, 1977.
———. *Buddhism: Flammarion Iconographic Guides*. N. Marshall, trans.; J. Havell, ed. Paris: Flammarion, 1995.
———. *The Art of Southeast Asia: Temples and Sculpture*. A. Rosin, trans. New York: Harry N. Abrams, Inc., n.d.
Gethin, R. *The Foundations of Buddhism*. Oxford: Oxford University Press, 1998.
Getty, A. *The Gods of Northern Buddhism*. Tokyo: Charles E. Tuttle, Co., 1962. First published 1914.
Girard-Geslan, M., et al. *Art of Southeast Asia*. New York: Harry N. Abrams, Inc., 1998.
Ghose, R., with Puay-peng Ho, and Yeung Chun-tong. *In the Footsteps of the Buddha: An Iconic Journey from India to China* (exh. cat.). Hong Kong: University of Hong Kong, 1998.
Gottlieb, W. P., and M. T. Lees, eds. *The Path to Enlightenment: Masterpieces of Buddhist Sculpture from the National Museum of Asian Arts/Musee Guimet* (exh. cat.). A. Quervel, trans. Fort Worth: Kimbell Art Museum, 1996.
Groslier, B. P. *The Art of Indochina, Including Thailand, Vietnam, Laos and Cambodia*. G. Lawrence, trans. New York: Crown Publishers, Inc., 1962.
Hallade, M., and H. Hinz. *Gandharan Art of North India and the Graeco-Buddhist Tradition in India, Persia, and Central Asia*. D. Imber, trans. New York: Harry N. Abrams, Inc., 1968.
Hiuen Tsiang. *Si-Yi-Ki: Buddhist Records of the Western World, translated from the Chinese of Hiuen Tsiang (A.D.: 629) by Samuel Beal*. Delhi: Motilal Banarsidass, 1981. First published 1884.
Humphreys, C. *Buddhism: An Introduction and Guide*. London: Penguin Books, 1990. First published 1951.
———. *A Popular Dictionary of Buddhism*. London: Arco Publications, 1962.
———. *Zen Buddhism*. London: Mandala Books, 1986. First published 1949.
Kim, I. *The Future Buddha Maitreya: An Iconological Study*. New Delhi: D. K. Printworld (P) Ltd., 1997.
La Plante, J. D. *Asian Art*. Dubuque, Iowa: Wm. C. Brown Publishers, 1968.
Lee, S. E. *A History of Far Eastern Art*. London: Thames and Hudson, 1964.
Lerner, M., and S. Kossak. *The Arts of South and Southeast Asia*. New York: The Metropolitan Museum of Art, 1994.
Ling, T. O. *A Dictionary of Buddhism*. New York: Charles Scribner's Sons, 1972.
Manupuria, T. C., and R. Kumar. *Gods & Goddesses: An illustrated account of Hindu, Buddhist, Tantric, Hybrid and Tibetan deities*. Lashkar, India: Smt. M.D. Gupta, 1998.
Matics, K. I. *Gestures of the Buddha*. Bangkok: Chulalongkorn University Press, 1998.
Menzies, J., ed. *Buddha: Radiant Awakening* (exh. cat.). Sydney: Art Gallery of New South Wales, 2001.
Mitra, D. *Buddhist Monuments*. Calcutta: Shishu Sahitya Samsad Pvt. Ld., 1980.
Morgan, K. W., ed. *The Path of the Buddha: Buddhism Interpreted by Buddhists*. Delhi: Motilal Banarsidass Publishers Private Limited, 1997. First published 1956.
Myers, B. S., and T. Copplestone, eds. *Asian Art: An Illustrated History of Sculpture, Painting & Architecture*. London: The Hamlyn Publishing Group Limited, 1988.
Pal, P. *A Collecting Odyssey: Indian, Himalayan, and Southeast Asian Art from the James and Marilynn Alsdorf Collection* (exh. cat.). New York: The Art Institute of Chicago, 1997.
———, ed. *Light of Asia: Buddha Sakyamuni in Asian Art* (exh. cat.). Los Angeles: Los Angeles County Museum of Art, 1984.
———, ed. *American Collectors of Asian Art*. Bombay: Marg Publications, 1986.
———, ed. *Asian Art: Selections from the Norton Simon Museum*. Pasadena, California: Norton Simon Museum in association with *Orientations*, 1988.
———, and J. Meech-Pekarik. *Buddhist Book Illuminations*. New York: Ravi-Kumar, 1988.
Rawson, P. *The Art of Tantra*. London: Thames and Hudson, 1978.
———. *The Art of Southeast Asia*. London: Thames and Hudson, 1995. First published 1967.
Roscoe, G. *The Triple Gem: An Introduction to Buddhism*. Chiang Mai, Thailand: Silkworm Books, 1994.
Rowland, B. *The Evolution of the Buddha Image*. New York: Asia Society, 1963.
von Schroeder, U. *Indo-Tibetan Bronzes*. Hong Kong: Visual Dharma Publications Ltd., 1981.

Schuhmacher, S., and G. Woerner, eds. *The Shambhala Dictionary of Buddhism and Zen*. M.H. Kohn, trans. Boston: Shambhala Publications, Inc., 1991.

Seckel, D. *The Art of Buddhism*. A.E. Keep, trans. Baden-Baden, Germany: Holle Verlag GmbH, 1964.

de Silva-Vigier, A. *The Life of the Buddha Retold from Ancient Sources*. London: The Phaidon Press, 1955.

Singh, Madanjeet. *Himalayan Art: Wall Painting and Sculptures in Ladakh, Lahaul and Spiti, the Siwalik Ranges, Nepal, Sikkim and Bhutan*. London: Macmillan and Company Ltd., 1968.

Siribhadra, S., and E. Moore. *Palaces of the Gods: Khmer Art & Architecture in Thailand*. Bangkok: River Books, 1992.

Skilling, P. "Symbols on the Body, Feet, and Hands of a Buddha: Part 1–Lists." *The Journal of the Siam Society*, vol. 80, part 2, 1992, pp. 67–79.

Skilton, A. *A Concise History of Buddhism*. New York: Barnes & Noble Books, 2000. First published 1994.

Snellgrove, D.L., ed. *The Image of the Buddha*. Tokyo and New York: Kodansha Int., 1978.

Snelling, J. *The Buddhist Handbook: A Complete Guide to Buddhist Teaching and Practice*. London: Random House, 1997. First published 1987.

Subhadradis Diskul, M. C., ed. *The Art of Srivijaya*. Oxford: Oxford University Press, 1980.

Thomas, E. J. *The Life of Buddha as Legend and History*. Delhi: Motilal Banarsidass Publishers Private Ltd., 1997. First published 1927.

Tucker, J., et al. *The Lion of the Shakyas: Buddha Images from South & Southeast Asia* (exh. cat.). London: Spink, 1998.

Walpola Sri Rahula. *What the Buddha Taught*. Bedford, England: The Gordon Fraser Gallery Ltd., revised edition 1967. First published 1959.

Wassman, B., and J. Cummings. *Buddhist Stupas in Asia: The Shape of Perfection*. Footscray, Australia: Lonely Planet Publications, 2001.

Williams, P. *Mahayana Buddhism: The Doctrinal Foundations*. London and New York: Routledge, 1989.

Zimmer, H. *The Art of Indian Asia: Its Mythology and Transformations*. 2 vols. J. Campbell, ed. New York: Pantheon Books Inc., 1960.

Zwalf, W., ed. *Buddhism: Art and Faith*. London: British Museum Publications Limited, 1985.

BURMA (MYANMAR)

Guy, J. "The Art of the Pyu and Mon." *Marg*, June 1999, pp. 12–28.

Hasson, H. *Ancient Buddhist Art from Burma* (exh. cat.). Singapore: Taisei Gallery, 1993.

Herbert, P. M. *The Life of the Buddha*. London: The British Library, 1993.

Karow, O. *Burmese Buddhist Sculpture: The Johan Moger Collection*. Bangkok: White Lotus Co. Ltd., 1991.

Lowry, J. *Burmese Art* (Victoria and Albert Museum). London: Her Majesty's Stationary Office, 1974.

Singer, N. F. "The Jeyasura and Detkhinatharkhar Buddhas of Myanmar." *Arts of Asia*, March–April 1996, pp. 132–141.

Stadtner, D. M. "A Fifteenth-century Royal Monument in Burma and the Seven Stations in Buddhist Art." *The Art Bulletin*, vol. 73, March 1991, pp. 39–52.

———. "Pagan Bronzes: Fresh Observations." *Marg*, June 1999, pp. 53–64.

———, ed. *The Art of Burma: New Studies*. Mumbai: Marg Publications, 1999.

Strachan, P. *Pagan: Art and Architecture of Old Burma*. Whiting Bay, Arran, U.K.: Kiscadale Publications, 1989.

CAMBODIA

Giteau, M. *Khmer Sculpture and the Angkor Civilization*. D. Imber, trans. London: Thames and Hudson, 1965.

Jessup, H. I., and T. Zephir, eds. *Sculpture of Angkor and Ancient Cambodia: Millenium of Glory* (exh. cat.). London: Thames and Hudson, 1997.

Krairiksh, P. "Khmer Ruins in Thailand." *Orientations*, Dec. 1981, pp. 22–33.

Lee, S. E. *Ancient Cambodian Sculpture* (exh. cat.). New York: The Asia Society, 1969.

Lobo, W. "Reflections on the Tantric Buddhist Deity Hevajra in Cambodia." *Southeast Asian Archaeology* 1994, Conference Proceedings, Vol. II. P.Y. Manguin, ed., pp. 113–127.

Montgomery, G. *Khmer Sculpture* (exh. cat.). New York: The Asia Society, 1961.

Roveda, V. *Khmer Mythology*. Bangkok: River Books, 1997.

CHINA AND CENTRAL ASIA

Andrew, F. H. *Wall Paintings from Ancient Shrines in Central Asia, Recovered by Sir Aurel Stein, K.C.L.E., Described by Fred H. Andrew, O.B.E.* SDI Publications, 1998.

Baker, J., ed. *The Flowering of a Foreign Faith: New Studies in Chinese Buddhist Art*. Mumbai: Marg Publications, 1998.

Cambon, P. "Fouilles anciennes en Afghanistan (1924–1925) Paitava, Karratcha [Early Excavations in Afghanistan (1924–1925) Paitava, Karratcha]." *Arts Asiatiques*, tome 51–1996, pp. 13–26.

Chen, K. S. *Buddhism in China*. Princeton: Princeton University Press, 1964.

Davidson, J. L. *The Lotus Sutra in Chinese Art: A Study in Buddhist Art to the Year 1000*. New Haven: Yale University Press, 1955.

Dunhuang Institute for Cultural Relics. *Art Treasures of Dunhuang*. Diana Yu, et al., trans. Hong Kong: Joint Publishing Co., 1981.

Henss, M. "The Woven Image: Tibeto-Chinese Textile Thangkas of the Yuan and Early Ming Dynasties." *Orientations*, Nov. 1997, pp. 26–39.

Howard, A. F. *Summit of Treasures: Buddhist Cave Art of Dazu, China*. Bangkok: Orchid Press, 2001.

Ji Chongjian. "Images of Guanyin." F. J. McDonald, trans. *Orientations*, May 1997, pp. 42–49.

Juliano, A. L. "Hidden Treasures: Little-known Buddhist Cave Temples in Northwest China, 5th to 7th Centuries." *Orientations*, Oct. 2001, pp. 62–71.

Murray, J-K. "Buddhism and Early Narrative Illustration in China." *Archives of Asian Art*, vol. 48, 1995, pp. 17–31.

Reynolds, V. "Buddhist Silk Textiles: Evidence for Patronage and Ritual Practice in China and Tibet." *Orientations*, April 1997, pp. 52–63.

Rice, T. T. *Ancient Arts of Central Asia*. London: Thames and Hudson, 1965.

Sichuan Museum, ed. *Zhang Daqian's Reproductions of Dunhuang Frescoes*. Hong Kong: Arts Publishing House of Sichuan, Peace Book Co. Ltd., 1984.

Soper, A. C. *Literary Evidence for Early Buddhist Art in China*. Ascona, Switzerland: Artibus Asiae Publishers, 1959.

Stevens, K. "Luohans on Chinese Altars: Enlightened Disciples of the Buddha." *Arts of Asia*, Jan.–Feb. 2001, pp. 74–89.

Swart, P. "Imperial Cave-chapels of the Northern Wei Dynasty: The Buddhist Caves at Gongxian—an interpretive description." *Orientations*, Oct. 1989, pp. 56–66.

Tregear, M. *Chinese Art*. London: Thames and Hudson Ltd., 1997.

Tsiang, K. R. "Chinese Images of the Dharma: Regional Formulations and National Revisualizations." *Orientations*, Feb. 1998, pp. 71–82.

Weldon, D. "The Perfect Image: The Speelman Collection of Yongle and Xuande Buddhist Icons." *Arts of Asia*, May–June 1996, pp. 64–73.

Whitfield, R., and A. Farrer. *Caves of the Thousand Buddhas: Chinese art from the Silk Route*. London: British Museum Publications Ltd., 1990.

Wood, F. *Chinese Illustration*. London: British Library, 1985.

INDIAN SUBCONTINENT

Craven, R. C. *Indian Art*. London: Thames and Hudson Ltd., 1997. First published as *A Concise History of Indian Art*, 1976.

Dehejia, V. *Early Buddhist Rock Temples*. London: Thames and Hudson Ltd., 1972.

———. *Discourse in Early Buddhist Art: Visual Narratives of India*. Delhi: Munshiram Manoharlal Pub., 1997a.

———. *Indian Art*. London: Phaidon Press Limited, 1997b.

———, and P. Pal, eds. *Unseen Presence: The Buddha and Sanchi*. Mumbai: Marg Publications, 1996.

Errington, E., and J. Cribb, with M. Claringbull, eds. *The Crossroads of Asia: Transformation in Image and Symbol in the Art of Ancient Afghanistan and Pakistan*. Cambridge: The Ancient India and Iran Trust, 1992.

Foucher, A. *L'Art Gréco-Bouddhique du Gandhara*. Paris: Imprimerie Nationale, 1905.

Frederic, L. *The Art of India: Temples and Sculpture*. E. M. Hooykaas and A. H. Christie, trans. New York: Harry N. Abrams, Inc., n.d.

Huntington, S. L. "Early Buddhist Art and the Theory of Aniconism." Art Journal, vol. 49, Winter 1990, pp. 401–408.

———, with J. C. Huntington. *The Art of Ancient India*. New York: Weather Hill, 1985.

———, and J. C. Huntington. "Leaves from the Bodhi Tree: The Art of Pala India (8th–12th Centuries) and Its International Legacy." *Orientations*, Oct. 1989, pp. 26–46.

Karetzky, P. "Hellenistic Influences on Scenes of the Life of the Buddha in Gandhara." *Oriental Art*, Autumn 1989, pp. 163–168.

Khandalavala, K., ed. *The Golden Age: Gupta Art—Empire, Province and Influence*. Bombay: Marg Publications, 1991.

Krishan, Y. "The Emergence of the Buddha Image: Gandhara versus Mathura." *Oriental Art*, Winter 1988/1989, pp. 255–275.

Lerner, M. *The Flame and the Lotus: Indian and Southeast Asian Art from the Kronos Collections*. New York: Metropolitan Museum of Art, 1984.

Pal, P. *Bronzes of Kashmir*. New York: Hacker Art Books, 1975.

Rhi Ju-Hyung. "From Bodhisattva to Buddha: The Beginning of Iconic Representation in Buddhist Art." *Artibus Asiae*, vol. 54, no. 3/4, 1994, pp. 207–225.

Rowland, B. *The Art and Architecture of India: Buddhist-Hindu-Jain*. Suffolk, U.K.: Penguin Books, 1981. First published 1953.

———. *Gandhara Sculpture from Pakistan Museums* (exh. cat.). New York: Asia Society, 1960.

———. *The Ajanta Caves: Early Buddhist Paintings from India*. New York: The New American Library of World Literature Inc., 1963.

Sivaramamurti, C. *The Art of India*. New York: Harry N. Abrams, Inc., 1977.

Stone, E. R. *The Buddhist Art of Nagarjunakonda*. Delhi: Motilal Banarsidass Pub., 1994.

Weiner, S. L. *Ajanta: Its Place in Buddhist Art*. Los Angeles: University of California Press, 1977.

Zwalf, W. *A Catalogue of the Gandhara Sculpture in the British Museum*. 2 vols. London: British Museum, 1996.

INDONESIA

Bernet Kempers, A. J. *Ancient Indonesian Art*. Cambridge, Massachusetts: Harvard University Press, 1959.

———. *Ageless Borobudur*. Servire/Wassenaar, 1976.

Fontein, J., R. Soekmono, and E. Sedyawati. *The Sculpture of Indonesia* (exh. cat.). New York: Harry N. Abrams, Inc., 1990.

Fontein, J., R. Soekmono, and S. Suleiman. *Ancient Indonesian Art of the Central and Eastern Javanese Periods* (exh. cat.). New York: The Asia Society, 1971.

Holt, C. *Art in Indonesia: Continuities and Change*. Ithaca and London: Cornell University Press, 1967.

Miksic, J. *Borobudur: Golden Tales of the Buddhas*. Jakarta: Periplus Editions (HK) Ltd., 1990.

Tranchini, M. "Borobudur: Art and Religion." *Arts of Asia*, Jan.–Feb. 1991, pp. 80–94.

JAPAN

Addiss, S. *The Art of Zen: Paintings and Calligraphy by Japanese Monks 1600–1925*. New York: Harry N. Abrams, Inc. 1989.

Barnet, S., and W. Burto. *Zen Ink Paintings*. Tokyo: Kodansha International Ltd., 1982.

Batchelor, M. "The Ten Oxherding Pictures." *Tricycle: The Buddhist Review*, vol. IX, no. 3, Spring 2000, pp. 31–41.

Brinker, H. *Zen in the Art of Painting*. G. Campbell, trans. London: Arkana, 1987.

Cunningham, M. R. "Spiritual Vows of Compassion: Eleven-headed Kannon Images from the Nara National Museum." *Orientations*, Sept. 1998, pp. 76–83.

Ford, B. B. *The Arts of Japan*. New York: Metropolitan Museum of Art, 1987.

Hisamatsu, S. *Zen and the Fine Arts*. G. Tokiwa, trans. Tokyo: Kodansha International Ltd., 1974.

Irie, T., and S. Aoyama. *Buddhist Images*. T. I. Elliott, trans. Osaka: Hoikusha Publishing Co. Ltd., 1993.

Ishizawa, M., et al, *Pageant of Japanese Art: Sculpture*. Tokyo: Toto Shuppan Company, Ltd., 1958.

Kobayashi, T. *Nara Buddhist Art: Todai-ji*. R.L. Gage, trans. New York: Weatherhill / Heibonsha, 1975.

Mason, P. *History of Japanese Art*. New York: Harry N. Abrams, Inc., 1993.

Matsunaga, D., and A. Matsunaga. *Foundations of Japanese Buddhism*. Vols. I & II. Los Angeles & Tokyo: Buddhist Books International, 1974.

Mizono, S. *Asuka Buddhist Art: Horyuji*. R.L. Gage, trans. New York: Weatherhill / Heibonsha, 1974.

Mori, H. *Sculpture of the Kamakura Period*. K. Eickmann, trans. New York: Weatherhill / Heibonsha, 1974.

Morse, A. N., and S. C. Morse. "Object as Insight: Japanese Buddhist Art and Ritual." *Orientations*, Feb. 1996, pp. 36–45.

Mosaku Ishida, et al. *Japanese Buddhist Prints*. Tokyo: Kodansha International Ltd., 1967. First published 1963.

Okazaki, J. *Pure Land Buddhist Painting*. E. ten Grotenhuis, trans. Tokyo: Kodansha International, 1977.

Saunders, E. D. *Mudra: A Study of Symbolic Gestures in Japanese Buddhist Sculpture*. Princeton: Princeton University Press, 1985. First published 1960.

Sawa, T. *Art in Japanese Esoteric Buddhism*. R.L. Gage, trans. New York: Weatherhill / Heibonsha, 1972.

Seo, A. Y. "The Art of Twentieth-century Zen." *Oriental Art*, vol. 44, no. 3, Autumn 1998, pp. 50–56.

Suzuki, D. T. *Zen Buddhism: Selected Writings of D. T. Suzuki*. W. Barrett, ed. New York: Doubleday, 1996. First published 1956.

Watanabe, M. "A Preliminary Study of 'Life of the Buddha' in Mediaeval Japan: The Metropolitan Museum Paintings." *Orientations*, Sept. 1996, pp. 46–56.

KOREA

Chun Shin-yong, ed. *Buddhist Culture in Korea*. Seoul: International Cultural Foundation, 1974.

Chung Young-ho. "Pagoda: Symbols of the Buddha Throughout Korean History." *Koreana*, vol. 6, no. 4. Winter 1992, pp. 32–39.

Joh Myung-gee, et al. *Buddhism and Its Culture in Korea*. Seoul: Dongguk University Press, 1964.

Kim, Chewon, and Lena Kim Lee. *Arts of Korea*. Tokyo: Kodansha International Ltd., 1974.

Korean Buddhist Chogye Order. *Korean Buddhism*. Seoul: Korean Buddhist Chogye Order, 1996.

Lefebvre d'Argence, R-Y, and D. Turner, et al. *5000 Years of Korean Art* (exh. cat.). San Francisco: Asian Art Museum of San Francisco, 1979.

McCune, E. *The Arts of Korea: An Illustrated History*. Tokyo: Charles E. Tuttle Company, 1962.

National Museum of Korea. Seoul: National Museum of Korea, 1991.

LAOS

Boun Souk, T. *L'image du Buddha dans l'art Lao*. Vientiane: L'imprimerie National, 1971.

———. *Luang Phrabang: 600 ans d'art Bouddhique Lao*. Paris: Quartz International, 1974.

Somkiart Lopetcharat. *Lao Buddha: The Image and Its History*. Bangkok: S.O.M. Co. Ltd., 2000.

MONGOLIA

Berger, P., and T. Tse Bartholomew, et.al. *Mongolia: The Legacy of Chinggis Khan* (exh. cat.). San Francisco: Asian Art Museum of San Francisco, 1995.

Youso, K. "The Art of Mongolia's Buddhist Renaissance." *Arts of Asia*, Nov.–Dec. 1995, pp. 78–89.

NEPAL

Huntington, J. C. "The Iconography of Svayambhu Mahachaitya: The Main Mandalas." *Orientations*, Dec. 2002, pp. 16–23.

Kramrisch, S. *The Art of Nepal* (exh. cat.). New York: The Asia Society, Inc., 1964.

Lavizzari, A. "The Art of Thanka Painting." *Arts of Asia*, Sept.–Oct. 1984, pp. 96–103.

Min Bahadur Shakya. *Sacred Art of Nepal: Nepalese Pauba Paintings: Past and Present.* Kathmandu: Handicraft Association of Nepal, 2000.

Pal, P. *Buddhist Art in Licchavi Nepal*. Bombay: Marg Publications, 1974.

———. *The Arts of Nepal*, Part I, Sculpture. Leiden, Netherlands: E.J. Brill, 1974.

———. *Nepal: Where the Gods are Young* (exh. cat.). New York: Asia House Gallery, 1975.

———. *The Arts of Nepal, Part II, Painting*. Leiden, Netherlands: E. J. Brill, 1978.

Waldschmidt, E., and R. L. Waldschmidt. *Nepal: Art Treasures from the Himalayas.* D. Wilson, trans. London: Elek Books, 1969.

SRI LANKA

Devendra, D. T. *The Buddha Image and Ceylon*. Kandy, Sri Lanka: K.V.G. DeSilva and Sons, 1957.

Gunasinghe, S. "Ceylon and the Buddha Image in the Round." *Artibus Asiae*, vol. 19, 3/4, 1956, pp. 251–258.

———. *An Album of Buddhist Paintings from Sri Lanka (Ceylon) (Kandy Period)*. Columbo: National Museums of Sri Lanka, 1978.

Listopad, J. "The Development of the Sri Lankan Buddha Image." *Arts of Asia*, Nov.–Dec. 2003, pp. 95–106.

Mahathera, N. *The Buddha and His Teachings: Illustrated with Paintings from Buddhist Temples in Sri Lanka*. Columbo: Lever Brothers Cultural Conservation Trust, 1987. First published 1980.

Paranavitana, S. *Art of the Ancient Sinhalese*. Columbo: Lake House Investments, Ltd., 1971.

Perera, H. R. *Buddhism in Sri Lanka: A Short History*. Kandy, Sri Lanka: Buddhist Publication Society, 1988.

von Schroeder, U. "Mahayana Buddhism in Sri Lanka." *Marg*, vol. 50, no. 4, June 1999, pp. 65–76.

THAILAND

Bowie, T., ed., with M.C. Subhadradis Diskul, and A. B. Griswold. *The Sculpture of Thailand* (exh. cat.). New York: The Asia Society, 1972.

Bunker, E. "The Prakhon Chai Story: Facts and Fiction" [A study of Khmer Buddhist bronze statues found in northeastern Thailand]. *Arts of Asia*, March–April 2002, pp. 106–125.

Chand, M.C., and K. Yimsiri. *Thai Monumental Bronzes*. Bangkok: Published by the authors, 1957.

Fickle, D. H. *The Life of the Buddha: Murals in the Buddhaisawan Chapel, National Museum, Bangkok, Thailand*. Bangkok: The Fine Arts Department, 1972.

———. *Images of the Buddha in Thailand*. Singapore: Oxford University Press, 1989.

Ginsburg, H. *Thai Manuscript Painting*. London: The British Library, 1989.

Hoskin, J. *Buddha Images in the Grand Palace*. Bangkok: The Office of His Majesty's Principal Private Secretary, 1994.

Jarunee Incherdchai, et al. *Phra Bot* [*Buddhist Banner Paintings*] (exh. cat.). Bangkok: The Fine Arts Department, 2002.

Kositpipat, C., P. Vijinthanasarn, and S. Budrat. *The Mural Paintings of Wat Buddhapadipa*. Bangkok: Amarin Printing Group Ltd., 1987.

Krairiksh, P. "A New Chronology of Buddhist Art in Thailand." *Muang Boran*, April–June 1999, pp. 10–43.

Le May, R. *A Concise History of Buddhist Art in Siam*. Tokyo: Charles E. Tuttle Co., 1962. First published 1938.

Luang Buribal Buribhand, and A.B. Griswold. *Thai Images of the Buddha*. Bangkok: The Fine Arts Department, 1990.

Matics, K. I. *Introduction to the Thai Mural*. Bangkok: White Lotus, 1992.

Painted Sculpture on Life of the Buddha. Bangkok: Matichon Publishing House, 1983.

Pattaratorn Chirapravati, M. L. *Votive Tablets in Thailand: Origins, Styles, and Uses*. Oxford: Oxford University Press, 1997.

Phimontharm Rachabundit, Phra. *Tamnan Phraphuttharup Pangtangtang* [*Legends of Various Types of Buddha Images*]. Bangkok: Haw Tri Foundation, 1990.

Prateep Yanyong, et al. *Thai Buddha Images* (exh. cat.). Bangkok: River City Art & Antiques Center, 2001.

Saneh Dhanaratnasaritsadi, *Phap Phuttha Prawat* [*The Buddha's History in Pictures*]. Bangkok: Amnuaysan Printing, 1989.

Silpa Bhirasri, et al. *The Origin and Evolution of Thai Murals*. Bangkok: The Fine Arts Department, 1959.

Smithies, M., et al. *The Mons: Collected articles from The Journal of the Siam Society*. Bangkok: The Siam Society, 1986.

Subhadradis Diskul, M.C. *Art in Thailand*: A Brief History. Bangkok: Amarin Press, 1981.

TIBET

Allinger, E. "The Green Tara as Saviouress from the Eight Dangers in the Sumtsek at Alchi." *Orientations*, Jan. 1999, pp. 40–44.

Beer, R. *The Encyclopedia of Tibetan Symbols and Motifs*. Boston: Shambhala, 1999.

Bryner, E. *Thirteen Tibetan Tankas*. Indian Hills, Colorado, U.S.A.: The Falcon's Wing Press, 1956.

Chutiwongs, N. "Visual Expressions of Tantric Buddhism." *The Journal of the Siam Society*, vol. 70, part 1, 1982, pp. 76–85.

Dagyab Rinpoche. *Buddhist Symbols in Tibetan Culture*. M. Walshe, trans. Boston: Wisdom Publications, 1995.

Deng Ruiling, et al. *The Potala Palace of Tibet*. Liu Biqi, et al., trans. Hong Kong: Joint Publishing Co., 1982.

Doboom Tulku, and G. H. Mullin. *Compassion and Reincarnation in Tibetan Art* (exh. cat.). New Delhi: Tibet House, n.d.

Fisher, R. E. *Art of Tibet*. London: Thames and Hudson Ltd., 1997.

Goepper, R. "Akshobhya and His Paradise: Murals in the Dukhang of Alchi." *Orientations*, Jan. 1999, pp. 16–21.

Gordon, A. K. *The Iconography of Tibetan Lamaism* (Revised Edition). Rutland, Vermont & Tokyo: Charles E. Tuttle Company, 1958. First published 1939.

Klimburg-Salter, D. E. "A Thangka Painting Tradition from the Spiti Valley." *Orientations*, Nov. 1997, pp. 40–47.

Lee, R. "Chinese Textiles related to Tibetan Buddhism in the Hong Kong Museum of Art." *Arts of Asia*, July–Aug. 1995, pp. 70–76.

Liu Lizhong. *Buddhist Art of the Tibetan Plateau*. R. Kiggell, ed. and trans. San Francisco: China Books & Periodicals, Inc., 1988.

Neumann, H. F. "Wall Paintings of Western Tibet: A Stylistic Analysis." *Orientations*, Oct. 1999, pp. 74–83.

Reynolds, V., A. Heller, and J. Gyatso. *Catalogue of the Newark Museum Tibetan Collection*, vol. III: Sculpture and Painting. Newark: The Newark Museum, 1986.

Rhie, M. M., and R. A. F. Thurman. *The Sacred Art of Tibet* (exh. cat.). London: Thames and Hudson Ltd., 1991.

Snellgrove, D. L. *Buddhist Himalaya: Travels and Studies in Quest of the Origins and Nature of Tibetan Religion*. Oxford: Bruno Cassirer (Publishers) Ltd., 1957.

Tucci, G. *The Theory and Practice of the Mandala*. A. H. Broderick, trans. London: Rider & Co, 1961.

Webb, B. "Chenrezig: The Embodiment of the Sangha." *Buddhism Today: The Diamond Way*, vol. 7, 2000, pp. 34–37.

Weiner, D. *Tibetan and Himalayan Woodblock Prints*. New York: Dover Publications, Inc., 1974.

Weldon, W., and J. C. Singer. *The Sculptural Heritage of Tibet: Buddhist Art in the Nyingjei Lam Collection*. London: Laurence King, 1999.

VIETNAM

Bezacier, L. *L'art Vietnamien*. Paris: Editions de L'union Francaise, 1954.

Guillon, E. *Cham Art: Treasures From the Da Nang Museum, Vietnam*. T. White, trans. Bangkok: River Books Ltd., 2001.

Hejzlar, J. *The Art of Vietnam*. T. Gottheiner, trans. London: Hamlyn Publishing Group Ltd., 1973.

Long, K. N. "A Vietnamese Pagoda: Buddhist Expression in Chua Thay." *Arts of Asia*, May–June 1994, pp. 68–79.

Minh Chi, Ha Van Tan, Nguyen Tai Thu. *Buddhism in Vietnam: From its Origins to the 19th Century*. Hanoi: The GIOI Publishers, 1993.

Nguyen Duc Dieu, senior editor. *Buddhist Temples in Vietnam*. Hanoi: Social Sciences Publishing House, 1993.

Pham Cam Thuong. *Ancient Sculpture of Vietnam*. Hanoi: Fine Arts Publishing House, 1977.

Unger, H. A., and W. Unger. *Pagodas, Gods and Spirits of Vietnam*. L. Dale, trans. London: Thames and Hudson, 1997.

LIST OF ILLUSTRATIONS AND PHOTO CREDITS

The location of an object in a museum or private collection is shown in square brackets.

Where no photographer's name is given, the location is also the source of the photograph.

Front cover: see fig. 12; background is a Tibetan painting of Sakyamuni Buddha's life. Photo: Trakarn Tilaganont. Graphic: Umaporn Soetphannuek.

Fig. 1. *Phra Bot (Buddhist temple banner). Top section shows Sakyamuni Buddha (center figure) with his two chief disciples, the monks Sariputra and Maudgalyayana. Lower section illustrates the shipwreck scene from the Mahajanaka Jataka.* Painting on cloth, 38⅝ x 106¼ in. (98 x 270 cm). Wat Mahathat Temple, Petchburi Province, Thailand. Photo courtesy of the National Museum of Bangkok's National Art Gallery.

Fig. 2. *The Enlightenment of Sakyamuni Buddha.* Gilt bronze, Buddhist lineage, Tibet, 1600–1699. [Collection of Rubin Cultural Trust, item #700130] Photo courtesy of the Rubin Cultural Trust: www.himalayanart.org.

Fig. 3. *Queen Maya's Dream.* Ink and colors on silk, 5⅞ x 6½ in. (15 x 16.5 cm). Dunhuang, China, Tang dynasty, 9th century. [The British Museum, London] Photo © Copyright The British Museum.

Fig. 4. *Queen Maya Giving Birth to Prince Siddhartha, the Future Buddha.* Gilt copper and brass, inlaid with semiprecious stones, H: 21½ in. (54.5 cm). Nepal, early 19th century. [Musee Guimet, Paris]

Fig. 5. *Prince Siddhartha Sees the Four Sights.* Acrylics on wood, 15⅛ x 10⅛ in. (38.4 x 25.6 cm). Thailand, 20th century. [Private collection]

Fig. 6. *The Great Departure (Prince Siddhartha Leaving His Palace).* Illustrated manuscript, 18½ x 29⅛ in. (47 x 74 cm). Burma, 19th century. [The British Library, London]

Fig. 7. *The Great Renunciation (Prince Siddhartha Cutting Off His Hair).* Stone wall carving, Borobudur, Indonesia, circa 9th century. Photo: K. Kawasaki.

Fig. 8. *Siddhartha Fasting.* Black stone, H: 33⅛ in. (84 cm). Gandhara, Pakistan, 3rd–4th centuries. [Lahore Museum, Lahore]

Fig. 9. *Monk's Fan. Painted with Sujata offering rice-milk to Siddhartha. Reverse side tells the event that the fan commemorates.* H (overall): 36¼ in. (92.1 cm). Thailand, 20th century. [Private collection] Photo: Trakarn Tilaganont.

Fig. 10. *Siddhartha Meditating Beneath the Bodhi Tree.* Wall painting (detail), Cave #2, Maharajavihara, Dambulla, Sri Lanka, circa 1760. Photo: J. Listopad.

Fig. 11. *The Buddha Subduing Mara.* Oil on canvas (Detail), 65 x 27 in. (165 x 68.6 cm). Thailand, 19th century. [Private collection]

Fig. 12. *The Enlightenment of Sakyamuni Buddha.* Gilt bronze, H: 16¼ in. (41.3 cm). Style of Lanna, Northern Thailand, 11th–18th centuries. [Private collection] Photo: Trakarn Tilaganont.

Fig. 13. *The Enlightenment of Sakyamuni Buddha.* Bronze, H: 57 in. (144.8 cm). Rangoon, Burma (Myanmar), circa 18th century. [Wat Benchamabopit, Bangkok] Photo: C. Chicarelli.

Fig. 14. *The Enlightenment of Sakyamuni Buddha.* Silver, H: 15 in. (38.1 cm). Tibet, 19th century. [Tomlinson Collection] Photo: C. Chicarelli.

Fig. 15. *Crowned Buddha protected by Muchalinda, the Serpent King.* Sandstone, H: 35¼ in. (89.5 cm). Angkor, Cambodia, approx. 1150–1175. [Asian Art Museum of San Francisco, museum purchase, B69S12. Used by permission.]

Fig. 16. *The Naga Raja in Human Form Offering Gifts to the Buddha.* Gilt copper, H: 23⅝ in. (60 cm). Southern Tibet, early 15th century. [Private collection] Photo courtesy of John Eskenazi, London.

Fig. 17. *The Buddha Preaching His First Sermon.* Sandstone, H: 63 in. (1.60 m). Sarnath, India, Gupta period, 5th century. [Archaeological Museum, Sarnath] Photo: K. Kawasaki.

Fig. 18. *The Buddha Preaching His First Sermon*. Carved, painted and gilded teakwood, 98 x 46 in. (2.48 x 1.17 m). Wat Palelai Temple, Singapore. Photo: C. Chicarelli.

Fig. 19. *The Buddha Performing Miracles at Kapilavastu*. Mural painting (detail), Wat Rajasittharam, Thonburi, Thailand, 18th century. Photo: K. Kawasaki.

Fig. 20. *The Buddha with His Alms Bowl*. Gilt wood, H: 11⅜ in. (28.9 cm). Cambodia, 18th century. [Frankel Collection]

Fig. 21. *The Buddha visits his Family in Kapilavastu*. Oil on canvas, 23½ x 34½ in. (59.7 x 87.6 cm). Burma (Myanmar), 19th century. [Wat Bovoranives Vihara Museum, Bangkok] Photo: C. Chicarelli.

Fig. 22. *The Buddha visits his Former Wife and their Son*. Phyllite, 10½ x 16½ in. (26.7 x 41.9 cm). Gandhara, Pakistan, approx. A.D. 100–300. [Asian Art Museum of San Francisco, The Avery Brundage Collection, B60S283. Used by permission.]

Fig. 23. *Standing Buddha, "Stopping his Relatives from Quarreling over Water."* Gilt bronze, H: 28¾ in. (73 cm). Ayutthaya, Thailand, 17th century. [National Museum of Bangkok] Photo: C. Chicarelli.

Fig. 24. *Standing Buddha, "Calming the Waters."* Gilt wood with glass inlay, H: 74¾ in. (1.90 m). Laos, 1700–1900. [Asian Art Museum of San Francisco, The Avery Brundage Collection, B60S18+. Used by permission.]

Fig. 25. *Anathapindada Purchasing the Jetavana Park*. Mural painting, Kamsansa Temple, Kyongju, Korea. Photo: K. Kawasaki.

Fig. 26. *The Miracle of Sravasti*. Mural painting (detail), Wat Suthat Thepwararam, Bangkok, Thailand, 19th century. Photo: Prajak Maolee.

Fig. 27. *The Buddha Descending from Heaven*. Mural painting (detail), Wat Thong Thammachat, Thonburi, Thailand, 19th century. Photo: L. Tettoni.

Fig. 28. *Udayana Style Buddha Image*. Gilt bronze, H: 7½ in. (19 cm). China, Yongle period (1403–1424). [Speelman Collection, London] Photo: P. J. Gates.

Fig. 29. *Miracle of the Monkeys*. Segment of a Prajnaparamita manuscript, palm leaf, H: 2 in. (5.0 cm). Bihar, India, circa 1075–80. [Cambridge University Library] Photo by permission of the Syndics of Cambridge University Library.

Fig. 30. *Angulimala and the Buddha*. Mural painting, Chogyesa Temple, Seoul, Korea, 20th century. Photo: C. Chicarelli.

Fig. 31. *The Buddha Taming the Elephant Nalagiri*. By Soliyas Mendis. Mural painting, Kelaniya Rajamaha Vihara, Gampaha District, Sri Lanka, 1946. Photo: G. Jayasinghe.

Fig. 32. *The Parinirvana of the Buddha*. Blue-gray schist, 10½ x 17½ in. (26.7 x 44.4 cm). Gandhara, Pakistan, 2nd–3rd centuries. [The British Museum, London] Photo © Copyright The British Museum.

Fig. 33. *The Great Stupa of Sanchi (Stupa 1) and its West Torana*. H: 54 ft., 1 in. (16.5 m). Sanchi, India, original brick core constructed 3rd century B.C., enlarged 1st century B.C. Photo: Takeo Kamiya.

Fig. 34. *The First Sermon, with the Wheel of the Law representing the Buddha*. Sanchi Stupa 3, south torana, west pillar, north face. Sanchi, India, 1st century B.C. Photo: D. Stadtner.

Fig. 35. *Buddha Seated on a Lion Throne*. Red sikri sandstone, H: 27⅛ in. (69 cm). Katra, India, Kushan period, circa 2nd century A.D. [Mathura Museum]

Fig. 36. *Gold stater of Kanishka I*. Diameter: 25/32 in. (2.0 cm), weight 7.04 g. Ahinposh, Jalalabad District, Afghanistan, issued circa A.D. 100–123. [The British Museum, London] Photo © Copyright The British Museum.

Fig. 37. *Meditating Buddha*. Schist, H: 12¾ in. (32.4 cm). Gandhara, Pakistan, Kushan period, A.D. 200–300. [Asian Art Museum of San Francisco, The Avery Brundage Collection, B60S541. Used by permission.]

Fig. 38. *Head of the Buddha*. Stucco, H: 7⅛ in. (18 cm). Gandhara, Pakistan, 4th–5th centuries. [National Museum, Karachi]

Fig. 39. *Bodhisattva Maitreya*. Schist, H: 41 in. (1.04 m). Gandhara, Pakistan, A.D. 100–300. [Asian Art Museum of San Francisco, The Avery Brundage Collection, B60S597. Used by permission.]

Fig. 40. *Relief Carving of a Stupa and two Elephants*. Stone, 12⅜ x 25⅝ in. (31.25 x 65 cm). Amaravati, India, 2nd century. [The British Museum, London] Photo © Copyright The British Museum.

Fig. 41. *Head of the Buddha*. Sandstone, H: 10¼ in. (26.0 cm). Sarnath, India, Gupta period, 5th century. [National Museum of India, New Delhi] Photo: C. Chicarelli.

Fig. 42. *Sakyamuni Buddha*. Copper alloy with color, H: 15½ in. (39.4 cm). Uttar Pradesh (?), India, Gupta period, late 6th century. [Los Angeles County

Museum of Art, Gift of the Michael J. Connell Foundation. M.70.17.] Photograph © 1997 Museum Associates / LACMA.

Fig. 43. *Scene from the Vessantara Jataka*. Mural wall painting in Cave 17, Ajanta, India, 5th–6th centuries. Photo: L. Tettoni.

Fig. 44. *Eight Great Miracles in the Buddha's Life*. Stone, H: 18¾ in. (47.5 cm). Eastern India, Pala-Sena period, 12th century. [National Museum of India, New Delhi] Photo: C. Chicarelli.

Fig. 45. *Lokesvara Seated Between two Tara Images and two Donor Figures*. Bronze alloy inlaid with silver and copper, H: 13⅝ in. (34.5 cm). Kashmir, India, late 10th or early 11th century. [Private collection] Photo courtesy of John Eskenazi, London.

Fig. 46. *Colossal Buddha of Bamiyan*. Carved sandstone, H: circa 175 ft. (53.3 m). Bamiyan, Afghanistan, 5th–6th centuries; destroyed 2001. Photo: Dr. R. Edwards.

Fig. 47. *Ksitigarbha with the Ten Kings of Hell*. Ink and colors on silk, 35⅞ x 25¾ in. (91 x 65.5 cm). Dunhuang, China, Five Dynasties, mid-10th century. [The British Museum, London] Photo © Copyright The British Museum.

Fig. 48. *Sakyamuni Buddha and Prabhutaratna Buddha*. Gilt bronze, H: 10⅛ in. (25.7 cm). China, Northern Wei dynasty, 518. [Musee Guimet, Paris] Photo: C. Chicarelli.

Fig. 49. *Greeting the Soul of a Righteous Man on the Way to the Pure Land of Amitabha*. Mineral pigments painted on canvas, 56⅛ x 37 in. (142.5 x 94 cm). China, Tangut State of Xi Xia, Khara Khoto, 12th–13th centuries. [©The State Hermitage Museum, St. Petersburg, Russia]

Fig. 50. *Tamo (Bodhidharma). By Guo Fa Cheng*. Carved wood, H: 23¼ in. (59 cm). China, 1999. [Private collection]

Fig. 51. *Sakyamuni Buddha*. White marble with traces of polychromy, H: 30 in. (76.2 cm). China, Tang dynasty, 618–906. [Lent anonymously to Los Angeles County Museum of Art]

Fig. 52. *Lokapala*. Painted pottery, H: 24¾ in. (62.8 cm). China, Tang dynasty, 8th century. [Tsui Art Foundation, Hong Kong]

Fig. 53. *Dvarapala*. Carved wood, H: 92⅛ in. (2.34 m). China, 18th century. [Private collection] Photo: C. Chicarelli.

Fig. 54. *Maitreya, the Future Buddha*. Gray limestone, H: 32½ in. (82.6 cm). China, Tang dynasty, dated 705. [Art Institute of Chicago; gift of Miss Alice Getty] Photo: C. Chicarelli.

Fig. 55. *The Monk Budai*. Glazed stoneware with paint, H: 9⅜ in. (23.8 cm). China, 20th century. [Private collection] Photo: C. Chicarelli.

Fig. 56. *Frontispiece of a Chinese translation of the Diamond Sutra*. Block printed on paper, H: 9⅞ in. (25 cm). Found at Dun-huang, China, dated A.D. 868. [The British Library, London]

Fig. 57. *Bodhisattva Guanyin*. Wood with paint, 95 x 65 in. (2.41 x 1.65 m). China, Northern Sung or Liao dynasty, 11th–12th centuries. [Nelson-Atkins Museum of Art, Kansas City, Missouri. Purchase: Nelson Trust]

Fig. 58. *Bodhisattva Guanyin*. Stoneware with polychrome glazes, H: 8⅛ in. (20.9 cm). China, 19th century. [Private collection]

Fig. 59. *Head of Bodhisattva Guanyin with Five Transcendent Buddhas in the Headdress*. Gray marble, H: 24⅜ in. (62 cm). North China, 14th–15th centuries. [Musee Guimet, Paris] Photo: C. Chicarelli.

Fig. 60. *A Luohan Seated in Meditation*. Earthenware with 3-color lead glaze, 40 x 31 x 26 in. (102 x 78.7 x 66.0 cm). China, Liao dynasty (907–1125) to Jin dynasty (1115–1234). [Nelson-Atkins Museum of Art, Kansas City, Missouri. Purchase: Nelson Trust] Photo: R. Newcombe.

Fig. 61. *Sakyamuni Buddha*. Gilt copper, H: 5½ in. (14 cm). Korea, Koguryo period, mid-6th century. [Collection of the Honorable Joseph P. Carroll, New York]

Fig. 62. *Bodhisattva Maitreya*. Gilt bronze, H: 36⅞ in. (93.5 cm). Korea, Three Kingdoms period, 7th century. [National Museum of Korea, Seoul]

Fig. 63. *Sakyamuni Buddha*. Granite, H (statue): 11 ft., 2⅞ in. (3.42 m). Sokkuram, Kyongju, Korea, Unified Silla period, circa 751. Photo: J. Listopad.

Fig. 64. *Amitabha Buddha*. Stone, H: 114¼ in. (2.90 m). Korea, Unified Silla period, 719. [National Museum of Korea, Seoul]

Fig. 65. *Bhaisajyaguru Buddha*. Gilt bronze, H: 9¼ in. (23.5 cm). Korea, Unified Silla period, 8th century. [Collection of the Honorable Joseph P. Carroll, New York]

Fig. 66. *Vairochana Buddha displaying the Bodhyangi Mudra*. Cast iron, H: 44⅛ in. (1.12 m). Korea, Koryo dynasty, 10th–11th centuries. [National Museum of Korea, Seoul]

Fig. 67. *Fourth of the Ten Kings of Hell*. Ink and paint on silk, 47¼ x 34 in. (120 x 86.4 cm). Tongdosa Temple, Korea, 1775. Photo: Korean Chogye Buddhist Order.

Fig. 68. *Amida Nyorai (Amitabha Buddha) flanked by two Bodhisattvas*—(right) *Kannon (Avalokitesvara) and* (left) *Daiseishi (Mahasthamaprapta)*. Gilt bronze, H (center figure): 14⅛ in. (35.7 cm). Japan, Hakuho/early Nara period, 7th century. [Tokyo National Museum]

Fig. 69. *Yakushi Triad*: (left) *Gakko, Bodhisattva of the Moon (Sanskrit, Chandraprabha)*; (center) *Yakushi Nyorai (Sanskrit, Bhaisajyaguru Buddha)*; (right) *Nikko, Bodhisattva of the Sun (Sanskrit, Suryaprabha)*. Yakushiji Temple, Nara, Japan, Hakuho/early Nara period, 697. Photos courtesy of Yakushiji Temple.

Fig. 70. *Birushanabutsu, the Great Buddha of Nara (Vairochana Buddha)*. Bronze, H: 49 ft., 3 in. (15 m). Todaiji Temple, Nara, Japan, 752. Photo: C. Chicarelli.

Fig. 71. *Senju Kannon Bosatsu (Thousand-armed Bodhisattva Avalokitesvara)*. Dry lacquer over a wooden core, H: 17 ft., 7 in. (5.36 m). Toshodaiji Temple, Nara, Japan, 8th century.

Fig. 72. *Jizo Bosatsu (Bodhisattva Ksitigarbha)*. Carved wood, H (figure only): 57 in. (1.46 m). Japan, late Heian period, late 11th–early 12th century. [Los Angeles County Museum of Art, Gift of Anna Bing Arnold. M.74.117.] Photograph © 2003 Museum Associates / LACMA.

Fig. 73. *Daibutsu, the Great Buddha of Kamakura (Amitabha Buddha)*. Bronze, H: 37 ft., 3 in. (11.36 m). Kotoku-in Temple, Kamakura, Japan, 1252. Photo: C. Chicarelli.

Fig. 74. *Ten Oxherding Pictures*. By Master Gyokusei Jikihara. Ink paintings on paper, each 30 x 24 in. (76.2 x 61.0 cm). Zen Mountain Monastery, Mt. Tremper, New York, 1983.

Fig. 75. *Shaka (Sakyamuni) Coming Down from the Mountain*. Ink on paper scroll, 35¾ x 16 in. (90.8 x 41.9 cm). Japan, Kamakura period, circa 1300. [Seattle Art Museum, Eugene Fuller Memorial Collection] Photo: P. Macapia.

Fig. 76. *Hui-k'o Presenting His Arm to Bodhidharma (Japanese, Daruma)*. By Sesshu Toyo. Ink and colors on paper, 78¾ x 44⅞ in. (2.00 x 1.14 m). Sainenji, Aichi prefecture, Japan, Muromachi period, 1496. Photo: K. Kawasaki.

Fig. 77. *Bishamonten* (or *Tamonten*), *Guardian of the North, One of the four Lokapala*. Wood, copper and pigments, H: 52 in. (1.32 m). Japan, 18th–19th centuries. [The British Museum, London] Photo © Copyright The British Museum.

Fig. 78. *Netsuke of Bishamonten and a Tiger*. By Kokoku. Boxwood, ebony and ivory, inlaid with tortoise shell, gold, and silver, H: 1¾ in. (4.3 cm). Japan, Meiji period. [Private collection] Photo courtesy of Orientations Gallery, New York.

Fig. 79. *The Western Paradise of Amida (Amitabha Buddha)*. Ink and gold and colors on silk, 27⅛ x 20½ in. (69 x 52 cm). Japan, 19th century. [The British Museum, London] Photo © Copyright The British Museum.

Fig. 80. *Bodhisattva Manjusri*. Silver, H: 6½ in. (16.5 cm). Nepal, 19th century. [Private collection]

Fig. 81. *Svayambhu Mahachaitya*. Kathmandu, Nepal, original brick and clay core constructed circa 4th century A.D. Photo: L. Tettoni.

Fig. 82. *Vajrasattva*. Carved wood, gilded and painted, H: 42⅛ in. (107 cm). Nepal, 19th or 20th century. [Private collection] Photo: C. Chicarelli.

Fig. 83. *Cover of a Sutra picturing Five Transcendent Buddhas*. Left to right: *Akshobhya, Ratnasambhava, Vairochana, Amitabha, and Amoghasiddhi*. Painted wood, H: 3¼ x 15¾ in. (8.3 x 40 cm). Nepal, 19th century. [Private collection] Photo: C. Chicarelli.

Fig. 84. *Dipankara Buddha*. Bronze with gilt and paint, H: 28 in. (71 cm). Nepal, 17th–18th centuries. [Patan Museum, Nepal] Photo: R. Steiner.

Fig. 85. *Goddess Prajnaparamita*. Bronze repousse inlaid with semiprecious stones, H: 16½ in. (42 cm). Nepal, 16th century. [Collection of Drs. Ann & Robert S. Walzer]

Fig. 86. *Amitayus Buddha*. Copper, gilded and inlaid with gemstones, H: 15¾ in. (40 cm). Nepal, 14th century. [Tibet House Museum, New Delhi] Photo: C. Chicarelli.

Fig. 87. *Wheel of Life*. Tempera on cloth, 15¾ x 11¾ in. (40 x 29.8 cm). Nepal, 20th century. [Private collection] Photo: Trakarn Tilaganont.

Fig. 88. *Padmasambhava (Main Form)*. Ground mineral pigments on cotton, 27¼ x 18⅞ in. (69 x 48 cm). Nyingma Lineage, Tibet, 1800–1899. [Collection of Shelley & Donald Rubin, item #188, acc. #P1997.12.1] Photo courtesy of the Collection of Shelley & Donald Rubin: www.himalayanart.org

Fig. 89. *Bodhisattva Maitreya*. Copper with traces of pigment, H: 14⅝ in. (37 cm). Tibet, circa 11th–12th centuries. [Nyingjei Lam Collection]

Fig. 90. *Akshobhya Buddha*. Gilt copper, H: 22⅞ in. (58 cm). Central Tibet, late 12th or early 13th century. [Private collection]

Photo courtesy of John Eskenazi, London.

Fig. 91. *The Buddha with Scenes from his Life*. Colors on cotton cloth, 31½ x 23½ in. (80 x 59.7 cm). Central Tibet, 12th century. [Zimmerman Family Collection]

Fig. 92. *Mandala of Tara*. Ground mineral pigments on cotton, 14¼ x 11½ in. (36 x 29 cm). Sakya Lineage, Tibet, 1400–1499. [Collection of Shelley & Donald Rubin, item #799, acc. #P1998.4.13] Photo courtesy of the Collection of Shelley & Donald Rubin: www.himalayanart.org

Fig. 93. Detail of fig. 92.

Fig. 94. *Bhurkumkuta*. Gilt-copper with pigments, H: 5⅝ in. (14.2 cm). Tibet, circa 15th–16th centuries. [Nyingjei Lam Collection]

Fig. 95. *Manuscript Cover*. Gilded polychromed wood, carved with figures of five deities. Left to right: Sakyamuni Buddha, Sadaksari Lokesvara, Prajnaparamita, Manjusri, and Syamatara (Green Tara), H: 10⅝ in. (27 cm). Tibet, 13th century. [Private collection] Photo courtesy of Carlo Cristi, Milan.

Fig. 96. *The Abbot Yongzin Ngawang Zangpo*. Gilt bronze with turquoise and silver inlay, H: 7¼ in. (18.5 cm). Tibet, 1600 or earlier. [Asian Art Museum of San Francisco. Gift of Raymond G. and Milla L. Handley, B86B8. Used by permission.]

Fig. 97. *Lama's Crown*. Embroidered in satin stitch with five transcendent Buddhas, l–r: Amitabha, Akshobhya, Vairochana, Ratnasambhava, and Amoghasiddhi; trimmed with gold-wrapped silk thread, H (each section): 7⅞ in. (20 cm). Tibet, late 16th century. [Private collection]

Fig. 98. *Tantric Buddhism Ritual Objects*. Tibet and Nepal. [Various private collections] Photos: C. Chicarelli.

Fig. 99. *Padmapani (Avalokitesvara)*. Gilt bronze with inlaid gemstones, H: 30¾ in. (78.1 cm). Tibet, 19th century. [Tomlinson Collection] Photo: C. Chicarelli.

Fig. 100. *Chenrezig (Avalokitesvara)*. Gilt copper, H: 15 in. (38.1 cm). Tibet or Nepal, 19th century. [Private collection]

Fig. 101. *Dambulla Viharaya Cave Temple*. Sri Lanka, Buddhist artworks installed circa 1st century B.C. on through the 18th century A.D.

Fig. 102. *Sakyamuni Buddha*. Bronze, H: 42½ in. (1.08 m). Sri Lanka, late Anuradhapura period, circa 3rd–7th centuries. [Ho Chi Minh City Historical Museum, Vietnam] Photo: L. Tettoni.

Fig. 103. *Bodhisattva Tara*. Gilt bronze, H: 57⅛ in. (1.45 m). Sri Lanka, late Anuradhapura period, 8th century. [The British Museum, London] Photo © Copyright The British Museum.

Fig. 104. *Pair of Colossal Statues carved from Stone*. (left) Standing image of the monk Ananda, H: 23 ft. (7 m). (right) Reclining image of Sakyamuni Buddha's Parinirvana, Length: 46 ft. (14 m). Gal Vihara, Polonnaruva, Sri Lanka, 12th century. Photo: K. Kawasaki.

Fig. 105. *Life-size Diorama of seated and standing images of Sakyamuni Buddha*. Stucco and wood. Nagavimanas Kandy Vihara, South wall, Kandy, Sri Lanka, 18th century. Photo: J. Listopad.

Fig. 106. *Votive Tablet illustrating Eight Great Events in the Buddha's Life and his Seven Stations of Enlightenment*. Terracotta, H: 7¾ in. (19.7 cm). Pagan, Burma (Myanmar), 7th–10th centuries. [Museum of Fine Arts, Boston; Marshall H. Gould Fund; 1976.62] © 2002 Museum of Fine Arts, Boston.

Fig. 107. *Standing Buddha Statue*. Lacquered and gilded wood, H: 31 ft., 5 in. (9.59 m). Ananda Temple, Pagan, Burma (Myanmar), circa 12th century. Photo: L. Tettoni.

Fig. 108. *Crowned Buddha in Royal Attire*. Gilt wood and lacquer with inlaid gemstones and glass. Shan States, Burma (Myanmar), circa 19th century. [Private collection] Photo: L. Tettoni.

Fig. 109. *Reclining Buddha*. White marble with gilt and paint, Length: 101 in. (2.56 m). Burma (Myanmar), circa 19th–20th centuries. [Hsi Lai Temple, Hacienda Heights, California] Photo: C. Chicarelli.

Fig. 110. *The Buddha Shielded by Muchalinda the Serpent King*. Gilt wood, H: 46 in. (1.17 m). Shan States, Burma (Myanmar), circa 18th century. [Private collection] Photo: C. Chicarelli.

Fig. 111. *Five Buddhist Monks*. Gilt and black lacquer on teakwood, H: 20 in. (50.8 cm). Burma (Myanmar), 18th century. [Suthiprapa Collection, Bangkok] Photo: C. Chicarelli.

Fig. 112. *Bhaisajyaguru Buddha*. Copper alloy, H: 10½ in. (26.7 cm). Shan States, Burma (Myanmar), 18th century. [Los Angeles County Museum of Art, Gift of Michael Phillips. M.80.228.3.] Photograph © 2003 Museum Associates / LACMA.

Fig. 113. *Buddha's Footprint*. Carved stone, engraved with auspicious emblems and gilded, 67⅜ x 39⅜ in. (1.71 x 1.00 m). Burma (Myanmar), 19th century.

[The British Museum, London] Photo © Copyright The British Museum.

Fig. 114. *Borobudur.* Constructed from stone, H: 115 ft., 9 in. (35.29 m), Width: 393 ft., 9 in. (120 m). Central Java, Indonesia, 8th–9th centuries. Photo: L. Tettoni.

Fig. 115. *Borobudur.* One of 72 Buddha statues on the upper three levels, with its covering stupa partially removed. Photo: Photobank Thailand.

Fig. 116. *Ratnasambhava Buddha seated in Varada Mudra.* Andesite volcanic stone, H: 52½in. (1.33 m). Style of Borobudur, Central Java, Indonesia, 8th–9th centuries. [Private collection] Photo: C. Chicarelli.

Fig. 117. Side view of fig. 116. Photo: C. Chicarelli.

Fig. 118. *Buddha seated European fashion, in the pose of Dharmachakra Mudra.* Stone, H: 9 ft., 10 in. (2.99 m). Chandi Mendut, Java, Indonesia, 8th–10th centuries. Photo: L. Tettoni.

Fig. 119. *Kubera.* Copper alloy, H: 4¾ in. (12.1 cm). Central Java, Indonesia, early 9th century. [Los Angeles County Museum of Art, Purchased with funds provided by the Phil Berg Collection. AC1992.204.1.] Photograph © 2003 Museum Associates / LACMA.

Fig. 120. *The Buddhist deities Avalokitesvara and Vasundhara.* Silver and bronze, 4¾ x 5⅛ in. (12.1 x 13.1 cm). Java, Indonesia, approx. 850–950. [Asian Art Museum of San Francisco, Gift of the Walter and Phyllis Shorenstein Fund, B86B1. Used by permission.]

Fig. 121. *Standing Buddha.* Sandstone, H: 35½ in. (90 cm). From Preah Theat, Cambodia, 7th century. [Musee Guimet, Paris] Photo: C. Chicarelli.

Fig. 122. *Angkor Wat.* Cambodia, 12th century. Photo: Venerable Kantasilo.

Fig. 123. *Queen Maya Giving Birth to Prince Siddhartha, the Future Buddha.* Stone, 29⅜ x 24¼ in. (74.6 x 61.6 cm). From Angkor Wat, Cambodia, 12th century. [National Museum of Bangkok] Photo: Sadayu Kooamornpatana.

Fig. 124. *Seated Buddha.* Bronze, H: 13 in. (33 cm). Angkor Wat style, Cambodia, 12th century. [Private collection] Photo courtesy of Spink & Son, London.

Fig. 125. *Goddess Prajnaparamita.* Bronze, H: 8⅝ in. (22 cm). Angkor Wat style, Cambodia, 12th century. [Private collection, Antwerp, Belgium]

Fig. 126. *Hevajra.* Bronze, H: 9½ in. (24 cm). Khmer-Lopburi art, 12th century. [National Museum of Bangkok] Photo: Sadayu Kooamornpatana.

Fig. 127. *Ritual conch with an image of Hevajra flanked by attendant figures and naga guardians.* Bronze, H: 8¾ in. (22.2 cm). Angkor Wat style, Cambodia, circa 12th century. [Private collection] Photo: Tira Vanichtheeranont.

Fig. 128. *Vajrasattva.* Bronze, H: 9 in. (23 cm). Khmer-Lopburi art, circa 12th century. [National Museum of Bangkok] Photo: Sadayu Kooamornpatana.

Fig. 129. *The Bayon.* Angkor Thom, Cambodia, constructed circa 1190. Photo: Venerable Kantasilo.

Fig. 130. *Asuras Pulling a Naga.* Sandstone. Angkor Thom, Cambodia, circa 1190. Photo courtesy of Jacques-Edouard Berger Foundation, Lausanne.

Fig. 131. *Radiating Avalokitesvara.* Sandstone, H: 62¼ in. (1.58 m). From Prasat Muang Singh, Kanchanaburi Province, Thailand; Lopburi art, influenced by Khmer Bayon style, 13th century. [National Museum of Bangkok] Photo: C. Chicarelli.

Fig. 132. *Apsaras.* Sandstone. The Bayon, Angkor Thom, Cambodia, circa 1190. Photo: J. Listopad.

Fig. 133. *Apsaras.* Sandstone. Angkor Wat, Cambodia, 12th century. Photo courtesy of Jacques-Edouard Berger Foundation, Lausanne.

Fig. 134. *Cambodian scripture cabinet illustrating the "Five Buddhas of this Auspicious Age."* [National Museum, Phnom Penh, Cambodia] Photo: O. de Bernon.

Fig. 135. *Wheel of the Law and a Deer.* Black stone, H: 82¾ in. (2.10 m). From Nakhon Pathom Province, Thailand, Dvaravati period, 6th–8th centuries. [National Museum of Bangkok] Photo: C. Chicarelli.

Fig. 136. *The Buddha Shielded by Muchalinda the Serpent King.* Black stone, H: 30 in. (76.2 cm). Prachinburi Province, Thailand, Dvaravati period, 8th–10th centuries. [National Museum of Bangkok] Photo: C. Chicarelli.

Fig. 137. *Bodhisattva Padmapani (Avalokitesvara).* Bronze, H: 24⅞ in. (63 cm). Surat Thani Province, Thailand, Srivijiya period, 8th century. [National Museum of Bangkok] Photo: C. Chicarelli.

Fig. 138. *The Buddha Descending from Heaven.* Gilt bronze, H: 49¾ in. (1.26 m). Ratchburi Province, Thailand, 12th–13th centuries. [National Museum of Bangkok] Photo: C. Chicarelli.

Fig. 139. *The Buddha Walking*. Gilt bronze, H: 21 in. (53.3 cm). Thailand, Sukhothai period, 14th century. [Private collection] Photo courtesy of Spink & Son, London.

Fig. 140. *The Enlightenment of Sakyamuni Buddha*. Bronze, H: 40⅛ in. (1.02 m). Thailand, Sukhothai period, 2nd half of 14th century. [National Museum of Bangkok] Photo: Sadayu Kooamornpatana.

Fig. 141. *The Enlightenment of Sakyamuni Buddha*. Bronze, H: 40⅝ in. (1.03 m). Thailand, U-Thong period, 13th–14th centuries. [National Museum of Bangkok] Photo: Sadayu Kooamornpatana.

Fig. 142. *Crowned Buddha Dispelling Fear*. Gilt bronze, H: 96½ in. (2.45 m). Bangkok, Thailand, Ratanakosin period, 19th–20th centuries. [National Museum of Bangkok] Photo: C. Chicarelli.

Fig. 143. *Queen Maya Giving Birth to Prince Siddhartha, the Future Buddha*. By Sangduen Rawijan. Acrylics on canvas, 46 x 31 in. (117 x 79 cm). Thailand, 2001. [Private collection] Photo: C. Chicarelli.

Fig. 144. *Buddhist Amulets and Miniature Figures*. Thailand, various styles. [Private collections]. Photos: C. Chicarelli.

Fig. 145. *Bodhisattva Tara*. Bronze, H: 47¼ in. (1.20 m). Dong Duong, Vietnam, 9th–10th centuries. [Da Nang Museum of Cham Sculpture, Vietnam] Photo: L. Tettoni.

Fig. 146. *Bodhisattva Vajrapani*. Bronze, H: 13 in. (33 cm). Cham art, Vietnam, 8th century. [Private collection] Photo courtesy of Alexander Goetz, London.

Fig. 147. *Amitabha Buddha*. Gilt lacquer with paint on wood, H: 33 in. (83.8 cm). Vietnam, circa 19th century. [Private collection] Photo: C. Chicarelli.

Fig. 148. *Bodhisattva Ksitigarbha seated atop a Lion*. Gilt wood, H: 22½ in. (57.2 cm). Vietnam, circa 18th–19th centuries. [Private collection] Photo: C. Chicarelli.

Fig. 149. *Bodhisattva Avalokitesvara*. Gilded and lacquered wood, H: 34½ in. (87.6 cm). Vietnam, circa 1750. [Pacific Asia Museum Collection, Pasadena, California; gift of Anna and Dana Bresnahan] Photo: C. Chicarelli.

Fig. 150. *The Enlightenment of Sakyamuni Buddha*. Gilded and painted wood with inlaid gemstones. Vietnam, 19th century. [Fine Arts Museum, Ho Chi Minh City] Photo: C. Nguyen.

Fig. 151. *The Monk Budai*. Gilt bronze, H: 18¼ in. (46.4 cm). Vietnam, 19th century. [Private collection]. Photo: C. Chicarelli.

Fig. 152. *Main Altar of a Mahayana Temple*. Giac Vien Temple, Ho Chi Minh City, Vietnam. Photo: C. Nguyen.

Fig. 153. *Sakyamuni Buddha seated in meditation beneath the Bodhi Tree*. Mother of pearl inlay with pigments and lacquer on wood, 23 x 15½ in. (58.4 x 39.4 cm). Vietnam, 20th century. [Private collection]. Photo: C. Chicarelli.

Appendix 1: Mudra, Asana, and Bhanga Terminology

Fig. 154. Mudra gestures often seen in Buddhist art.

Fig. 155. Asana terms in Buddhist art.

Appendix 2: The Five Transcendent Buddhas of the Mahayana and Vajrayana Faiths.

ACKNOWLEDGMENTS

This book is a product of some thirty-five years of studying Buddhism and Buddhist art in numerous countries, under the much-appreciated guidance of a great many teachers and specialists. Regrettably, it is impossible in the space available here to name and thank all those people and institutions who have taught and assisted me. But I do wish to thank some who have been especially helpful in my studies and in my writing: my wife Lek and our family; my teacher and friend, Venerable Kantasilo; Ms. Tanitta Viriyavanich; Dr. John Listopad; Mr. Ken Kawasaki; Acharn Helen Jandamit; Mr. Ed Reinke; Mr. Martin Perenchio; the Asian Art Museum of San Francisco; the Los Angeles County Museum of Art; the British Museum, London; the National Museum of Bangkok; The Siam Society; Sri Sang Color Lab; and Silkworm Books, particularly Ms. Trasvin Jittidecharak and Ms. Susan Offner. My gratitude is also extended to Zen Mountain Monastery, New York, U.S.A., for permitting me to include their Ten Oxherding Pictures and descriptions; and to Dharma Publishing, California, U.S.A., for permitting me to include the excerpt from their book, *The Voice of the Buddha: The Lalitavistara Sutra*, describing the "thirty-two signs of a great man."

INDEX

Page numbers in **bold** indicate prime information about or a definition of a subject.

Numbers in *italic* are illustration numbers.

C

D

E

F

G

H

U

V

W

X

Y

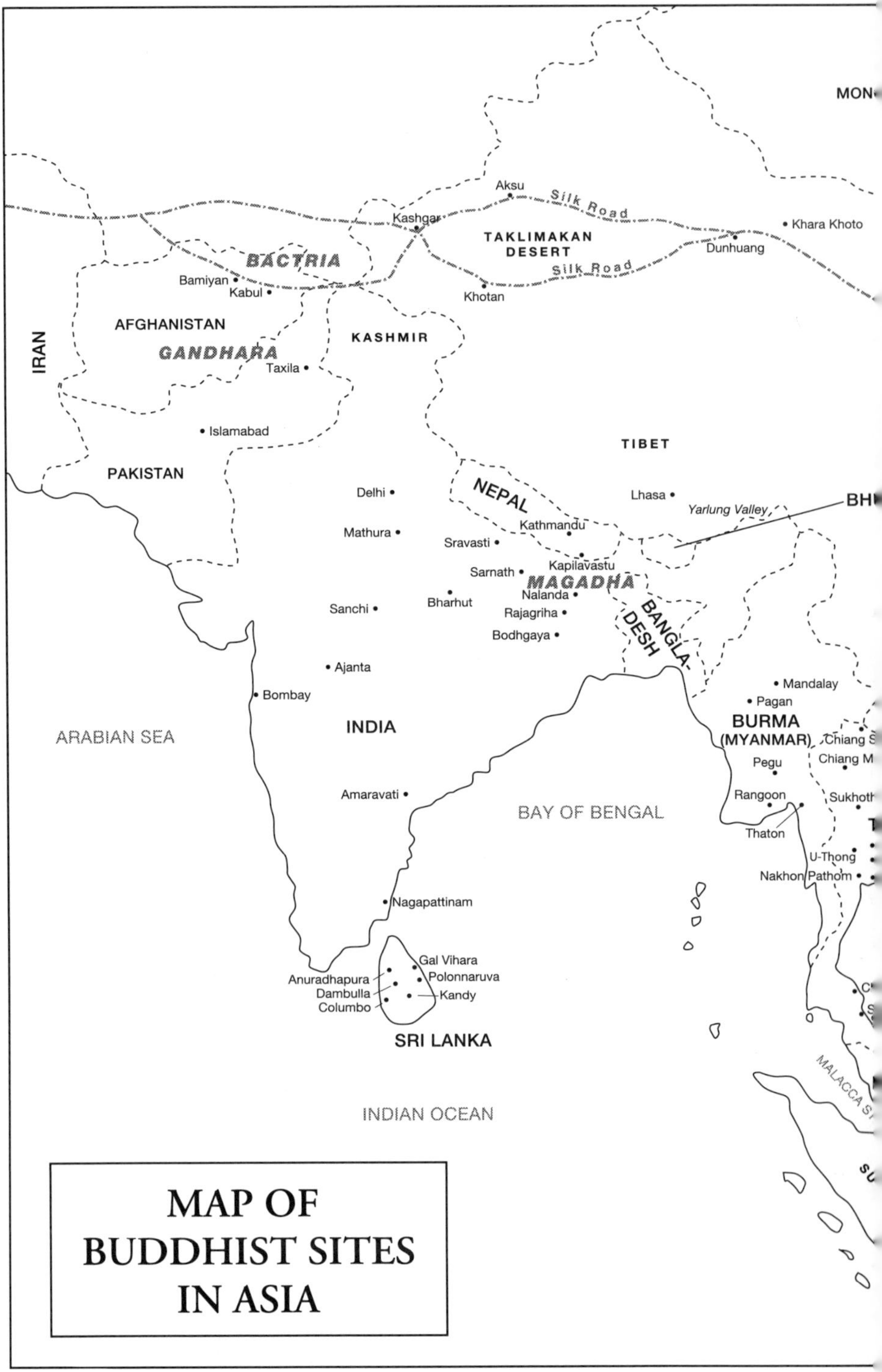

MAP OF BUDDHIST SITES IN ASIA